Seventh-day Adventism in Crisis

Seventh-day Adventism in Crisis

Gender and Sectarian Change in an Emerging Religion

Laura L. Vance

University of Illinois Press

Urbana and Chicago

Publication of this work supported by a grant from the
Georgia Southwestern State University Foundation.

This book is printed on acid-free paper.

Library of Congress Cataloging-in-Publication Data
Vance, Laura Lee.
Seventh-day Adventism in crisis : gender and sectarian change in
an emerging religion / Laura L. Vance.
    p.   cm.
Includes bibliographical references and index.
ISBN 0-252-02434-6 (alk. paper)
ISBN 0-252-06744-4 (pbk. : alk. paper)
1. Seventh-day Adventists—History. 2. Adventists—History.
3. Sabbatarians—History. 4. Women clergy. 5. Ordination of women.
6. Sex roles—Religious aspects—Christianity. I. Title.
BX 6115 .V36   1999
286.7'32'09—ddc21
98-19765
CIP

For Jennifer,
who sees with the heart
and understands what is essential

Contents

Acknowledgments

I express my sincere gratitude foremost to the Adventist women and men who participated in this research endeavor as interviewees and survey respondents. This work would not have been possible without their willingness to share knowledge, experience, and insight. I am greatly indebted to those Adventist congregations with whom I attended worship services, painted school buildings, and studied—I thank them for welcoming me into their communities and lives. I thank also the pastors and associate pastors who permitted and encouraged me to attend worship and other services and who assisted me in locating and contacting interview participants. I am especially grateful to Henning Guldhammer, John Cress, and Nancy Canwell for the time that they each generously set aside, despite busy schedules, to share thoughts and suggestions.

This research could not have been completed without the resources made available to me during the spring and summer of 1993 at the Peterson Memorial Library of Walla Walla College. I particularly wish to thank Violet Maynard-Reid, reference librarian, for her patient explanations and assistance, and Sheila Clark, of access services, for her interest in my research and her willingness to permit me access to restricted collections. I also wish to thank the periodical staff of the library for allowing me access to special collections of older *Review and Heralds*.

I am especially indebted to Elizabeth Dulany and Pat Hollahan, my editors at the University of Illinois Press, for comments and suggestions on earlier drafts of this work. I am also indebted to Roger Dudley, Catherine Wessinger, Robert Wyllie, Derryl MacLean, and Katheryn Anderson for their criticisms of earlier drafts of the manuscript. To John Whitworth, my doctoral supervisor, for his consistent ability to share knowledge and expertise while still allowing me autonomy as a scholar, I express my gratitude. I appreciate also the guidance and inspiration offered me by Kathy Young, Joyce Hammond, Constance Faulkner, and Robert Marshall—exceptional and dedicated teachers all. While

I am grateful for the suggestions and guidance that others have provided me, I take responsibility for this work and any shortcomings it may contain.

I am grateful to Simon Fraser University for research, fellowship, and scholarship funds which financed this endeavor and to the Georgia Southwestern State University Foundation for a generous grant.

Last, Jennifer Langton has encouraged this work at every juncture. My thanks to her, I think, cannot be expressed but only lived.

Seventh-day Adventism in Crisis

Introduction:
Religious Identity and Gender

Seventh-day Adventism emerged in nineteenth-century America among a group of believers in Christ's second coming known best (albeit unfairly) for donning white ascension robes, leaving crops unharvested, and climbing atop houses to await Christ's coming. In the disappointment resulting from Christ's failure to appear, the movement first floundered, then coalesced around a young girl, Ellen (Harmon) White, who experienced dramatic waking visions and thereby offered not only an explanation of the failure of the anticipated parousia but assurance that predictions of Christ's expected return were not incorrect, only in error in their timing of the event. As time continued, Adventists commenced building an increasingly temporal religious movement, interpreting their earthly success in the construction of medical, educational, and religious institutions as hastening the expected advent.

Although the movement has been largely ignored by secular scholars, Seventh-day Adventism boasts more than nine million members worldwide and an immense and growing system of hospitals, primary and secondary schools, universities, colleges, and other institutions. In the context of the birth and growth of this increasingly institutionalized religious movement, women played a crucial role. Most obviously, the words and, later, writings of Ellen White provided the glue which bound the movement together and propelled it on a certain course. But in examining contributions of Ellen White, whose leadership and teachings are recognized as inspired due to her unique spiritual gifts, scholars too often ignore contributions of more ordinary Adventist women. Less-celebrated women, however, held positions of authority in, and contributed in crucial ways to, the burgeoning movement, and were acknowledged, as much as were the men with whom they labored, as having been called of God.

These women, their work and contributions, are largely forgotten in Adventism today. Indeed, one of the major crises facing Adventism at the dawn of the twenty-first century is a debate regarding whether women may be ordained to serve in pastoral capacities. Adventism has been beset for decades by contention concerning the propriety of women's public participation in leadership. It is this paradox, this incongruity of historical authority replaced by contemporary disenfranchisement, which must be examined in order to understand not only the changing place of women in the movement but institutionalization and maturation of Seventh-day Adventism as a whole. To address this discrepancy also sheds light on consequences of institutionalization and denominationalism for women in other marginal religions: How can movements which originally welcome women's participation; which rely so extensively on their pastoral leadership, teaching, proselytizing and prophesying; which listen to them preach, read their admonitions, and respect their ideas—eventually disallow women's access to public positions of leadership and become engaged in debate about the extent to which to allow them public religious participation?

Sectarian Development

Of particular relevance in addressing these questions is analysis of the tendency of new, marginal religious movements to originally eschew secular society only to demonstrate, later, increasing accommodation to "the world." The consequences of this process are of particular import for women: Sociological theory of sectarian development hints that religious maturation and change may affect the allotment of authority on the basis of gender. The theory provides foundation for analysis of these questions first in the work of Max Weber, who distinguishes the church from the sect. According to Weber's theory of "religion of the non-privileged classes" (a theory never fully developed by Weber), "the religion of the disprivileged classes [sects] . . . is characterized by a tendency to allot equality to women" (Weber 1963:104). Weber argues that as sectarian movements become bureaucratized and seek accommodation to secular society the positions of authority and leadership available to women in the initial phase of sectarian development diminish. In short, Weber asserts that while women and members of other disprivileged groups are allowed increased authority early in sectarian development, "only in very rare cases does this practice continue beyond the first stage of a religious community's formation, when the pneumatic manifestations of charisma are valued as hallmarks of specifically religious exaltation. Thereafter, as routinization and regimentation of community relations set in" public authority previously allotted women is limited and, eventually, disappears entirely (ibid.).

Weber left examination of the evolution of religious movements responsible for limitation of women's religious authority to later theorists. These theorists do not specifically address questions of gender and religious leadership posed briefly by Weber but instead concentrate on explicating distinctions between types of religious movements and on the evolution of religious movements. This explication, however, provides the foundation for application of Weber's hypothesis in examination of women in religion. Understanding the sect as a marginal religious movement whose members identify themselves in opposition to secular society and the church as an accommodating body allows insight regarding the relationship between religious identity and response to secular society and allotment of religious authority on the basis of gender.

In his 1912 work, for example, Ernst Troeltsch expounds Weber's definitions of the church and sect, identifying the church as a conservative institution that accepts and legitimates the existing secular social and economic order and identifying the sect as a disenfranchised group in tension with the extant social order. While the church has the ability to administer grace, the sect is a holy community, set apart from "the world."[1] In his influential 1929 work, H. Richard Niebuhr insists that sects begin as radical protest groups, though eventually they become concerned with socializing, training, and educating children of the group. Thus, over time, sectarians, who are initially socially and economically disenfranchised, become increasingly involved in secular matters—including the acquisition of property and social status—and consequently develop more formalized structures of religious worship, and decreased spontaneity.[2]

In his 1942 work, Liston Pope insists that a group must organize to exist over time and that in organizing, a sect (comprised of economically disprivileged, socially disenfranchised individuals who emphasize spontaneity, lay leadership, and authentic religious experience in worship) becomes a church (made up of wealthy, socially enfranchised individuals who hire a trained ministry and emphasize passive listening and institutionalized norms and procedures in worship). Although sect members initially view themselves as distinct from the world, Pope argues (with Niebuhr) that the sect eventually attempts to accommodate the predominant social order. Some members of the sect are able to accrue wealth (and concomitant social status) and subsequently exert increased influence over the financially struggling sect. Consequently, the sect experiences, according to Pope, a gradual shift toward institutionalization and concern with secular matters. Pope concurs with Niebuhr that "by its very nature the sectarian type of organization is valid for only one generation" (Pope

1942:19). In his 1946 discussion, Milton J. Yinger observes the limitations inherent in the presumed inevitability of sect/church evolution as understood by Niebuhr and Pope, and posits, distinguishing the "established sect" from the "sect," that sectarian movements may persist for several generations. Yinger recognizes that although sects may adopt churchlike qualities (a trained ministry, for example) in order to recruit or retain members, some sects continue to maintain an identity distinct from those outside of the group (to be "seen as a group apart" from institutional churches [Yinger 1961 (1946):22]) and to maintain tension with secular society.

According to Bryan Wilson, the commitment of the sectarian "is always more total and defined than that of the member of any other religious organization" (1959:4). Because the sectarian withdraws, to varying degrees, from the world in order to participate in the sect, which she believes to have exclusive access to truth, sects "experience different types of tension" with other religious groups and with secular society (ibid.). Wilson observes that sects desire to maintain tension with the world and may do so by rejecting social symbols and rituals, disagreeing with society as to what constitutes true knowledge, refusing to accept the legitimacy of the state's legal system, withdrawing from the state's political arena, and/or becoming indifferent to or opposing the secular economic system. Recognizing that the maturation, socialization, and conversion of the second (and subsequent) generation(s) poses a threat to the rigor necessary to maintain sectarian distinction, Wilson observes further that sects continue their separation from the world (identity) through *isolation* (both spatial and cultural—linguistic, etc.) and *insulation* (rules pertaining to dress, diet, appropriate sexual norms, etc.) and thus might retain distinctness indefinitely. In addition to the maturation of the second generation, sectarian accommodation may be encouraged by a shift in the balance of the sect's membership (a large number of converts), a change in secular circumstances (the outbreak of war, for example), or a change in the socioeconomic, educational, or other status variables of sect members (Wilson 1975:37). Moreover, accommodation might result from sectarian institution of bureaucracy: Sects require oversight and the development of organizational, most often hierarchic, structures in order to coordinate membership and worship. These structures must minimally: (1) determine the place and content of group meetings; (2) have some authority to call meetings and appoint members to preside over them; (3) make arrangements for administration and decision making; (4) establish agencies to "maintain essential agreement of belief and practice"; (5) make arrangements to accept new members; (6) define procedures for disciplining members; (7) designate group members to be specifically concerned with the socialization of new members; and (8) administer secular concerns (property ownership, education, taxes, etc.) (Wilson 1967:14). Sects thus develop structures of bureaucracy and organization which, although most often associated with denominations, may actually be used by sects to prevent denominationalization by structuring and enforcing a specific group identity (Wilson 1959).

In a marked departure from his earlier work, and from the work of other theorists, Wilson, in the 1980s and 1990s, insists that sects do not arise in "specific protest" against the church, but instead arise in protest against, and retain distinction from, the world (1981:90). Sects proscribe activities, prescribe behaviors, and advocate a belief system which is presented as being unique in its complete representation of truth. Sharing a history of distinctness in (to varying degrees) dress, behavior, diet, belief, and jargon, "each sect sustains an explicit culture" (ibid.:48). Rodney Stark and William Sims Bainbridge note that sects "disagree" with the larger society "over proper beliefs, norms, and behavior" (1985:49) and thus maintain "a state of tension" with their "surrounding sociocultural environments" (ibid.:23). Sects are forced, in order to preserve their identity, sense of destiny, and unique purpose and mission, to sustain a feeling of apartness—to cultivate a certain hostility toward secular society. Sectarians, however, who believe themselves to be in possession of unique, complete truth, are compelled to share with the world that truth which originally necessitated the development and maintenance of the sect's distinguishing characteristics. Thus, sectarians may choose to share their truth, but in so doing, threaten the distinctions to which that truth gave rise (see Teel 1980).

Sects, which arise in protest against secular society, are therefore originally framed as a radical departure from tradition, and may seek to reassert moral precepts which the sect deems to have been ignored by secular society. Rejection of secular norms and standards may allow the sect, in the context of a society which limits women's authority, to embrace participation by women in public religious leadership. A sect's "deviance," it must be noted, is influenced by the plurality of the society in which it arises, and its relationship with the world (its hostility or accommodation toward the world) may be shaped, in part, by changing social norms, beliefs, and behavioral expectations: "As society undergoes change, so do its margins and its concepts of marginality" (B. Wilson, 1990:21).

Though Weber's theory of religion of the nonprivileged classes is rarely employed by sociologists of religion and has not been previously applied in explication of Adventism, there is evidence that the theoretical framework provided by the church-sect typology, in conjunction with Weber's theory, is practicable for analysis of women in marginal religious movements such as Seventh-day Adventism. In one application of this theoretical approach, for example, Charles H. Barfoot and Gerald T. Sheppard (1980) found that Pentecostal women played a significant, even indispensable, role in the founding of the movement and its early growth. The authors found further that as the movement underwent the process of denominationalism, women were increasingly denied access to positions of leadership and authority that had previously been theirs. In another application, Hans Baer examined black spiritual churches and concluded that religious movements which "appeal to the disinherited often grant equality to women" (1993:66). Sociological theory of sectarian development points the way to understanding religious change and the ways in which movement from sectlike status to increasing denominationalism affects the gendered allotment of religious authority.

Analyses of Adventism

Previous explication of Seventh-day Adventism is limited, particularly with regard to discussion of the place or contribution of women in the movement. Most studies of Adventism are historical in approach and content, and even these, until the mid-1970s, omit serious examination of the historical, social, or political context of the origin or development of the movement. Though Adventists published widely, even from the movement's earliest years, the literature proffered concentrates on promulgating the message to believers and warning unbelievers of Christ's imminent coming.[3] It is not until the participation by large numbers of Adventist students in secular graduate programs in the late 1960s and thereafter that a body of serious scholarly work on Adventism emerges.

Early literature by Adventists, notably periodical publications such as the *Second Advent Review and Sabbath Herald* and the *Present Truth,* is religiously motivated and ignores explanations which might require secular examination of the movement's history (Graybill 1975; see Loughborough 1892). Those outside of the movement, moreover, did not attempt to examine Adventism except in flagrant and often harsh criticism of former Millerites. Later literature about Adventism is characterized by apologetic works by Adventists who attempt to defend the movement from internal detractors and external critics.[4] Studies of Adventism, then, especially prior to the 1970s, were primarily left to apologists and uncritical historians. Consequently, these explanations of the origins and development of the movement tend to be defensive, to dwell on divine explanations of historical progress and growth, and to emphasize the insider's explanation of history and disregard important elements of analysis.

The last three decades of the twentieth century saw a veritable explosion of works on both Adventism and its parent movement, Millerism, which demonstrate marked attention to secular academic standards of scholarship. Of import are Gary Schwartz's *Sect Ideologies and Social Status* (1970), Ronald Numbers's *Prophetess of Health: A Study of Ellen G. White* (1992 [1976]), P. Gerard Damsteegt's *Foundations of the Seventh-day Adventist Message and Mission* (1977), Ingemar Lindén's *The Last Trump* (1978), David L. Rowe's *Thunder and Trumpets* (1985), Steve Daily's "The Irony of Adventism: The Role of Ellen White and Other Adventist Women in Nineteenth Century America" (1985), Gary Land's *Adventism in America: A History* (1986), *The Disappointed: Millerism and Millenarianism in the Nineteenth Century* (1987) by Ronald L. Numbers and Jonathan M. Butler, *Seeking a Sanctuary: Seventh-day Adventism and the American Dream* (1989) by Malcolm Bull and Keith Lockhart, and Michael Pearson's *Millennial Dreams and Moral Dilemmas: Seventh-day Adventism and Contemporary Ethics* (1990). Most significantly, many works published during these decades move beyond accepted Adventist explanations to attempt to provide more objective analyses of Ellen White and Seventh-day Adventism. Specifically, recent scholars of Adventism undertake critical examination of Adventist history, including serious explication of Ellen White's role and prophetic writings and of contemporary Adventism. Though there is occasional reference to the place of women in the context of Adventist history and development in some of these works, however, none gives protracted attention to Adventist women, their contributions or their struggles to secure positions of authority within the movement.[5] The following analysis is unique, therefore, in its attempt to apply the sociological model of sectarian development to Seventh-day Adventism, while at the same time incorporating analysis of changing gender ideals.

Methodology

In order to assess the relationship between Adventism's changing response to the world and evolving gender ideals, I have employed multiple research methods. For a period of over a year, I participated extensively in four Adventist congregations in two primary research locations. Participant observation included taking part in a wide variety of Adventist gatherings and activities, including Sabbath worship services, prayer meetings, vespers, camp meeting, work parties, potlucks, student activities, community service, and women's meetings. This research was completed openly, with the knowledge and consent of selected congregations' pastoral staffs. Participant observation was supplemented most extensively by interviews with fifty active Adventists (thirty-nine women and eleven men) using a formal interview schedule. Interview participants were selected from rural and metropolitan congregations based on demographic data pertaining to Adventists in North America (see Sahlin 1989) using quota sampling methods.[6] In order to gain sufficient understanding of Adventist history, belief, and organization, and of the place of women within the movement, I consulted numerous Adventist publications and completed content analysis of almost one and one-half centuries of the *Adventist Review* (discussed in chapter 5). Last, in order to address questions pertaining to women's participation in the SDA pastorate, I completed a survey of all women and a random sample of men serving in pastoral capacities in North America (the North American Division; see chapter 9).

Seventh-day Adventism in Crisis: Gender and Sectarian Change in an Emerging Religion explores various facets of Seventh-day Adventism, including Adventist history, practice, belief, and crises of belief, and examines the complex relationship between Adventism's changing response to the world and the roles and positions available to Adventist women at different points in the movement's history. Part 1 outlines Adventism's emerging response to the world through a discussion of the history of the movement, institutionalization of the movement, and Adventist belief and crises of belief. Part 2 discusses the evolution of gender and gender ideals and expectations with reference to specific aspects of Adventist experience—the family, sexuality, wage labor participation, and the ministry—with particular attention to the relationship between sectarian change and concomitant ideals advocated for Adventist women. The work provides information pertaining to Adventist history; belief; organization; and ideals of gender, the family, and sexuality; and foremost, attempts to understand the evolution of women's position and authority in the context of this dynamic, growing religious movement.

Notes

1. As Wilson notes, Troeltsch's data were gathered primarily from sects that emphasized the advent and the coming millennium and in that respect are biased (1970).

2. Critics observe, however, that the seeming inevitability of denominational maturation inherent in Niebuhr's analysis cannot account for sects which persist over time (Martin 1962; Wilson 1970:233).

3. As Land observed in 1986, "Although a dynamic . . . entity on the religious scene, Seventh-day Adventism has a history that is neither well known nor well understood. This situation has come about largely because, until recently, Seventh-day Adventists, who look to an imminent Second Coming of Christ, took little serious interest in their own history" (1986b:vii).

4. Notable works include M. Ellsworth Olsen's *History of the Origins and Progress of Seventh-day Adventists* (1926) and Arthur Whitefield Spalding's four-volume *Origin and History of the Seventh-day Adventists.* LeRoy E. Froom, a major Adventist apologist, completed *The Prophetic Faith of Our Fathers,* a history (and defense) of Seventh-day Adventism.

5. The only exception is found in Daily's "The Irony of Adventism: The Role of Ellen White and Other Adventist Women in Nineteenth Century America" (1985), which explores the relationship between Ellen White's leadership and nineteenth-century notions of propriety and social change as they pertained to Adventist women, and the positions and roles available to Adventist women generally. Daily observes briefly the "direct correlation between growth of [Adventism's] hierarchical . . . structure and the decline of female participation and lay involvement in the decision making processes of the church" without offering any substantive explanation or examination of this process (1985:234).

6. Although Adventism is a worldwide religion, this examination considers the movement in North America and choice of research sites, each of which was located in the United States, reflects that bias. While this choice limits the generalizability of findings, it is not without justification. Despite wide geographic distribution of Adventist membership, SDA belief and practice remain highly consistent and uniform worldwide (Bull 1988:145). Originally a product of nineteenth-century American religious ferment, Adventism "is essentially an American phenomenon. Although [more than] 75 percent of the current world membership now resides in the third world, the ethos of the movement is unmistakably American" (Pearson 1990:9).

Part 1

Seventh-day Adventism Examined

1

Millerism and the Origins of Seventh-day Adventism

Historical Context: The Era of "Good Feeling"

Like many other sectarian movements indigenous to the United States, Adventism arose in the context of the Second Great Awakening of early nineteenth-century America. Dramatic national expansion in combination with the shift toward a more participatory democratic government during the Jacksonian era initiated religious fervor and revivalism in the young country (Dick 1986). In the midst of the optimism generated by the seemingly indefatigable expansion of the new nation, the notion that society could be made perfect took root: social and religious thinkers (perhaps most notably Charles Grandison Finney) shook Calvinism with the idea that perfection not only of the individual but of society was possible (see Johnson 1978).

Postmillennialism popularized the concept of free agency and the possibility of perfection that had been precluded by the predestination of Calvinism, and the implications of these possibilities lent purpose and momentum to both the religious revivals and the social reform movements of the nineteenth century. The prevailing notion of postmillennialism (that social perfection would usher in the millennium) gave rise to humanitarian reform movements and offered a compelling incentive for mass religious conversion (see Mustard 1988). The best known and most successful proponent of universal conversion, Charles Finney (1792–1875), employed innovative and evocative techniques, including the anxious seat, private and public prayer, and "direct and colloquial preaching," to create an emotion-laden, personal religious climate in which religious revival burgeoned. (The number of Protestants in the United States doubled between 1800 and 1855 largely as a result of Finney's efforts [see Dick 1986].)[1] America was "'drunk on millennialism': Joseph Smith preached a premillennial eschatology; the Shakers shared the message that Christ had returned in Mother Ann Lee, and John Humphry Noyes of the Oneida community insisted that the millennium had occurred in A.D. 70" (Lindén 1978:3). In the secular realm too, people became enthusiastically dedicated to ushering in a utopian age. No longer interested in gradually evolving social change, many secular reformers "were convinced that revolution was essential, and worked for quick results" (ibid.). Social reformers, including abolitionists, suffragists, temperance workers, and health and education reformers, as well as those attempting to organize labor unions, enact penal reform, and institute more humane treatment of the mentally ill, saw in society the possibility not only of dramatic and meaningful social reform but ultimately of social perfection. Especially after 1830, social reform movements and religious revivals looked "less to the salvation of the individual only; [instead the movements took as their goal] nothing less than working in an organized fashion for the salvation of the whole world" (Lindén 1978:8).

This "era of good feeling," however, was splintered under the economic pressures of the depression of 1837 and the social tension and controversy surrounding slavery. The unity and purpose of the movements of the first decades of the nineteenth century gave way, by the late 1830s and early 1840s, to divisiveness. Finney and a plethora of revivalists connected with reform movements expected soon-to-be-achieved social perfection; the enthusiasm and hope generated by religious revivals led, under the pressure of disappointment stemming from failed expectations, to the emergence of new religious sects (see Damsteegt 1977).

Heralding Christ's Soon Coming: William Miller and the Millerites

William Miller was born the eldest of sixteen children in Massachusetts in 1782, but spent his childhood and youth in Low Hampton, New York, where he assisted his father on the family's farm. Although a prolific reader and curious student, Miller was able to attend public schools only until age nine; his insatiable love of literature did not go unnoticed, however, and Miller was granted access to the private libraries of two of the Millers' neighbors (Judd 1987), through which he studied European history.[2] In 1803 Miller married Lucy Smith and the couple moved to Poultney, Vermont, where Miller had access for the first time to a public library. Despite having been groomed by his mother for the Baptist ministry, Miller's studies in Poultney led him to conclude that the Bible was inconsistent and that the history of Christianity was one of oppression (see ibid.). Following a pattern not uncommon in Vermont at that time, Miller left his Baptist heritage to embrace Deism.

As a volunteer captain in the war of 1812, Miller was disillusioned with God and humanity. Haunted by the constant death that surrounded him on the battlefield, Miller began to hope for the possibility of immortality, even if it presupposed the "heaven and hell of the scriptures" (Judd 1987). Miller found the evidence of divinity that he sought when fifteen hundred American troops and four thousand volunteers defeated fifteen thousand British troops at the Battle of Plattsburg. Attributing the unlikely victory to divine intervention, Miller was poised after his discharge in 1815 to commence a personal spiritual struggle (Dick 1986).

Upon his return from military service, Miller began regularly to attend Baptist religious services and, on occasion, to read prepared sermons to the congregation. In one instance, reading a sermon on parenting, Miller became overwhelmed with emotion and was impressed that "there might be a being so good as to himself atone for our transgressions, and thereby save us from suffering the penalty of sin" (Judd 1987:20). Following this 1816 personal conversion experience, Miller accepted Christ as a divine personal savior, joined the Baptist church, and on occasion served as a Baptist lay minister. After his conversion Miller was mocked by Deist friends who cited to him the same proofs of biblical error and inconsistency he had previously recited. Confronted by these evidences, Miller set out to prove to his Deist friends that the Bible was accurate and consistent; he determined that he would "harmonize all those apparent contradictions" of the Bible or renounce his newfound faith and reclaim Deism (ibid.:7).

In his examination of the Bible, Miller adopted hermeneutic principles of interpretation based on a Protestant tradition that held the Bible to be self-authenticating and solely sufficient (Damsteegt 1977:17, 18). This method—Biblicism—"the principle that the Bible is to be considered wholly homogenous and that any passage can be used to clarify the significance of any other irrespective of context," was a method of biblical interpretation commonly used by Miller's Protestant contemporaries (Lindén 1978:28).[3] Miller's rules of scriptural interpretation assumed that all biblical prophecies had been or would be literally and completely fulfilled, that the Bible (accompanied by Cruden's Concordance) was sufficient for full understanding of God's word, and that the most important rule of study was faith.[4] Miller "began reading the Bible in a methodical manner; and by comparing scripture with scripture and taking notice of the manner of prophesying and how it was fulfilled" he found repeatedly "that prophecy had been literally fulfilled" and, further, that "God had explained all the figures and metaphors in the Bible, or had given rules for their explanation. . . . And in every case where time had been revealed every event was accomplished as predicted. . . . Therefore I believed that all would be accomplished" (Miller in Bird 1961:9). Employing the year/day principle (the not-uncommon assumption that a biblical reference to one day could be literally interpreted as one year) Miller determined in 1818 that the 2,300 days of Daniel 8:14[5] had commenced in 457 B.C. with the rebuilding of Jerusalem by Artaxerxes' decree and that Christ would return to the sanctuary (earth, according to Miller), the wicked would be condemned, and the righteous would be saved "on or around" 1843 (Dick 1986:4).[6]

Unsure of his ability to disseminate the message that he had uncovered, Miller was nonetheless hounded by a sense of personal responsibility to warn others of Christ's soon coming and the judgment which would follow.[7] After protracted personal turmoil over perceived divine prompting to share his findings, Miller, one morning, feeling strongly impressed that he should share his discovery, covenanted with God that if provided an opportunity to preach he would "perform [his] duty to the world" and tell others of the coming advent (Judd 1987:19). Within half an hour Miller's nephew arrived with an invitation to preach to the Baptists of Dresden, New York. Miller accepted, was warmly received by the congregation, and thus commenced to herald the advent.

"Conditions [were] . . . eminently favorable [in the early 1830s] to the acceptance of Miller's apocalyptic views" (Lindén 1978:40). A number of supernatural events, including the "Dark Day" of May 1780[8] and a great meteor shower of November 13, 1833, were widely regarded as signs that the end of the world was fast approaching. Miller's message stirred interest and religious revivals followed his speaking engagements. For one and one-half years Miller remained in Low Hampton, and although he met with unexpected success in sharing his message in that locale, he would have remained an obscure figure had he not met his eventual supporter and enthusiastic promoter, Joshua V. Himes.

Himes originally extended an invitation to Miller to speak to his Boston Christian Connection congregation in spite of his uncertainty about the accuracy of Miller's advent message. After meeting with Miller, however, and hearing him speak, Himes became convinced of the urgency (if not *accuracy*) of Miller's message (Dick 1986). In Himes, Miller found the publicist he needed to promote him in telling the world of Christ's imminent advent—active in the temperance, suffrage, nonresistance, and anti-slavery movements, Himes was well versed in the art of promoting an idea. He immediately embraced the nineteenth-century technology available to him in an effort to tell the world about Miller's parousia.

Himes took Miller from rural Low Hampton and arranged his speaking engagements in urban New England. He oversaw the publication and mass distribution of tracts, pamphlets, and hymnals, established adventist libraries in cities across the United States, coordinated, raised, and administered funds, and provided leadership to the genesis and burgeoning of the Millerite movement.[9] Perhaps most important, Himes commenced publication and distribution of periodicals in conjunction with Miller's speaking engagements. In addition to publishing several long-term periodicals, Himes regularly published and distributed an adventist paper for a short period in a specific locale prior to renting a public hall or auditorium in which Miller was to speak.[10] Miller's presentations were well publicized and Miller began to attract thousands of listeners to urban lecture series (Lindén 1978:51).[11] Miller quickly garnered a reputation for stirring religious revival and was a much-sought-after visiting preacher, leaving renewed religious commitment and numerous conversions in his wake.[12]

Miller and Himes were by no means alone, however, in warning the world of the soon coming parousia. Converts to Miller's message included religious leaders with ties to a variety of denominations, but especially Methodists and Baptists (as well as, to a lesser extent, members of the Christian Connection) who felt compelled to assist in warning the world of Christ's imminent return. These ordained and lay ministers relied upon adventist publications, including periodicals and prophetic charts (graphic illustrations portraying scenes from Daniel and Revelation), to warn any who might potentially comprise an audience to prepare for Christ's soon coming. Although Miller insisted adamantly and repeatedly in the 1830s and 1840s that he had no intention of organizing a distinct religious body, leaders necessarily emerged among Miller's followers in order to ensure that the logistical requirements of publishing and distributing periodicals were met, that halls and auditoriums were rented, that lecture series were advertised, and that all of the necessary components of what was becoming a mass movement within mainstream Protestantism were coordinated.

Regardless of repeated references in sociological and historical literature to "Millerites," however, Miller's following was comprised of a broad cross section of Protestants from various denominations who rarely severed their original ties of denominational affiliation (especially before 1844). Researchers have suggested that there were between ten thousand and one million Millerites. This vast numerical discrepancy arises from the ambiguity inherent in identifying Millerites: because they remained within Protestant churches, Millerism was only one component of most Millerites' identities (Doan 1987a). Conservative estimates based upon records of active participation in the movement suggest that there were at least 25,000–50,000 active Millerite adherents by 1844 (Rowe 1987);[13] a much larger number of people undoubtedly read about, heard of, and were influenced by Miller's message (Doan 1987a).[14] The only indicator, initially, of adherence to Millerite millennial convictions was a sense of urgency surrounding the desire to prepare for the advent. Miller and other Millerite leaders originally embraced a broad, ecumenical following. Miller wrote, for example, that "our fellow laborers are among the choicest of the faithful in Christ from among all denominations."[15] "We know no sect, or party, as such while we respect all. . . . We have no purpose to distract the churches . . . or to get ourselves a name by starting another sect among the followers of the lamb. We neither condemn nor rudely assail, others of a faith different from our own, nor seek to demolish their organizations; nor build new ones of our own" (in Doan 1987b:96).

Early Millerites saw the advent hope as uniting Christians across denominational barriers and prided themselves on their refusal to form a new religious organization. Millerites boasted that they had "no constitution, bye-laws, or anything bearing the stamp of organization" (Doan 1987a:123). But as even the formation of the Millerite General Conference demonstrates, Miller's adherents were forced to organize themselves in order to oversee the practical matters involved in spreading the advent message (Doan 1987a). The Millerite General Conference, which was formed in 1840, continued to meet through 1842 and was replaced in 1843 by organized local gatherings of Millerites which were more widely accessible to a greater number of believers. The General Conference increased its emphasis, beginning in 1841, on promoting worship services (prayer meetings and Bible classes) specifically for Millerites. This emphasis, coupled with Millerite camp meetings and publications, contributed to an increasing sense of unique, shared identity (Dick 1986:18). Though Millerite leaders continued to insist that they had no intention of "taking a name" or assuming a unique Protestant identity and thereby instigating a new and separate religious sect, mainline denominations were increasingly threatened by the organizational and evangelical successes of the Millerites. In the face of emerging denominational hostility, Millerites were, by 1842, prevented in many cases from renting public spaces for meetings and were forced to rely on tents purchased for the purpose of camp meetings.[16] In the same year, Millerites, facing enmity in their local congregations, began to raise questions about the possibility of separating from the mainline denominations; they were advised in Millerite publications, however, to remain in their congregations (Mustard 1988).

Nevertheless, the belief in an imminent advent made eventual Millerite separation from mainline Protestant denominations inevitable: "Adventism . . . evoked such a fervent commitment from its adherents that sectarian withdrawal was an historical inevitability" (Judd 1984:3). Although Miller's parousia evoked strong responses and inspired religious revival, the Millerite tendency, especially after 1842, to set dates for the expected advent that were "scandalously imminent" threatened and angered mainstream Protestant leaders.

Prior to 1842 prominent Millerite leaders, including William Miller, "solemnly protested" "against the setting of the hour, day, or month, of the end of the world" (Damsteegt 1977:37). The failure of Miller's original expectation that the sanctuary was to be cleansed in 1843 was not met with severe disappointment, in part because Miller consistently discouraged the emphasis of a specific date for the parousia.[17] After the 1843 disappointment, Miller adjusted his expectation, basing it on the Jewish calendar (which according to Miller's calculations extended 1843 until the spring of 1844) and Millerites continued to warn the world of Christ's soon coming. When April 18, 1844, passed and again there was no sign of Christ's coming, Millerite leaders expressed disappointment, and some Millerites became disillusioned and left the movement, but the larger part of Miller's following "continue[d] on with renewed courage and hope" (Dick 1986:26). Millerites had created a movement within Protestantism that was dedicated to convincing all of Christ's soon coming, and while the faith and dedication of that commitment did not fail in the face of initial disappointment, the group had coalesced around the hope of Christ's return "on or about" 1843, and when that central organizing tenet was lost, confusion threatened the movement (Doan 1987a).

A specific expectation for the advent around which to organize was presented to the group by Samuel S. Snow at a New Hampshire camp meeting on August 12, 1844.[18] Snow presented to the gathered Millerites "a message the people were thirsty for" (Dick 1986:27). Christ would return to the earth on the Jewish Day of Atonement, Snow insisted, the tenth day of the seventh month of the year—October 22, 1844. Snow's new date was welcomed by the group, which had begun to flounder without a specific expectation for Christ's return. The seventh month movement was an "immediate success" (Lindén 1978:60): "The influence of this time message went forth like the released waters of a mighty river when the dam has given way" (Dick 1986:27–28). This, Millerites agreed, was the "true midnight cry."[19] By the autumn of 1844, Snow's date was almost universally accepted by Millerites (Damsteegt 1977). Even William Miller, who had expressly opposed further date-setting, was "swept away" by the enthusiastic reception Snow's prediction received (Teel 1984:20).[20]

If the seventh-month movement set Millerites aflame with religious fervor, it also exacerbated the fears of mainline Protestantism. Millerites were increasingly perceived as a threat to the denominations when, in the enthusiasm generated by the seventh-month movement, they became "more active, more precise, and . . . perhaps most important of all . . . more popular" (Doan

1987b:27). Millerites, expecting Christ's imminent return, led successful evangelical efforts in which the date of Christ's expected coming was stressed more than adherence to any particular Protestant belief system. Protestant leaders, threatened by this emphasis on the advent, began to denounce Miller from their lecterns and to disfellowship Millerites from their congregations.

Prior to 1843, Millerite ecclesiology identified Catholicism as the Laodicean ("lukewarm") church; with increased persecution of Millerites within mainline Protestant denominations in 1843 and 1844, however, Millerite periodicals identified Protestant denominations as the "daughters of the Harlot" because they continued to expect a pre-advent, earthly millennium and to deny Christ's soon coming (Damsteegt 1977:80). Tension continued to mount until Charles Fitch, a prominent Millerite preacher, delivered a sermon (widely published and distributed among Millerites) in which he identified Catholicism as the Anti-Christ and Protestantism as "Babylon," and admonished: "If you are a Christian, come out of Babylon! If you intend to be a Christian when Christ appears, come out of Babylon, and come out now!" (ibid.). Fitch's 1843 message, though it was not accepted by the majority of Millerite preachers "with any degree of unanimity" until 1844, had a profound impact upon other Millerites (Mustard 1988:59). Departure from Protestant denominations came to be seen as necessary in order to achieve salvation (Damsteegt 1977:81). Further, the cry, "Come out of Babylon," came to represent, for adventists, not only a separation from Protestantism and Catholicism but from the "established order in general: 'not only the churches, but the governments of the world, too, were a part of Babylon'" (Teel 1984:20).

The Great Disappointment

It would be difficult to overstate Millerite belief in and hope for the October 22, 1844, parousia. On October 16, 1844, *Advent Herald* editors wrote that "our work is finished and . . . all we have to do is go out and meet the Bridegroom and to trim our lamps accordingly" (Damsteegt 1977:99). Much has been made of the bizarre behaviors in which Millerites are said to have participated as they prepared, in the autumn of 1844, to meet Christ. The popular press of the time relied upon secondhand accounts to report about Millerites dressed in white ascension robes, sitting on housetops and in trees, eyes heavenward, watching the clouds to catch the first glimpse of Christ. Certainly Millerites did engage in emotional expressions of religious feeling (including falling prostrate, crying out, and swooning), but accounts of rampant insanity among Miller's followers have been overstated (see Numbers and Numbers 1992), and examples of fanaticism among Millerite leaders were the exception rather than the rule (Dick 1986). As Whitney Cross noted, our understanding of the Millerite movement, and particularly of the Great Disappointment, has become "shrouded in the fantastical images of critics' imaginations": "Thievery, murder, lasciviousness and insanity; the preparation of ascension robes in such numbers as to boom the textile markets; gatherings in cemeteries . . . the indictments against Adventists, grown in folklore, have commonly been written into history without close examination" (Cross in Lindén 1978:63).

Nonetheless, Millerites, expecting Christ to return to the earth on October 22, 1844, made preparations for that eventuality. Millerites, in the summer and autumn of 1844, failed to harvest crops, paid off debts, disposed of earthly possessions, and, on October 22, closed their businesses and stayed away from work to watch for Christ's coming (Lindén 1978; Dick 1986). Believers waited all day and into the night for the parousia; Miller sat atop a hill close to his home so that he could easily glimpse the descending Christ. When midnight passed with no sign of the advent, Miller and his followers experienced bitter disappointment; believers "wept till the day dawned" (Dick 1986:30). As Ellen White later wrote:

> The earnest, sincere believers had given up all for Christ, and had shared his presence [in preparing for the advent] as never before. They had, as they believed, given their last warning to the world; and expected soon to be received into the society of their divine master and the heavenly angels; they had, to a great extent, withdrawn from the society of those who did not receive the message. With intense desire they had prayed, "Come Lord Jesus, and come quickly." But he had not come. And how to take up again the many burdens of life's cares and perplexities, and to endure the taunts and sneers of a scoffing world, was a terrible trial of faith and patience. (White 1911 [1888]:404)

Resumption of earthly responsibilities was particularly difficult for Millerites who refused to prepare for winter in their eagerness to demonstrate their unwavering faith in Christ's imminent return. Himes began, immediately following the Great Disappointment, to organize the delivery of foodstuffs and other necessities from Millerites who had stockpiled goods for the upcoming winter to those who had not. Although the physical strain of meeting immediate needs was exacerbated by the hostility demonstrated toward Millerites by those outside the movement in the national press and in mainstream Protestant churches (Millerites were mocked as extremists and lunatics), Millerite leadership, under Himes's guidance, began to regroup. On April 29, 1845, Millerite leaders converged in Albany, New York, in an attempt to coalesce and reunite advent believers. Using the conference to reiterate their doctrinal position, to encourage believers, and to initiate a lose organization under which believers could gather in worship, Miller, Himes, and other Millerite leaders also attempted to use the meeting to distinguish and distance themselves from "extremist" groups emerging from the rubble of the Great Disappointment (see Lindén 1978). Among these factions was a group of sabbatarian adventists associated with a seventeen-year-old named Ellen Harmon.

Ellen White and the Emergence of Sabbatarian Adventism

Born on November 27, 1827, in Gorham, Maine, Ellen Harmon was indelibly affected by the religious revival sweeping through the northeastern United States in the 1820s and 1830s. As a child Ellen participated with her family in daily Bible study, prayer, and witnessing activities among neighbors and acquaintances. The Harmons were actively involved in their Methodist congregation, and it was there that Ellen's penchant for enthusiastic religious worship was nurtured by her own and her mother's identification with the congregation's "shouters" (ecstatic worshipers who shouted "amen" and "hallelujah" and otherwise participated unreservedly in religious worship) (Butler 1991). Prophecy, glossolalia, and visions were common in the Methodism of Ellen White's childhood (Lindén 1978). In addition, Ellen watched women participate in religious worship as Methodists, unlike their contemporaries, "permitted . . . females to exhort their churches" and allowed women "an equal right to take part in the religious manifestations" at religious gatherings held in private homes (ibid.:145, 146).

In addition to the religious devotion of her childhood home and the religious excitement of her public worship experience, two incidents of Ellen's childhood set her on a course of spiritual contemplation. At age nine, while walking home from school with her twin, Elizabeth, Ellen was hit in the head by a stone thrown by a schoolmate "angry at some trifle" (Lindén 1978:149). Ellen arrived at home hemorrhaging seriously and fell unconscious for three weeks (Daily 1985:43; Butler 1991). Though she was not initially expected to survive, Ellen eventually recovered enough to be able to sit up in bed and resume shaping crowns for her father's hat-making business. Ellen, who had been at least an above-average student prior the incident, was unable to pursue her studies as a result of the physical effects of her injury. In this predicament, Ellen began to concentrate on death, on seeing Christ at death, on spiritual preparation for redemption, and on cultivating a personal, intimate relationship with God (Butler 1991); she began to pray earnestly, sometimes all night, speaking "intimately with Jesus and the angels" (Lindén 1978:149).

Ellen's spiritual concerns were fed by a fear of the end of the world. In 1836, upon finding a scrap of paper on the ground announcing the imminent end of the world, Ellen was "seized with terror" and "could [scarcely] sleep for several nights and prayed continually to be ready when Jesus came" (Lindén 1978:150). Concerned about her unreadiness for Christ's return, Ellen felt a brief emotional reprieve when she experienced personal conversion at a Methodist camp meeting in Baxton, Maine. Following her conversion experience, Ellen presented herself for baptism and membership in the Methodist church, but was troubled by the prospect of testifying about her conversion experience in a public meeting, as young converts were expected to do. Unsure of her own righteousness, Ellen hesitated to share her experience until, while attending a religious meeting at her uncle's house, she underwent the first of hundreds of religious trances.[21] Standing in a prayer circle with other worshipers, Ellen was silent until: "My voice rose around in prayer before I was aware of it. . . . As I prayed the burden of agony of soul that I had so long endured, left me. . . . Everything seemed to be put out from me but Jesus and his glory, and I lost consciousness of what was passing around me" (White in Lindén 1978:148).

When William Miller visited Portland, Maine, in the early 1840s, Ellen Harmon was prepared to hear his message of the imminent advent—her protracted spiritual struggles in combination with her poor health made her especially receptive to Miller's idea of the soon coming Christ. Ellen first heard Miller's message at a camp meeting that she attended in Portland, Maine, with her parents in 1840. Though poor health prevented Ellen from attending many later Millerite lectures, Miller's message was discussed extensively in the Harmon household. When the Harmons accepted Miller's message in the early 1840s, they were asked by their minister to withdraw their memberships from the Methodist church; when they refused, in 1843, the Harmons were excommunicated. The Harmons, in turn, joined with other Portland Millerites in preparing for Christ's soon return.

When the Great Disappointment shattered the hopes of many Millerites, Ellen was discouraged, but she did not lose her faith in Christ's soon coming. As other Millerites attempted to explain the apparent failure of October 22, 1844, Ellen, firm in her faith that Christ would soon appear, was in precarious health, suffering from a collapsed lung and heart trouble. In December of 1844, attending a prayer meeting at a friend's home, Ellen experienced her first vision. As she later described it, she saw the "travels of the Advent people to the holy city" and saw that Miller's message had been the truth for salvation (White 1915:64). Ellen saw that those 144,000 who remained on the path (remained faithful to Miller's message) were welcomed into the Kingdom of God, and she interpreted her vision as meaning that William Miller had been correct—adventists must simply persist in their conviction that Christ would return soon.[22]

In the context of religious fervor and failed expectations following the Great Disappointment, Ellen Harmon's confirmation that Millerites had been correct in their hope for the advent was welcomed by adventists hungry for renewed religious hope. Ellen Harmon's claim of inspiration was accepted following her first visions by about sixty Portland adventists who testified to the divine nature of her prophecies. In the context of heightened religious activity (Pearson 1990:58) following the Great Disappointment, Ellen Harmon, an introverted, "frail" young woman, garnered the role of prophet (Butler 1991:15). One week after her first vision, Harmon had a second vision in which she was shown the trials through which she must pass. Realizing that she was being called by God to serve, Harmon "shrank in terror from the thought of being a prophet" (ibid.:12). For days she pleaded with God to relieve her burden, but Harmon could not rid herself of her calling. Notwithstanding her poor health, youth, and limited financial resources, Harmon was convinced that God had given her responsibility to share her visions with adventist believers.

Consequently, in the winter of 1844–45, despite failing health and other difficulties, Harmon traveled across New England reassuring believers that their convictions of the advent were correct and that "time could last but a little longer" (Lindén 1978). While traveling in Orrington, Maine, Ellen met James White, a Millerite lay preacher who, after becoming convinced of the truth of Harmon's visions, joined Harmon and her sisters in their travels. In spite of their convictions that the advent was imminent, the two attempted to curtail rumors arising out of the assumed impropriety of their unchaperoned travel, and married on August 30, 1846.[23]

Ellen White emerged as a divine messenger in a context of intense emotional upheaval following the Great Disappointment (Bull 1988). Emotionalism was an important and prominent characteristic of early Adventism (Daily 1985:35), though Adventists were not atypical in this respect (Bull and Lockhart 1989: 89).[24] The leadership provided by Ellen White served to calm the religious intensity of early adventists and to encourage them to make the transition from a scattered band of believers to a body of organized worshipers. White's early visions were not mundane: while in vision Ellen White would fall to the floor in a trance-like state, rise to walk about the room, limbs stiff, and speak in a loud voice of things others couldn't see.[25] Yet White's visions served to legitimate more organized, mundane worship as White used her increasing authority to legitimate specific beliefs and practices and to settle points of doctrinal dispute. In her early years as a prophet, Ellen White entered a vision crying

"GLORY! Glory! glory!" She is said to have possessed superhuman strength while in vision and to have walked about the room, eyes open, head raised "toward heaven."[26] Yet in this context of religious excitement, Ellen White used the faith that she inspired to promote consensus. When adventist leaders were unable to reach agreement upon the meaning of Scripture, Ellen White, who "couldn't understand" the Bible on her own, had visions in which she was shown the meaning of the disputed passage(s). It came to be necessary, as the scattered believers in the advent came together, to organize into a collective body of believers—to rely upon "the spirit of prophecy" to interpret and understand Scripture (Bull and Lockhart 1989:26). Ellen White thus created, as a divine messenger, unity in an emerging and otherwise divided movement (Lindén 1978:133).

As she matured, Ellen White evolved from a young visionary who was completely absorbed and physically influenced by the "spirit"—rolling on the floor and so on—to a more conservative prophet who increasingly distrusted emotionalism in worship (Bull and Lockhart 1989:65). The dramatic waking visions of the 1840s and 1850s declined in frequency during the 1860s and were replaced entirely, in the 1870s, by religious dreams (see Graybill 1983). The mature Ellen White spoke out against emotional displays in religious worship and instead encouraged sobriety in worship (see also Lindén 1978).

The Rise of Seventh-day Sabbatarians: Understanding the Heavenly Sanctuary and the Sabbath

It would be inaccurate, however, to portray the emergence of Adventism as coming about effortlessly, or even easily, from the ashes of the Great Disappointment. The disappointment of October 22, 1844, "was a humiliating thing and all felt it alike" (Arthur 1974:5). As Millerites explained at the time, "all hopes were fixed on that day," and when Christ did not appear they experienced "absolute disappointment" and an "all pervading feeling of emptiness": "All were silent save to inquire, 'Where are we?' and 'What next?'" (ibid.). Following the Great Disappointment, Millerite adherents were forced to reevaluate their beliefs and to reinterpret Miller's message. It was a time of confusion, perplexity, and disillusionment (Adams 1981:19). Four distinct groups emerged from the post-1844 confusion. The first attributed Miller's predictions to human fallibility or satanic influence, gave up their adherence to Miller's message, and returned to their original (pre-Millerite) church affiliation or renounced religion; the second group, comprised of the most prominent and best-educated Millerites (including William Miller and Joshua Himes), concluded that the October 22 date was in error, that Christ was still "at the door," and continued activities to prepare for the soon coming advent; the third group persisted in their belief that the October 22 date had been correct and insisted that Miller had been inaccurate in his prediction of events. This group, deemed Spiritualists, believed that Christ had returned to the earth in spirit form on October 22, 1844, and following that date, dwelt within them, rendering their flesh holy and their bodies immortal. Spiritualists practiced foot washing, observed the seventh-day Sabbath, and formed "spiritual couples" or "spiritual matrimony without sexual connection" (Arthur 1974:7; Adams 1993:20).[27]

The fourth group to emerge from the Great Disappointment was comprised of the most enthusiastic faction of Millerites who, like the Spiritualists, maintained that Miller's expected event rather than his predicted date had been in error (Butler 1991). On the morning following the Great Disappointment, Hiram Edson, a Millerite lay preacher who had spent October 22 in prayer waiting for Christ's coming, and when midnight came and Christ had not appeared, in scriptural study trying to make sense of the failed advent, received a vision from which contemporary Adventist eschatology has grown. Edson was walking through a cornfield on his way to comfort fellow believers when he saw in vision that the sanctuary to be cleansed on October 22 was a *heavenly*, rather than an earthly, sanctuary. He later wrote: "I saw distinctly and clearly that instead of our high priest coming out of the Most Holy of the heavenly sanctuary to come to this earth on the tenth day of the seventh month, at the end of 2,300 days, that He for the first time entered on that day the second apartment of that sanctuary; and that he had a work to perform in the Most Holy Place before coming to this earth" (in Damsteegt 1989:17). Edson's new understanding of the cleansing of the sanctuary was presented to Millerites by F. B. Hahn and Owen R. L. Crosier in an 1846 Millerite journal (of which James White and Joseph Bates each received a copy).[28]

The original adventist understanding of the heavenly sanctuary explained Christ's failure to appear in the autumn of 1844, reinforced belief in Miller's chronology, and created new expectations (though simultaneously discouraging further date-setting) of Christ's coming (Adams 1981). Instead of returning to earth on October 22, 1844, Christ had entered the second apartment of the heavenly sanctuary; he had left the Holy Place to commence work in the Most Holy Place; he began the final judgment of humanity (Butler 1991:10). When this final, exacting judgment was complete, Christ would come again to the earth (Pearson 1990:6; for discussion of SDA understanding of the heavenly sanctuary and the investigative judgment, see chapter 2).

Their emerging understanding of the sanctuary allowed adventists to rene-gotiate their perception of the Great Disappointment. Christ had not failed adventists, they had simply misunderstood his intention: "The subject of the sanctuary was the key which unlocked the disappointment of 1844" (Dam-steegt 1989:171). Further, the sanctuary doctrine gave believers in the advent new purpose. In 1844, "the people were not yet ready to meet their Lord. There was still a work of preparation to be accomplished among them. Light was to be given, directing their minds to the temple of God in heaven; . . . new du-ties [were to] be revealed" (White 1911 [1888]:425).

Because Seventh-day Adventism emerged from Millerism instead of from one established Protestant belief system, early adventists had no single unit-ing doctrine or event and therefore no one group from which to distinguish themselves, or to which they could return (Bull and Lockhart 1989:86).[29] Their belief in the sanctuary, however, provided adventists with a foundation on which to build a shared belief system. Less crucial, but also serving to provide a basis for a distinct, shared identity, was the adventist adherence to the seventh-day (Saturday) Sabbath, introduced to Adventists by Seventh-day Baptists.[30] Belief in the seventh-day Sabbath was joined with the adventist understand-ing of the heavenly sanctuary to create a more complete, shared conception of the Great Disappointment: Christ did not return in 1844 because he needed to complete his heavenly ministry and because the Sabbath (the seventh-day Sabbath, the *true* Sabbath) had to be restored prior to the advent. For early adventists, the delay of Christ's return, the cleansing of the heavenly sanctu-ary, and the seventh-day Sabbath were interrelated; Christ's work in the heav-enly sanctuary and the restoration of the seventh-day Sabbath became the justification for, and the explanation of, the Seventh-day Adventist theology of mission (Damsteegt 1989:164). Adventists were no longer simply disap-pointed believers in the advent; they were fast becoming a group (though still geographically isolated) of believers in the advent hope sharing a specific eschatology. The introduction of Saturday worship did not render early adventists outsiders—they had been outsiders as Millerites; it did set them apart from other Millerite factions (Bull and Lockhart 1989:86).[31]

This coalescence of sabbatarian adventists was augmented by an 1848 series of Bible conferences, at which fifty adventists met to study the seventh-day Sabbath and the sanctuary doctrine. Disagreements over the sanctuary doc-trine and the divine nature of Ellen White's visions ("the spirit of prophecy") were settled (Anderson 1986) and the 1848 conferences enabled the adventist remnant to "develop a new unity and identity" especially in regard to the issues discussed above (Mustard 1988:99). While attending the conferences, Ellen White received a vision in which she was instructed that James should commence to "print a little paper"—a regular publication of adventist theology and news, to unite sabbatarian adventists.[32] The conferences, in conjunction with the new periodical (the *Second Advent Review and Herald of the Sabbath*), were "pivotal to the survival of the Sabbatarian Advent movement" (ibid.).

Early Controversy: The Shut Door and Evangelism

In part as a result of the unity surrounding the 1848 conferences and, more especially, as a consequence of the shared disappointment experienced by adventists in 1844 (not only when Christ failed to return but when advent believers were humiliated in the press and from Protestant pulpits), by the late 1840s adventists had developed the idea that the "door to salvation" had been "shut" in 1844, and that only those who had accepted Miller's message prior to the Great Disappointment had any hope for salvation (see Pearson 1990).[33] The prospect of salvation for those "in the world" (non-Millerites and, later, nonsabbatarian adventists) was gone, "shut door" proponents argued, after 1844. Because the door to salvation was closed, according to James and Ellen White, evangelism was not possible. Believers were encouraged only to continue to prepare and wait for Christ's imminent coming (Arthur 1974:6; Mustard 1988). Many sabbatarian adventists were not convinced, however, that salvation was available only to those who had accepted Miller's message prior to the Great Disappointment. Children born after 1844 had no opportunity to accept Miller's message and, despite their lack of evangelical effort, Sabbath-keepers found that some who had not participated in the Millerite movement, upon hearing the message of the advent, the sanctuary, and the Sabbath, desired to join Sabbath-keeping adventists.

Conflict surrounding the "shut door" doctrine resulted. In May of 1850, when James White commenced publication of the *Advent Review,* Ellen White, who had had visions confirming that the door to salvation was closed in 1844, was denied an audience. Although James did consent to publish five articles by Ellen between 1851 and 1855, there was no mention in the *Review* of her prophetic role or of her visions (Anderson 1986). As James made the editorial decision not to publish Ellen's visions, they became less frequent until, in 1855, Ellen concluded that her work for the movement was complete (Haloviak 1985:2).[34]

Adventists abandoned the "shut door" in the early 1850s as the belief proved increasingly untenable. First, sabbatarian adventists were induced to acknowl-

edge that the children of believers might achieve salvation; then former Millerites (not leaders of the movement but those who had been "led astray" by
the movement's leaders after the Great Disappointment) who attended
adventist gatherings and accepted the sanctuary doctrine as well as the seventh-day Sabbath were allowed the possibility of salvation (Damsteegt 1977).
Perhaps the greatest factor in opening the door of salvation and, in effect, allowing those not previously associated with Millerism to join the sabbatarian
adventist movement was the realization by adventists that successful evangelism was possible. Adventist publications (the *Present Truth* and, a few years
later, the *Advent Herald*) led some who had had no connection with Millerism
to desire to join Sabbath-keepers in preparing for Christ's soon coming.

Acknowledging that some members of mainline Protestantism could yet
"come out of Babylon," accept the adventist message, and be saved, adventists
eventually moved away from the "shut door" altogether, thus opening the way
for evangelical efforts. By the late 1840s Ellen White increasingly spoke of future missionary work among nonbelievers. In addition, there was growing
concern among sabbatarian adventists (who numbered about one hundred at
that time) that they needed to increase the number of believers to the 144,000
who were, according to Revelation, to receive salvation at Christ's return. In
1849 both James and Ellen White made statements encouraging missionary
efforts among nonbelievers.[35] Although adventist evangelical efforts were most
encouraged (and most successful) among ex-Millerites, Ellen White's visions
of future missionary success were primarily responsible for the adventists'
eventual shift in emphasis toward evangelism among those unfamiliar with
the advent message (Damsteegt 1977:162). By 1851 James White considered it
possible for some who had *rejected* the 1844 message to join the sabbatarian
adventist movement and thereby have access to salvation (Mustard 1988).[36]

As controversy surrounding the open/shut door was resolved in favor of the
possibility of salvation for, and, concomitantly, of the necessity of evangelism
among, nonbelievers, Ellen White again emerged as a divine witness among
sabbatarian adventists.[37] At a conference of sabbatarian adventists held in Battle
Creek, Michigan, in 1855, leaders of the movement "confess[ed] that we as a
people have [failed to] appreciate the glorious privilege of claiming the gifts
[of prophecy as manifested in Ellen White]" (Haloviak 1985:2). The absence
of discussion or publication of Ellen White's visions in adventist periodicals
led adventist leaders to publicly confess fault for not having promoted the
visions (Graybill 1983), and a coalition of Ellen's supporters accused James of
working to prevent the dissemination of the visions (Lindén 1978). Ellen had
a vision at the close of the conference which members voted to publish in the

Review, and prominent adventist leaders were advised by a majority vote of the delegation to address Sabbath-keepers on the prophetic gifts. The delegation closed by voting to support a statement making explicit their belief that Ellen White's visions were from God and that adventists were "under obligation to abide by their teachings" (Anderson 1986). Ellen White, whose visions had almost ceased following her husband's editorial decision to exclude them from publication in the *Review,* began again, after the 1855 Battle Creek conference, to have numerous visions.[38]

Courting Babylon, Coalescing a Remnant: Seventh-day Adventist Organization

Sabbatarian adventists continued, through the 1850s, as a "scattered flock of believers." Though the "little remnant" had, by 1850, generally agreed on shared tenets of belief and practice (including the seventh-day Sabbath, conditional mortality, the spirit of prophecy, the imminent, personal advent of Christ, baptism by immersion, and foot washing [Anderson 1986]), Sabbath-keepers were often geographically isolated and alone in their religious study and worship. United principally by the regular publication of the *Review,* sabbatarian adventists considered themselves God's remnant people—outside of an organized religious institution and therefore outside of Babylon. The memory of rejection by mainline Protestantism was fresh in the minds of sabbatarian adventists who had judged the denominations to be Babylon less than a decade previously and "come out" of them. Sabbatarian adventists generally associated formal organization with the development of creeds and unbiblical belief and were therefore hesitant to organize and thereby appear to assume the very characteristics to which they were so strongly opposed. Further, adventists were united in their conviction of Christ's soon coming: to formally organize would be, many insisted, to deny the imminence of the advent and to detract from the central goal of preparing for, and sharing the message of, the advent (Pearson 1990:19; Daily 1985:42; see also Dick 1986).

As early as 1851, though, local groups of believers began to move toward formal organization by designating and setting apart leaders and thereby attempting to limit those who publicly represented sabbatarian adventism. In addition, local groups attempted to define belief and control membership by instituting disciplinary actions against wayward members, thus unwittingly introducing at least limited informal organization into the movement (Anderson 1986). James White, unlike many other leaders of the movement, deemed formal organization and the assumption of a legal structure and name necessary for sabbatarian adventists, and used his position as editor of the *Review* to advocate organization (see the *Review,* 1850–63). James White noted that "large bodies of intelligent brethren [were] being raised up" in adventism and argued that "without some regulation . . . [they would] be thrown into confusion" (Anderson 1974:31–32). James White insisted that while no divine pattern for organization was outlined in Scripture, adventists had experienced initial success in their evangelical labors and should continue to spread the message of Christ's soon coming and the seventh-day Sabbath. He implored adventists in his *Review* columns to consider the necessary requirements of worship that demanded formal organization: the ability to regulate those ministering in the name of adventists; the capability to collect and distribute, in an organized fashion, funds for the financial support of sabbatarian adventist ministers and to meet other needs; the ability to control membership based on uniform standards of admittance; the faculty to create and maintain uniformity in the sabbatarian adventist message; and most important, the capacity to maintain ownership of meetinghouses and other property (most especially James White's small publishing facility) (Theobald 1980:91–92; Anderson 1986; Bull and Lockhart 1989:100). In short, James White favored organization because he believed that it would provide unity, consistency, and control of belief, as well as property rights to the young movement (Haloviak 1988:5).

In the face of persistent opposition from those, like R. F. Cottrell, who continued to portray organization as the path to an unbiblical, creedal Babylon, James White was able, especially in the late 1850s, to coalesce support around the banner of formal, legal organization (see Cottrell 1860, 1862). Undoubtedly, his most effective proponent was Ellen White, whose visions helped to solve organizational problems and to enforce (as well as to make) organizational decisions (see Graybill 1983:141–42).[39] In 1859, Ellen White wrote that "God is well pleased with the efforts of his people in trying to move with system and order in his work. I saw that there should be order in the church of God, and arrangement in carrying forward the last great message of mercy to the world" (White in Butler 1987:203–4).

In 1857, adventists held a series of General Conferences at Battle Creek, Michigan, at which they discussed publishing and other movement concerns. Sabbatarian adventists agreed at that time to organize their publishing enterprise but rejected formal, movement-wide organization. Later, however, in 1860, at a September 29 General Conference (also held at Battle Creek), adventists, after protracted debate, agreed to adopt a name and to legally organize. Though some persisted in objections that the assumption of a name

would lead the movement to become a denomination ("Babylon") and encourage the destruction of the peculiarities of the sabbatarian adventist movement, James White countered that "we are classed with [the denominations]
already, and I don't know that we can prevent it, unless we disband and scat-
ter, and give up the thing altogether" (Anderson 1974:31). At James White's
urging, a majority of delegates eventually resolved that a shared name and legal
organization were necessary to avoid confusion within, and the eventual dis-
integration of, the "scattered remnant." Possible names, including the Church
of God (which supporters called "biblical" and opponents dismissed as "mean-
ingless") were discussed until sabbatarian adventists decided to call themselves
Seventh-day Adventists, agreeing that this title conveyed the essential elements
of their message (ibid.). Ellen White embraced the name as "marking"
Adventists as a "peculiar people," as a "standing rebuke to the Protestant
world," and as "drawing a line between the worshipers of God and those who
worship the Beast and receive his mark" (ibid.:32). Adventists also resolved, at
the 1860 Battle Creek conference, to organize a legal association (the Seventh-
day Adventist Publishing Association) that would better allow them to maintain control of their publishing assets.

The legal organization established in 1860 proved insufficient, however, for
the growing movement. Groups of Adventists residing in specific locales were
able to pool funds in order to build meetinghouses but were unable, due to
the lack of movement-wide organization, to legally own the buildings they
constructed.[40] Consequently, James White persisted in pleading with Adventists
to undertake more than the legal organizational association that they had established in 1860. If Adventists would create an organized, recognized religious
group, he contended, their ministers could more easily rent and use public
facilities (public halls, schools), they could have greater control over their
ministers, they would be better able to arrange their assets (as finances and
capital could be overseen through one central office), and Adventists, who were
opposed to participation in war (based on their understanding of the seventh
commandment), would be able to claim conscientious objector status in the
then ongoing Civil War (Lindén 1978:18).[41] For these reasons, despite previous denunciations of organization, the General Conference of Adventists was
founded in May of 1863. Twenty delegates from 125 churches (with a total
membership of approximately thirty-five hundred) ratified a constitution and
elected officers.[42] James White was nominated for the office of president but
declined, claiming pressing responsibilities as the *Review*'s editor and probably hoping to avoid the appearance of having sought formal organization in
order to claim a position of personal power (Jordan 1986:65).[43]

After Formal Organization: Continuing until the Advent

In overcoming hostility toward organization present among sabbatarian Adventists following the Great Disappointment and in encouraging Adventists to adhere to a name and to a legal and a formal religious organizational structure, James White was able to remove Adventists from the ambiguity and instability of their post-Disappointment position and to place them firmly in a position conducive to institutional development. Original Adventist organization (1860) coalesced around the object of maintaining ownership of Adventist publishing facilities in the event of James White's death. When Adventists created a formal organizational structure in 1863, they were poised not only to continue and to expand publishing interests but, after Ellen White's 1865 health vision, to institute a system of sanitariums and, relatedly, educational institutions in which to train first health practitioners and later Adventist schoolteachers, secretaries, pastors, and other denominational employees. The distinction and stability provided Adventists by official association and the resulting continued development of a shared theology as well as institutional growth "would enable them to maintain a degree of separation from the world" (Anderson 1986:38).

As (to use Adventist phraseology) "time continued" at the end of the nineteenth century, formal organization provided Adventists with new understanding of and explanations for the delayed advent. Ellen White began to attest to the unreadiness of "God's people" (Adventists) "to receive him." She wrote in 1868 that "the long night of gloom is trying; but the morning [advent] is deferred in mercy, because if the Master should come, so many would be found unready. God's unwillingness to have his people perish has been the reason for so long delay" (279). The doctrine of the sanctuary (with its ongoing investigative judgment) had shifted the blame for the delay of Christ's coming from those outside Adventism to Adventists themselves: Christ had entered the second apartment (the Most Holy Place) of the heavenly sanctuary and could not return to earth until his work there was complete (Butler 1987:201). Legal organization served to clearly delimit believers in the advent who, in turn, were increasingly presented with visions and testimony delineating correct health practices, attire, diet, social activities, marriage partners, sexual behaviors, and so on. Called "standards," these behavioral expectations could be more readily communicated and enforced in a formally organized religious structure. In this milieu, Adventist leaders were able to attribute Christ's delay to the failure of Adventists to "live up to the light" (truth) that they had been given. In the late 1860s and 1870s, Ellen and James White began to refer to Adventism as the

Laodicean ("lukewarm") church. They emphasized that not all who belonged to the "remnant" would be saved, and evaluated Adventists and Adventism increasingly critically (Damsteegt 1977). Ellen White acknowledged in 1883 that "It is true that time has continued longer than we expected in the early days of this message. Our Savior did not appear as soon as we hoped." "But," she added, "has the word of the Lord ever failed? Never!" (White 1915:67, 69). Adventists were instructed to enact Sabbath reform, to share the adventist message with all the inhabitants of the earth, and to purify their souls "through obedience to the truth" (Douglass 1979:162).

Adventists were interested in more than critical self-evaluation in their attempt to understand Christ's delay, however, and began to develop, especially during the 1870s, non-apocalyptic justifications for evangelical endeavors.[44] Missionary work was encouraged not only as a way to warn others of Christ's soon coming but to: (1) become like Christ; (2) share the light of Adventist truth with the world; (3) promote "works" (in working to save others, Adventists were told, they provided for their own salvation); and (4) share talents (Damsteegt 1977:268). As converts were attracted to Adventism, Christ's delay was interpreted as allowing Adventists time to ready themselves for the advent, and as allowing time for further evangelical successes (Butler 1987).

James and Ellen White (and to a much lesser extent, Joseph Bates) were able to provide the leadership necessary to fashion the "scattered flock" of approximately two hundred disappointed adventists in 1850 into a formally organized religious body of thirty-five hundred by 1863 and of one hundred and twenty-five thousand by 1915 (at Ellen White's death). James, as Adventism's editor and publisher, served as Ellen's publicist and defender, and Ellen, as Adventism's prophet, had visions which promoted and defended James. Before James's 1866 stroke and subsequent incapacity, the Whites had shaped the emotionalism and failed expectations of a small group of advent believers into a quickly emerging, highly organized and institutionalized religious structure. From the onset of James's lessening capacity in 1866, and following his death in 1881, Ellen's influence in Adventism increased (Graybill 1983:29); she bolstered and directed Adventist institutional growth (especially medical and educational development), admonished and encouraged Adventist membership and leadership, traveled to Europe and (more extensively) Australia (from where she continued to communicate with General Conference leadership), and assisted (in 1903) in establishing international Adventist headquarters in Washington, D.C. After 1851 (in what Lindén [1978] refers to as her "mature period"), Ellen White wrote her *Testimonies* (five thousand pages reproving and exhorting Adventists) and, perhaps most important, the "Controversy" series—*Patriarchs and Prophets, Prophets and Kings, The Desire of Ages, The Acts of the Apostles,* and *The Great Controversy.* Following her death in 1915, the leadership void created by the prophet's departure was filled by the prolific publication of Ellen White's numerous writings. Before her death, White had declared that the Bible, in conjunction with her writings ("additional light" to the Bible), provided the guidance that Adventists needed to lead them in preparation for Christ's coming. After her death, Adventism used Ellen White's prolific written legacy to continue to frame, order, and guide belief and practice. In this way James and especially Ellen White assisted not only in formulating original belief but in encouraging institutional organization and growth.

Notes

1. The strongest thrust of the Second Great Awakening (also called "the Great Revival" or "the Finney Revival") occurred in the decade between 1825 and 1835.

2. Despite his lack of formal education, Miller "read well and was well read"; in his informal studies, he pursued the works of Hume, Voltaire, Volney, and Thomas Paine (see Dick 1986; Jordan 1986; Lindén 1978).

3. The Bible, according to Miller's method, was a whole, complete unit, each part equally divine and entirely inspired by God (Lindén 1978:38). Thus, each word had to be considered separately as each had its own scriptural meaning; sentences too were to be studied separately and interpreted literally if to do so made sense in the contexts in which the sentences were found.

4. Miller's method involved gathering all scriptures pertaining to a specific topic and "then let[ting] every word have its proper influence," resulting in an interpretation which, according to Miller, "cannot be in error" (Judd 1987:20).

5. Daniel 8:14 reads, "Unto two thousand and three hundred days; then shall the sanctuary be cleansed."

6. Despite Miller's conclusion that the advent was only slightly more than two decades away, his exegesis "achieved no startling novelty"; other than in his emphasis on the end of the world, Miller's conclusions "virtually epitomized orthodoxy" (Cross 1986:5).

7. Convinced in 1818 that the advent was imminent, Miller made no concerted effort to share his findings; instead he continued earnest examination of the Bible until 1823, and although he did cautiously share his conclusions with neighbors and friends, he attempted to convince ministers in his acquaintance to warn their congregations of Christ's soon coming and thereby relieve himself of the onerous responsibility of warning others of the imminent parousia.

8. The Dark Day of 1780 consisted of a fifteen-hour eclipse of the sun (Jordan 1986:27–31).

9. Camp meetings, which originated as an evangelical revival method to reach frontier settlers, were also used by Millerites beginning in 1842 as an evangelical tool (see Lindén 1978:33).

10. Relatively long-term adventual publications of Himes and other Millerites included *Signs of the Times* (Boston), the *Midnight Cry* (Boston), the *Trumpet of Alarm* (Philadelphia), the *Christian Palladium* (Rochester, N.Y.), the *Voice of Truth and Glad Tidings of the Kingdom at Hand, Jubilee Trumpet* (succeeded by the *Day Star*), the *Hope of Israel*, the *Second Advent Harbinger* (Bristol, Eng.), the *Western Midnight Cry* (Cincinnati), and the *Advent Message to the Daughters of Zion*. According to Lindén, "probably no other religious movement or denomination produced so vast a quantity of printed matter in so short a time" (1978:50).

11. Five thousand attended one lecture in Philadelphia; thirty-five hundred attended another in New York. As Wayne Judd pointed out in 1987, the Millerites' success can only be understood in the context of the immediacy with which they perceived the end of time: "To understand the meaning of William Miller's life and the lives of those who were called Millerites, it is critical to remember the great, overriding touchstone of their existence. For them there was no future. Miller had settled the question of ultimacy. The world was coming to an end in 1843" (Judd 1987:21).

12. Miller was granted a Baptist minister's license in 1833.

13. In his 1987 attempt to paint a "shadow portrait" of Millerites, David Rowe defined Millerites as those who acted on Miller's message of an imminent advent—by contributing money to Miller's cause, writing letters in support of Miller, preaching Miller's message, or assisting in prayer meetings. Rowe's "shadow portrait" was based on active participants in the Millerite movement living in upstate New York.

14. Millerites came from all types of communities (commercial, rural, industrial), and although they have been portrayed as poor and economically disenfranchised, Rowe's 1987 study found "no evidence that Millerites were predominantly poor or even that the poor accounted for a large minority of Millerites" (11). Rowe suggests that Millerites may have claimed poverty inaccurately in some cases to set themselves apart from those outside of the movement—accumulation of worldly possessions was, after all, an indication of concern with the now, not the hereafter.

15. Other empirical studies have suggested that a majority of Millerites were Methodists (44 percent), while Baptists participated in the movement to a lesser extent (27 percent), in addition to Congregationalists (9 percent), Christians (of the Christian Connection) (8 percent), and Presbyterians (7 percent) (Dick 1986).

16. In the early 1840s the Millerites purchased the world's largest tent, called the "Great tent," which had a seating capacity of four thousand and attracted curiosity-seekers to Millerite camp meetings.

17. Miller did cite various calendric points at which the advent might be expected (March 21, 1843, originally), but he preferred to stress Christ's "soon coming" rather than to focus primarily upon the date of that coming.

18. George Storrs coauthored, with Snow, the first article outlining fundamentals of

belief that inspired the seventh-month movement, but he is not widely associated with the popularization of those ideas into a mass movement as is Snow.

19. The excitement generated by the belief that Christ would return on October 22, 1844, contributed not only to a sense of evangelical urgency but to increased fanaticism. Large, fervent crowds attended what were believed to be the final meetings of Christ's followers before his coming; people swooned, fainted, cried out, and donated generously when offering plates were passed.

20. David T. Arthur has suggested that Himes accepted Snow's date for the parousia not because he believed the prediction to be correct but because he was "interested in the effects" of the seventh month movement (1987:52).

21. According to Jonathan Butler (1991), Ellen White fits the profile of "someone suited to the prophetic role"; i.e., she experienced periods of severe depression intermittent with periods of ecstatic spirituality.

22. It was not unknown in nineteenth-century New England to experience visions, trances, intense religious anxiety, prostration, and spirit possession in the context of wider religious experience (Daily 1985:30). Visions like those White experienced were claimed by, among others, Paulina Bates, Peter Cartwright, Mary Baker Eddy, Eric Johnson, Barbara Heinemann, Michael Kransent, Ann Lee, Joseph Smith Jr., Joseph Smith Sr., and Jemima Wilkinson. Even modern Seventh-day Adventists, who regard Ellen White as a divinely inspired messenger, insist that God tried to call two others— William Foy (accounts of whose visions Ellen White read) and Hazen Foss (Ellen's relative by marriage) as messengers before turning to Ellen Harmon.

23. James White had criticized a couple who announced their plans to marry in 1845, telling them that to do so was to deny the imminence of the advent (Pearson 1990:19).

24. According to Bull (1988), early Adventists were relatively economically affluent despite their emotionally charged worship services.

25. White often lost her sight following a vision and sometimes required up to three hours to regain it (Lindén 1978).

26. Adherents claimed that White did not breathe during visions, and believers would sometimes cover her mouth and nose to demonstrate the truth of this claim.

27. Spiritualists also crawled on their hands and knees to "become like little children." Ellen White, who was, on occasion, accused of being a Spiritualist, was sensitive to charges that Adventism resembled Spiritualism and therefore was careful to emphasize distinctions between the two movements (see Hoyt 1985).

28. One week following the article, Ellen White sent a letter to the periodical's (the Day Star) editor claiming to have had the same knowledge of a heavenly sanctuary one year previously and endorsing Edson's vision enthusiastically (Lindén 1978:103–31).

29. Even the Great Disappointment did not unite all adventist believers as some joined the movement following October 22, 1844.

30. Rachel Oaks, a Seventh-day Baptist residing in Washington, New Hampshire, introduced the seventh-day Sabbath to an adventist community calling themselves the Christian Brothers in the early 1840s. Frederick Wheeler, a circuit-riding advent

preacher, visited the congregation and became convinced of the validity of the seventh-day Sabbath. Together, Oaks and Wheeler convinced T. M. Preble to keep the Sabbath, and Preble, in turn, published an article advocating the seventh-day Sabbath in the *Hope of Israel,* an adventist periodical. Joseph Bates read the article, visited a Sabbath-keeping congregation, became convinced of the truth of the seventh-day Sabbath in 1845, and, in 1846, published and distributed his first Sabbath tract (Review and Herald Publishers 1956:56; see Young 1975). James and Ellen White read the tract and, after becoming friends with Bates, were convinced of the urgency of the Sabbath message when, in 1846, Ellen White had a vision in which she was shown that in failing to honor the seventh-day Sabbath, adventists had disobeyed the fourth commandment (Review and Herald Publishers 1956).

31. The belief in the unconscious state of the dead, introduced to the group by Millerite George Storrs, further distinguished adventists. (It also allowed Ellen White to silence a rival prophet who claimed to be able to communicate with the dead) (Butler 1987).

32. The resulting publication, the *Review and Herald,* later the *Adventist Review,* continues to be the most widely read Adventist periodical.

33. Based on the parable of the ten virgins, the "shut door" hypothesis was first presented by Apollos Hale and Joseph Turner, who argued that Christ, when he entered in to the Most Holy Place to complete his final preparations for the advent, had finished his work for humanity and therefore ended the possibility of salvation for any who did not believe at that time (Arthur 1974:6). James White, who was most likely introduced to the "shut door" by Turner and Hale's *Advent Mirror* article, had accepted the doctrine by the late 1840s (Lindén 1978).

34. *Review* readers were promised that extra editions of the periodical, which were to include Ellen White's visions, would be published bimonthly, but only one extra edition was ever published (see Daily 1985).

35. At the same time that James and Ellen White realized the limiting nature of the "shut door," James deemed revision of past statements supporting the doctrine necessary. In September of 1851 James White published a revised version of Ellen White's visions—omitting references supporting the "shut door"—in pamphlet form. Advocation of the "shut door" was so interwoven throughout Ellen White's visions, however, that total revision was impossible, and James was able only to revise Ellen's most obvious statements of support (Lindén 1978:101).

36. Salvation was possible if those potential converts had been living "up to the light they had" at the time of the Great Disappointment (Mustard 1988).

37. Although Ellen White denied ever having had a vision which supported the "shut door" doctrine (a claim contradicted by her own account of her first [December 1844] vision), James White later wrote that "It is vain for any man to deny that it was the universal belief of [a]dventists, in the autumn of 1844, that their work for the world was done forever" (Mustard 1988:104; Lindén 1978:105).

38. According to Max Weber, it is "recognition on the part of those subject to" the authority of a charismatic leader which validates and legitimates that authority. Thus when Ellen White's visions were not recognized by adventists, they ceased. When the visions were again acknowledged and encouraged, they resumed (see Weber 1968:49).

39. One historian has contended that after James introduced the plans for formal organization, "Ellen added prophetic endorsement" (Graybill 1983:144).

40. In the event of the death of an individual on whose property a meetinghouse had been constructed, for example, ownership of the collectively financed place of worship reverted to the deceased person's next of kin (see Pearson 1990).

41. Bryan Wilson notes that James White's persistent advocacy of formal organization is uncommon among leaders of sectarian movements (see Teel 1980).

42. The newly organized Seventh-day Adventists recognized, beginning in 1863, evangelists (those who traveled to preach the gospel), pastors (heads of congregations), deacons (those who served the temporal needs of the congregation), and elders (those who oversaw the spiritual needs of the congregation). Lay members were to continue to participate in Seventh-day Adventist worship, but following formal organization in 1863, Adventists recognized a clear distinction between laity and appointed, ordained leaders (Damsteegt 1977:257), and Adventist lay participation declined (Anderson 1986:65).

43. James White did eventually serve as the Seventh-day Adventist General Conference president from 1865 to 1867, 1869 to 1871, and 1874 to 1880.

44. John Nevins (J. N.) Andrews became the first official SDA missionary to visit a country outside of North America when he sailed to Europe in 1874.

2

Adventist Belief

Contemporary Adventist belief is comprised of a complex of interlocking tenets, each of which contributes to a paradigm of understanding shaped with reference to what Adventists describe as "the Great Controversy"—an ongoing struggle between the forces of good and evil in the universe. From this basic conception of the division and conflict between good and evil, Adventists derive a series of beliefs depicting and explaining the past and the future through what is understood to be an ongoing process of revelation. In addition, revelation undergirds not only basic tenets of SDA belief but less pivotal beliefs which serve to distinguish and define Adventism. Though Adventist belief has become the subject of much debate of late (see chapter 4), Adventists with whom I worshiped and spoke generally framed their understanding of Adventism within the context provided by the beliefs discussed below.

The Great Controversy

Adventist theology may be ascertained fully only within the context of an understanding of the Great Controversy (Battisone 1986).[1] According to Adventist belief, the universe was originally without sin; God and numerous holy angels dwelt in peace, and other planets were inhabited by people who loved and praised God. Lucifer, an angel in this utopian universe, was originally a "special, beautiful angel," second only to Christ. "Little by little," however, "Lucifer became proud and began to indulge in the desire for self-exaltation; he wanted to share God's throne and glory" (White 1913 [1890]:40). In his desire to rule in God's place, Satan rebelled against God and thereby introduced sin into the universe. God allowed Satan to advance open rebellion so that the universe (especially the obedient angels), could "understand his deceit": "Satan had claimed from the first that he was not in rebellion. The whole universe must see the deceiver unmasked" (ibid.:42).

God attempted to convince Satan of his sin and rebellion, even allowing Satan and his followers a hearing before the unfallen angels, but Satan declared that he wouldn't submit to God's authority and so was cast out of heaven. God chose not to destroy Satan because "the inhabitants of heaven and of the worlds, being unprepared to comprehend the nature or consequences of sin, could not have seen the justice of God in the destruction of Satan. Had he been immediately blotted out of existence, some would have served God from fear rather than from love" (White 1913 [1890]:42). Instead, Satan was allowed to introduce sin into the universe so that all could watch the destruction it wrought and, eventually, see the awful consequences of sin, "that the justice and mercy of God and the immutability of his law might be forever placed beyond all question" (ibid.).[2]

After being cast out of heaven, according to Adventist theology, Satan introduced the Great Controversy between good and evil to earth by tempting Eve to eat the fruit of the tree of knowledge of good and evil. In response, God initiated a plan of redemption in order to allow for the possible salvation of earth's inhabitants and thereby to vindicate his reputation as the God of all good. God established the *Antediluvian* church (led first by Adam and later, Noah), so that any who believed in him could find solace and guidance. Later, God established Abraham's descendants (Israel) as his followers, but when they became obsessed with idols, God, through Christ, established the Apostolic church. After the apostles died, Adventists believe, Christianity lost sight of its mission, and although various Protestant reformers (Wycliff, Luther, the Waldenses) attempted to guide Christianity back to its original mission, God's message was lost until Adventism was formed from the ashes of the Great Disappointment (Weiss 1977:69). Seventh-day Adventists, therefore, identify themselves as God's remnant people, the last warning to the world before Christ returns to the earth; not the only people who will receive salvation but the core around which the faithful will congregate at Armageddon.[3]

As God's people—as the remnant that will vindicate God, the last manifestation of God's church on the earth—Adventists have a unique warning for the world, found in the "three angels' messages": (1) judgment is come; (2) come out of Babylon; and (3) keep the commandments. The first angel's message, according to Adventist belief, "symbolizes God's remnant carrying an everlasting gospel to the world" (Ministerial Association 1988:167), and is accomplished by Adventist preaching of an imminent advent throughout the world (Teel 1984); the second angel's message was of especial importance to early Millerites (who were told to "come out" of Babylon before leaving their

Protestant congregations) but continues to serve as a warning against connection with the world; and the third angel's message "proclaims God's most solemn warning" against Sunday worship and points to the central role that Adventists must assume in sharing the message of (and thereby restoring) the seventh-day Sabbath before the advent (Ministerial Association 1988:166; see below).

Adventists have evolved a complex of beliefs which, although similar in some ways to many mainline Protestant denominational teachings, retain facets that are unique to Adventism. Adventists believe in the literal (seven day) creation of the earth, that people were created in a sinless state, and that through the Fall, alienation, sin, and depravity were introduced to humanity. They believe that Christ's sacrifice on the cross is sufficient for the salvation of all, but will only benefit "those who avail themselves of its provision" (Knechtle and Sohlmann 1971:133; see below); that Christ was resurrected following his death, ascended literally into heaven where he serves as an advocate for those who accept him, and will literally, personally return to earth ("soon"; see below). Adventists teach that the Ten Commandments, the Decalogue, are an unchanging standard of right conduct and that people (usually not younger than twelve years of age), after being baptized by immersion, may follow the commandments, lead a sanctified life, come to know Christ, and by so doing, be glorified at the advent. Adventists reject the idea of an eternal hell, arguing instead that the "righteous dead sleep in Christ" (are unconscious), and that following God's final judgment, the wicked will be made "as though they had never been."

The Spirit of Prophecy

Ellen White, who provided early Adventists conciliatory confirmation of the distinct beliefs that came to delineate and define Adventism, was identified by them (and claimed to be) God's "messenger" sent to lead the final movement of God's people on earth prior to the advent. As the recipient of hundreds of visions, and later as an inspired and prolific writer, Ellen White settled doctrinal controversies which threatened to divide early Adventism by providing divine sanction for certain beliefs (the seventh-day Sabbath, the sanctuary doctrine) and practices (dress and dietary guidelines, foot washing). Early Adventists heralded her as the final manifestation of the "spirit of prophecy" before Christ's return and believed that she provided "new light" to aid in understanding of the Bible (Lindén 1978:286). While White did not call herself a "prophet," she was widely regarded as such by Adventists who went to great lengths to demonstrate that "Mrs. White's" inspiration was not merely another manifestation of nineteenth-century Spiritualism but was in fact evidence of God's divine guidance. The *Review and Herald* explained in 1928 that: "Seventh-day Adventists hold that Ellen G. White performed the work of a true prophet during the seventy years of her public ministry. . . . As Samuel was a prophet . . . as Jeremiah was a prophet . . . so we believe that Mrs. White was a prophet of the Church of Christ today" (Gerstner 1989:104).

Ellen White, though she referred to herself as a "messenger" and called her writings the "lesser light" (as opposed to the Bible, the "greater light"), encouraged the preeminence given her visions and writings. White taught that the *Testimonies*—personal counsel, often highly critical, given by White to her SDA contemporaries—were divinely inspired and insisted that to disregard the counsel therein was to take the first step toward apostasy, and ultimately damnation: "It is Satan's plan to weaken the faith of God's people in the *Testimonies*. Next follows skepticism in regard to the vital points of our faith, the pillars of our position, then doubts as to the Holy scriptures, and then the downward march to perdition" (White in Lindén 1978:282–83).

Adventists often note in worship services that Ellen White's writings provide them "an advantage" in attempting to interpret and understand the Bible: "In the writings of Ellen White, the Lord's chosen messenger to His remnant church, we have revealed not what man thinks about God and His word and its meaning, but what God thinks about these things. The author of the holy Bible thus reveals His purposes, intent, and meaning by the same kind of divine revelation that brought forth the word in its original form" (Lindén 1978:287). Though her writings are ostensibly meant to guide and supplement Bible study, in practice, White's "counsel is considered to have the same impact of authority—not only in principle, but frequently in literal interpretation—as the Bible" (Sturges 1972:66).

While many Adventists are uncomfortable with the apparent equality with Scripture, at least in practice, accorded White's writings, Adventist tradition has consistently recognized the need to secure White's authority and thereby to safeguard against attacks on doctrines, distinct to Adventism, that find divine sanction in her words.[4] Intellectual criticism of White or her writings has been discouraged. Francis D. Nichol, a popular SDA writer, contended that if White's writings appeared internally contradictory, "we need not intellectual stultification, but only intellectual humility, in order to view those contradictions as simply apparent, not real" (1964:105). Ronald Numbers's 1976 book, *Prophetess of Health,* which placed White in the context of the nineteenth-century health reform movement and demonstrated her tendency to borrow ideas and words from her secular contemporaries, forced an evolution of the official explanation of White's inspiration and has had a long-term impact on White's authority as the movement's figurehead (see chapter 4). Nonetheless, "for the overwhelming majority of Adventists, the writings of Mrs. White [continue to] serve to sanctify their basic beliefs, to resolve the ambiguities and contradictions in scripture, and, more generally, to furnish a blueprint for the complete Adventist life" (Theobald 1980:99).[5]

"Present Truth": Progressive Revelation

Adventists' conception of "truth" is not static. While Ellen White is an important source of guidance for biblical interpretation, and while some Adventists use her writings in a manner that would suggest that they are perceived as being inerrant, Adventism has a tradition of belief that is dynamic—growing and changing as God continues to reveal more of his plan (see Schwartz 1970:94). Ellen White, speaking at an 1888 General Conference session, maintained that "that which God gives his servants to speak today would not perhaps have been present truth twenty years ago, but it is God's message for this time" (Teel 1980:31). "Present truth," according to Adventists, is the idea of truth as a constant unfolding of biblical revelation not inconsistent with earlier belief but leading to a fuller knowledge of God's plan (Damsteegt 1977:297); it is truth that is made newly alive and becomes more fully understood within the context of present experience (Land 1986b:218–19). As one interviewee explained, "It's very true that there have been changes [in Adventist belief]. It's one thing that I, being somewhat scholarly . . . like about Seventh-day Adventism . . . that we do not have some rigid code. We allow considerable variation of belief— our belief *grows*—as long as we remain biblical" (emphasis in original). Adventist theology, then, evolves with increased understanding. Fundamentals of Adventist belief, however (such as the sanctuary doctrine and Ellen White's position as a messenger of God), have evolved only after meeting considerable resistance from Adventist leadership (see chapter 4).

Cleansing the Sanctuary

The beliefs which most arrest the attention of Adventists in worship services, in publications, and in media presentations are those beliefs that define Adventism; those beliefs which have historically set Adventists apart from other Protestant bodies and continue to provide Adventism boundaries of distinction from secular society. One important Adventist identity marker is the sanctuary doctrine. Hiram Edson's reinterpretation of Daniel following the Great Disappointment led Adventists to a unique understanding of Daniel's twenty-three hundred days and the "cleansing of the sanctuary" which "remains at the heart" of Adventist theology (Theobald 1985:116).

Adventists believe that Christ's Atonement was not completed on the cross. Instead, after his resurrection and ascension, Christ commenced work in the Holy Place, or "outer apartment," of the heavenly sanctuary, and on October 22, 1844, Christ entered the "inner apartment," or Most Holy Place, of the heavenly sanctuary to complete the work necessary for the redemption of humankind. The Adventist conception of the sanctuary is modeled on their interpretation of the biblical (earthly) tabernacle. The Old Testament tabernacle had two compartments—the Holy Place and the Most Holy Place (see figure 1 [compiled using data from field notes]). According to Adventists, each day in the Holy Place (outer compartment) worshipers would come to the sanctuary with a sacrifice, place their hands upon the sacrifice, and confess their sins. In this way, the person's sins were symbolically transferred to the sacrificial animal. Because the penalty for sin was death, the animal was then killed, transferring the blood, which now bore the confessor's sins, to the sanctuary (Ministerial Association 1988). Next, the high priest would undertake to cleanse the sin that had accumulated in the sanctuary by annually purifying the Most Holy Place of the sanctuary. Two goats were taken by the high priest to the temple and the first, the Lord's goat, was killed and its blood used to cover the ark of the ten commandments (housed, according to Adventists, in the Most Holy Place; see figure 1) "to satisfy the claims of God's holy law" (ibid.:318). The high priest then applied the blood of the Lord's goat to places in the sanctuary where the blood of the confessors' animals had been applied daily. Last, the high priest took upon himself the sins of the sanctuary and transferred them to the second goat (the "scapegoat"), which was then driven into the wilderness.

The Investigative Judgment

According to Adventists, the rituals of the earthly sanctuary serve as a model for the divine work of cleansing the heavenly sanctuary. The symbolic transfer of "sin . . . to the earthly sanctuary pointed to a *real* transmission of the same from the earthly penitent to the heavenly sanctuary through the blood of Jesus" (Adams 1993:85; emphasis in original). In entering the inner apartment of the heavenly sanctuary on October 22, 1844, Christ commenced the final work of atonement. During the typical day of atonement the cleansing of the earthly sanctuary removed the sins accumulated there, so too the "heav-

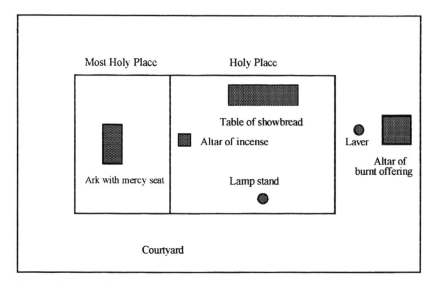

Figure 1. Terrestrial Sanctuary

enly sanctuary is cleansed by the final removal of the record of sins in the heavenly books" (Ministerial Association 1988:320). This act of "cleansing the heavenly sanctuary" involves a process of judgment. Before the records are finally cleared, they will be examined to determine who, through repentance and faith in Christ, is entitled to "enter His eternal kingdom" (ibid.). The "investigative judgment," must be completed, Adventists believe, before Christ can return again to the earth. Christ's work in the heavenly sanctuary consists first of pleading on behalf of, and serving as an advocate for, believers (a work commenced immediately following his ascension), and, after October 22, 1844 (when Christ entered the Most Holy Place), of "cleansing" the sanctuary by undertaking to examine all names and accompanying records of believers kept in divine books in the sanctuary, and thereby determining who is worthy to receive the gifts of the atonement (Theobald 1985:116).

The work of cleansing the sanctuary—the investigative judgment—is a methodical process whereby all sin is first recorded in the books of heaven and then examined. Ellen White wrote that: "Every man's work passes in review before God, and is registered for faithfulness or unfaithfulness. Opposite each name in the books of heaven is entered, with terrible exactness, every wrong word, every selfish act, every unfulfilled duty, and every secret sin, . . . all [are] chronicled by the recording angel" (White 1911 [1888]:482). In his work of cleansing the sanctuary, Christ will "plead the cases of those who believe in him" while Satan stands as the accuser of all. "Every name is mentioned, every case closely investigated," until all have been reviewed (ibid.). Then, if Christ can prove that a person has repented, her sin is blotted out; if not, her name is removed from the Book of Life.[6]

Although Adventists have begun, particularly since the 1950s, to adapt the concept of salvation as a "free gift of God's love," the investigative judgment, with its recording angels and extensive records of sin, injects an element of tension into Adventist experience. God must complete the investigative judgment before returning to earth. Further, the advent is not a distant possibility but a present reality. Christ will come *soon* to the earth, Adventists reiterate frequently, and when he comes the eternal fate of all will already have been decided.[7]

Christ's Soon Coming—Adventist Millennialism

Seventh-day Adventists came together as a scattered band of believers looking forward to Christ's soon advent, and have, as time continued beyond their expectations, renegotiated their understanding of the "imminence" of Christ's return. As early as 1884, Ellen White began to frame discussions of the advent in the context not only of continued expectation but of reasons for delay. Adventist theology has gradually evolved an understanding of Christ's coming that is concomitantly "soon" and "not yet"—that is at once imminent and delayed. The *Review and Herald* commented in 1892 that "you will not be able to say that he will come in one, two, or five years, neither are you to put off his coming by stating that it may not be for ten or twenty years" ("Father Which Seeketh" 1892:20). Thus, in the absence of a specific advent expectation (date), and in the face of apparent delay, Adventist leadership sought to maintain hope and belief in the imminence of Christ's return while simultaneously discouraging adherence to a specific time line.

While preparations for the advent generated by the expectancy of the Millerite movement have not been duplicated by modern Adventists, to deny the immediacy of Seventh-day Adventist adventual expectations would be to ignore an essential component of the movement's ethos. In conversations and interviews with Adventists, informants, on several occasions, stated that they had not expected to reach adulthood, marry, have children, or grow old because, as one woman explained, "I always thought Jesus would return before I'd have the chance to do [those] things."[8] Adventists call on Christ publicly and often to "come soon!" While some older Adventists express dismay that the advent "is stressed [emphasized] less" than it was in their youth, when I spoke with Adventists and attended SDA gatherings it was clear that the Adventist's temporal future (most especially the older Adventists' future) is a conditional future—events will continue to take place "if time continues."

Adventists are not without divine reminders of Christ's soon coming; the SDA "historicist hermeneutic" is consistently used to interpret events in the context of the impending advent—modern earthquakes, famines, floods, and other natural disasters are (and have been, throughout Adventist history) seen as signs of the end. Specifically, Adventists view increased incidence of crime and violence, war, materialism/avarice, apostasy, natural disasters, and persecution of Sabbath-keepers as indicators that the advent is near, "even at the door" (see Schwartz 1970; Theobald 1985; Ministerial Association 1988).

Adventist theology has developed four primary explanations for what is most often referred to as the "delay" in Christ's coming. Some argue that Christ cannot return until the investigative judgment is completed. The delayed advent, then, allows people time to repent and accept Christ, thus demonstrating Christ's ultimate compassion. This explanation has become increasingly less popular as time has continued, as it seems to imply limitations to God's omniscience and ability to complete judgment in a relatively short period of time. An explanation advocated by Ellen White and still widely accepted by Adventists is the insistence that the Adventist message must be "preached to all the world" before Christ will return. This message rose in conjunction with SDA evangelical work and continues to inspire missionary efforts. A more recent, though widely disputed, explanation is the "Harvest Principle"—the notion, promulgated most effectively by Herbert Douglass, that when Adventists have become "ripe" (righteous) and are "ready for harvest" (have become "perfect in Christ") Christ will return. Advocates of the Harvest Principle (especially Douglass) are active in the controversy within Adventism surrounding the relative importance of justification and/or sanctification for salvation, and are most often recognized as emphasizing sanctification (though they insist that justification also plays an important role in salvation; see chapter 4). A final explanation offered for the apparent delay in Christ's coming is based upon a specific understanding of biblical revelations that are to occur before Christ's return and the recognition that not all of these have been fulfilled. In the *Review and Herald,* as early as 1851, James White edited an article that insisted that the "seven last plagues" had not yet "been accomplished" (1). Contemporary Adventists maintain that these plagues have not transpired and therefore that Christ's coming, though soon, cannot take place until these final signs have come to pass. In one interview, an Adventist woman offered this explanation for the delay in Christ's coming:

VANCE: I know that Adventists place a lot of hope in the soon return of Christ to the earth. How imminent is the advent? Is it something that could happen tomorrow? Is it something that could happen this afternoon? Or is it more distant?

INFORMANT: It can't happen tomorrow or this afternoon the way I understand it because of some of the events that are to occur, according to the Bible. There are some plagues and they're actually named specifically. [Pause] And of course those haven't occurred. So it could be months, that would probably be the soonest.

VANCE: So there are signs, then, that haven't been fulfilled?

INFORMANT: That's right. There's just those very last things [that] haven't been fulfilled.

In this way, Adventists maintain a vivid, real, and present hope that Christ will return *soon;* although the exact delimitation of "soon" remains vague, Adventists live in a present which is shaped by the constant expectation that Christ *will* come. Adventists plan for their individual futures, and those of their children, but do so, within the institutional structures created and maintained by Adventism, in a context that simultaneously recognizes, for example, the importance of a college degree while time continues and insists that time will not continue for long. Though this may be a seeming contradiction to the outsider, my informants recognized their earthly work as *preparation for* (and *a hastening of*) the advent. Adventists believe that "Christ's work as a high priest is nearing its completion. The years of human probation are slipping away," but acknowledge that "no one knows just when God's voice will proclaim, 'It is finished'" (Ministerial Association 1988:327).

Adventist eschatology claims that immediately prior to Christ's coming, after the heavenly sanctuary has been cleansed, Satan will be allowed, for a short time, to "stir up God's people." Following this last "time of trouble," during which all will experience great suffering (though the "righteous will be cared for by God"), darkness will fall over the earth, the clouds will part, and Christ will appear personally to all earth's inhabitants. At his accession, Christ will call forth those who "sleep in Christ" (the righteous dead) and they will rise out of their graves[9] and be "made whole."[10] The living righteous will then be taken up to a heavenly paradise. Satan, who will be made the scapegoat for all sin, will be banished to the now desolate earth where he will wander for the millennium. Following this thousand years, the wicked will be raised at the second resurrection to receive their judgment. Christ, the redeemed, and the angels will return to earth, and though Satan will marshal to attack God and attempt to claim victory, Christ's goodness will be made apparent to all, and all will see that the expulsion of the wicked "from heaven is just" (White 1911 [1888]:668). The advent, for Seventh-day Adventists, provides hope not only for salvation, immortality, and heaven but for a public, universal vindication. All will recognize the truth of the advent message and the seventh-day Sabbath: "The redeemer's return brings to a glorious climax the history of God's people. It is the moment of their deliverance" (Ministerial Association 1988:346).

To emphasize only Adventists' hope for Christ's soon return without giving some attention to the tension introduced into the lives of individual Adventists, and into the movement as a whole, by the delay of Christ's coming would be to overlook the continuing struggle within Adventism—most pronounced at the level of individual Adventists—to understand the always future advent, not in the context of theology but in terms of everyday problems, plans, and realities. Adventists publicly long for Christ's appearance; in personal conversation this hope is no less fervent, but it is cause for perplexity. When asked if her life now was consistent with what she had expected as a young person, one seventy-one-year-old woman replied: "No! I didn't think I'd live this long. I thought Christ would come. I never thought I'd grow old; I never thought I'd die. I didn't even think I'd live long enough to have children. My *mother* didn't think she'd live long enough to have children. . . . And here we are" (emphasis in original).

According to Pearson, "the longer the delay in the fulfillment of the advent hope, the greater the emphasis on occupation rather than preparation" (1990:21). It would be an oversimplification, as Bull and Lockhart observed in 1989, to insist that Adventism evolved gradually and persistently from preparation for and expectation of the advent toward an emphasis on continuing time, but Adventism as a whole, and individual Adventists, have been forced, as time continues, to reinterpret the meaning of Christ's "soon" coming. Whereas early Adventists emphasized that "this generation shall not pass" before the advent, by 1950 the *Adventist Review* published a caption reading "the youth now living *may* witness with their own eyes the culmination of the Controversy of the Ages and the coming of the Lord" (129[51] [Oct. 26]:14; emphasis added). In 1960, the *Review* explained that "a Seventh-day Adventist is a person who weighs the opportunities of time on the scales of eternity, *and then walks the pathway of life* with conviction, courage and confidence" (137[5] [Feb. 4]:17; emphasis added). The 1990 *Review* carried articles detailing how to "deal with the delayed advent" and calling teachings that focus exclusively on Christ's soon coming, "pie-in-the-sky theology" (Jones-Haldeman 1990:6–7). Formal and informal informants generally saw continued and even increasing institution building as important for creating conditions necessary for Christ's return (though many older Adventists did bemoan what they per-

ceived to be an increasing lack of attention in worship services and in publications to the soon coming advent). Informants indicated, in response to questions not directly addressing the parousia, that because "no man knows the
day or the hour of the advent," one must prepare for the advent but also make
preparations for a temporal future.

After the Advent: Heaven

In part, Adventists' hope for Christ's return is encouraged by a seemingly tangible cognition of the heaven which is to follow the millennium. In heaven,
Adventists believe, relationships with friends and relatives will not only continue but will be enhanced by ability to achieve full intellectual and spiritual
growth. The Adventist heaven is a utopian (but very real, to SDAs) place in
which the saved may touch, smell, hear, and feel; enjoy music and nature; live
in (literal) houses in cities prepared for them by Christ constructed of precious
stones, gold, platinum, and silver; and continue pursuits which were of interest to them during life.[11] Although there is a definite disjunction between life
on earth and life in heaven for Adventists—life in heaven is without sin and is
orderly, run according to God's theocracy, while life on earth is contentious,
filled with evil and constant temptation—the heaven foreseen by Seventh-day
Adventists does not herald a release from the responsibilities they now face.
Indeed, life on earth is a preparation, a "training" even, for the new responsibilities SDAs will undertake in heaven. For Adventists, "there is no radical dis-
location between earth and heaven" (Bull 1988:153). Thus, as informants explained, Adventists must develop righteous lives not only in preparation for
the advent but so that they will be prepared to live in heaven following the
millennium.

The Sabbath

In addition to the expectation of the advent, the recognition of the seventh day
of the week as God's divinely appointed day of worship "has been the doctrine that has given [Adventism] its particular tone, and has been [Advent-
ism's] most visible identity marker" (Weiss 1987:33). Bull and Lockhart noted
in 1989 that the seventh-day "Sabbath is the key to understanding the Adventist
relationship with America": "In its peculiarity [the seventh-day Sabbath]
makes sacred the Adventist alienation from the American way of life, but in
its conformity to the American expectation that there should be one holy day
a week, it aligns Adventists with wider society" (Bull and Lockhart 1989:166).

Thus Adventists recognize *a* Sabbath in much the same manner as their religious contemporaries, but set side a *different* Sabbath, thereby distinguishing themselves.

As North American society has increasingly been perceived as neglecting Sunday worship, however, Adventists have become staunch advocates not only of the seventh-day Sabbath but of the recognition of at least one day each week as a time of rest and worship. Modern Adventists define themselves less in opposition to other religious bodies than to secular society as a whole ("the world"); this being the case, absence of a day of religious worship is recognized as expressing far greater disregard for the divine than is Sunday worship.

The Seventh-day Adventist understanding and observance of the Sabbath is developing in other ways as well (Rice 1978:68). Adventists generally recognize the Sabbath (beginning at sundown Friday evening with a family or small group vespers service and ending at sundown Saturday with prayer and/or scripture reading) as a time for shared worship, rest from daily work, helping and healing others, and celebration and praise of God. Adventists ideally prepare for the Sabbath during the week so that before Friday sundown their homes are clean, meals are prepared, and family members can rest and worship without being compelled to devote attention to "worldly things." While in the past (even as recently as the 1960s and 1970s, and among some "conservative" Adventists, still), Sabbath worship was deemed incompatible with specific (often recreational) activities, informants (especially those in institutional and urban settings) stressed the incompatibility of "rules" for Sabbath worship and "true, genuine, sincere, and personal worship of the Creator." Adventists are beginning to question the unwritten, but generally known, code for Sabbath worship—that hiking and walking are acceptable Sabbath activities, while biking is not acceptable; that wading in shallow water (below one's knees) is compatible with Sabbath worship, while swimming is unacceptable; that running and playing are allowable as long as no ball is used (Scriven 1987:47)—and to insist that veritable worship and praise of God may result from engaging in activities formerly deemed incompatible with Sabbath worship. It would be inaccurate to imply that all North American Adventists are rethinking Sabbath worship; certainly some Adventists contend unequivocally that Sabbath worship necessarily involves specific proscription of activity. Many informants, however, argued that to follow specific rules is not accordant "with a true celebration" of the Sabbath. Instead they explained that traditional Adventist rules of worship should be employed as "guidelines" to discover one's own most appropriate and "spiritually nurturing" mode of Sabbath celebration.[12]

Despite some disagreement in regard to appropriate Sabbath worship activities, celebration of the seventh-day Sabbath is an essential component in construction of the Adventist ethos. Adventists identify the Sabbath as the symbolic reminder of creation; God rested on the seventh day, following creation, and people must rest from regular routine, and worship God on the Sabbath to glorify and remember him. The Adventists with whom I attended worship services identified the Sabbath as a day of "joy," a time to "celebrate" and commemorate creation by exploring nature, a time to be with family and friends.

The Adventist Health Message

In addition to identity markers discussed above, Seventh-day Adventists find and demonstrate distinction through the health message—a series of dietary and health guidelines received in vision by Ellen White. Presented in the milieu of the nineteenth-century health reform movement (which promoted the "reform diet"—vegetarianism; increased use of nuts, grains, fruits, and vegetables; elimination of dairy products and tea and coffee; and limited use of spices and condiments), White's health message is in many respects identical to guidelines advocated by leaders of the health reform movement (see Lindén 1978; Numbers 1992 [1976]).[13] The American health reform movement, strongest between 1830 and the late 1860s, attempted to explicitly associate health and diet with "moral reform." Thus health reformers, who saw spices, dairy products, and especially meats as increasing the partaker's "animal nature" (sexual desire), proscribed these foods in an attempt to curb sexual activity. Masturbation, in particular, was deemed harmful to one's health and was emphatically discouraged. The Adventist health message incorporated the dietary guidelines of the health reformers (Ellen White discouraged meat-eating and the use of "stimulating foods" [including spices and condiments], proscribed the use of tobacco and alcohol, and encouraged Adventists to avoid prescription medications) and encouraged Adventists to exercise often, breathe fresh air, rest adequately, employ hydropathy as a curative method, and wear nonrestrictive clothing (i.e., avoid corsets and hoops). White's health message (especially after her *Appeal to Mothers* [1864]) also recognized a connection between sexual desire and diet, and warned graphically of the dangers of masturbation (see chapter 7).

The Adventist health message became a lasting ingredient of the Adventist way of life (unlike the nineteenth-century health reform movement in society generally) because it was integrated in Adventist theology—Adventists began to refer to the body as a "temple" which must "be made spotless" in preparation for the advent. Adventists came to recognize specific control of "physical appetites" as allowing inculcation of a spiritual outlook conducive to righteous growth. Thus, the avoidance of gambling, card-playing, novel-reading, theater attendance, immodest dress, and use of cosmetics and jewelry was not unlike avoiding meat, coffee, or condiments as both indicated proper self-control and unwillingness to indulge in base appetites. Each of these prohibitions "functioned, together with Sabbath observance, as powerful markers of Adventist identity" (Pearson 1990:43). Indulgence in "nonhealthy" appetites was associated with an inability to discern spiritual things; self-denial was held up as ideal, and "temperance in all things" was deemed necessary to prepare for Christ's coming.

Because Adventists associated the ability to discern spiritual truths with correct health, diet, and lifestyle choices, it became necessary not only to implement health reform among believers but to share the health message with others and, in so doing, prepare unbelievers to receive the truth of the Adventist message. Adventists thus constructed sanitariums, and later, hospitals, which originally had a strong evangelical component (but now are almost exclusively medically focused), in which SDAs and non-SDAs seek treatment that ideally encourages not only the healing of specific maladies but consideration of health in the context of life (dress, diet, religious, recreational) choices and attempts to heal the whole person.

Contemporary Adventists and "Standards"

While the Adventist identity remains predominantly unambiguously associated (in regard to health) with adherence to dietary guidelines, other components of nineteenth-century temperance advocated by Ellen White and other early adventist leaders (proscription of card-playing, novel-reading, theater attendance, use of cosmetics and jewelry) are in the process of being replaced within Adventism by less distinctive (and less restrictive) interpretations of SDA standards.[14] Young Adventists (Baby Boomers and their children) in particular have noted the apparent inconsistency in, for example, avoiding the theater but watching rented videos, or prohibiting the use of playing cards only to play card games designed and marketed for Adventists. Young Adventists have defined rigid adherence to SDA "standards" as one element of "immature faith"; to define spirituality by adherence to rules, they insist, is to fail to comprehend the "principles" from which the rules were derived, and to participate in a religious experience which can never progress beyond simple adherence to external codes of behavior. Although Adventists who reject strict, unquestioning adherence to standards (as demonstrating a lack of "mature faith") often adopt at least a revised (still recognizably Adventist) standard of behavior, they claim to base their adherence to that standard not on Adventist tradition alone but on a love for Christ out of which grows a desire to adhere to correct principles. Thus, Adventist women may use cosmetics but wear muted colors; Adventists may watch television but limit their viewing of secular television programs, or watch only Adventist programming; Adventists may wear wedding rings but avoid piercing their ears. Without oversimplifying the vast and complex range of Adventist adherence to "standards," it is apparent that younger Adventists in particular are redrawing the behavioral boundaries which have traditionally served to distinguish Adventism.

Conclusions

Adventists understand the world as a stage for a universal conflict between good and evil which will end with Christ's return and the universal vindication of God. Although Adventist belief has roots in Ellen White's role as a prophet, the sanctuary doctrine, the hope of the advent, and the seventh-day Sabbath, Adventist theology has grown and evolved in response to changing circumstance. The Adventist conception of present truth allows, encourages even, this renewal and, in many cases, rethinking of theology. The beliefs adumbrated above remain within the confines of the fundamental Adventist assumption that there exist in the universe two basic orientations—good and evil (good being associated with adherence and obedience to divine command, and evil consisting ultimately of disobedience)—and that salvation is available to those who obey God not out of a sense of obligation, duty, or desire for recognition but out of love for God. Adherence to the commandments and to SDA standards alone is not adequate to ensure salvation. Instead, Adventists are to believe in God, develop a personal relationship with Christ, and, as a consequence of the love that they develop for God, adhere to specific behavioral expectations. Any backsliding on the part of the believer is evidence of immature belief. As Adventists grow in love for and knowledge of Christ, wrongs are confessed and repentance sought, and consequently, fewer missteps are (ideally) made (see Schwartz 1970:104). But the possibility of salvation is, for Adventists, ambiguous: increasingly less comfortable defining morality in terms of adherence to a traditional regimen of behaviors, Adventists have begun to explore and embrace the idea that salvation is "a free gift" of "God's grace" (see also Pearson 1990). Adventism is poised, consequently, between a desire to interpret obedience to "God's law" as evidence of salvation, and a hesitancy to attribute salvation to anything other than "God's saving grace." While formal and informal informants negotiated a tenuous balance between these seemingly antithetic positions (see chapter 4), the tension created by this theological tug-of-war continues to create space in which Adventists may re-examine traditional SDA standards and beliefs and rethink what it means to be a Seventh-day Adventist.

Notes

1. "For Seventh-day Adventists, the great controversy between Christ and Satan is vivid and real. Satan is earnestly working to destroy earth's inhabitants; and Christ is working to save humankind, committing His people to a message of salvation and a warning against being deceived by Satan" (Gordon 1993:13).

2. "To make clear the eternal differences between God's government of love and law and that of selfish, arrogant greed and force is the central point of the cosmic controversy" (Douglass 1979:71).

3. According to one SDA writer, "the Seventh-day Adventist church, it may be humbly claimed, is nothing less than God's ecumenical movement of truth, providentially bringing together truths of the ongoing Reformation, relevant to our time. In fact, in its modern manifestation, it is the 'final remnant' of His true church [spanning] the centuries" (Emmerson 1983:7).

4. Despite her insistence upon her unique position as God's contemporary messenger, however, Ellen White did make statements insisting that only the Bible could serve as an infallible source of guidance, and encouraging Adventists to give the Bible ultimate preeminence over her writings.

5. "In fact, [Ellen White's] writings seem to have a similar degree of infallibility [as the Bible], a quotation from them invariably serving as the definitive statement on this or that question raised by scripture" (Theobald 1980:98).

6. "When any have sins remaining upon the books of record, unrepented of and unforgiven, their names will be blotted out of the book of life," they will loose the possibility of salvation, and "the record of their good deeds will be erased from the book of God's remembrance" (White 1911 [1888]:483).

7. "Some Adventists even suggest that at whatever moment this heavenly assize takes up the case of any living person, it passes the final verdict and there and then closes the probation of that individual" (Adams 1993:121–22).

8. In the December 1935 "Girl's Problems" section of the *Review and Herald,* two women wrote to ask whether they should marry as time was "to end soon."

9. The November 7, 1985, *Adventist Review* cover depicted a realistic rendition of people climbing from their graves, hugging and greeting the living (vol. 162, no. 50).

10. "Death is not a complete annihilation; it is only a state of temporary unconsciousness while the [righteous] person awaits the resurrection" (Ministerial Association 1988:352).

11. At one vespers service at which I was in attendance, the speaker spent nearly an hour outlining in detail activities in which those who are deemed righteous will participate after death.

12. Some SDA Sabbath traditions, such as refraining from working for wages on the Sabbath, remain unchallenged.

13. Lindén (1978) and Numbers (1992 [1976]) argue that Ellen White was aware of the tenets of the health reform movement's dietary restrictions prior to her health vision, although she denied any knowledge of guidelines advocated by the health reform movement and expressed surprise when she "learned," following her vision, that others "supported her ideas" (Lindén 1978:317).

14. Many of the inactive Adventists with whom I spoke noted that they continue to avoid food proscribed by the SDA health message.

3

Seventh-day Adventist Organization

Adventism has grown, from its beginnings as a "scattered remnant" of less than one hundred disappointed Millerites, into an international organization coordinating religious, educational, medical, and publishing institutions, diverse media programs, book distribution centers, and international financial holdings. Because the tenuous organizational structure originally achieved by James White in the face of opposition from "anti-Babylon" (anti-organization) Millerites was unable to deal adequately with the rapid institutional growth of Adventism in the 1880s, or the national financial crisis of the 1890s (due primarily to a lack of centralized fiscal planning [Graybill 1983]), Adventist leadership called for reorganization by the turn of the century (Schwarz 1986). Between 1855 and 1901 Seventh-day Adventism built and/or gained control of twelve publishing houses, seventeen educational institutions, and fourteen medical facilities, each of which was independently operated.[1] In response to the confusion ensuing from independent financial control of so many facilities, Adventist leaders, in 1901, collected all SDA institutions under the umbrella of a centralized organization (the Adventist General Conference) and institutional leaders were appointed to serve on electoral and executive committees within the General Conference. The organizational structure instituted in 1901 continues to serve as the basis for Adventist organization worldwide.

Overview of Adventist Organization

The primary unit in Adventist organization, Adventists explain, is the individual, who, with anywhere between twenty-five and over four thousand other individuals, forms a congregation, or "home church." Congregations within loosely drawn geographical boundaries, in turn, comprise a Local Conference, which oversees local elementary schools, Junior Academies (middle schools), Academies (high schools), and a number of Local Conferences, again, within given geographical boundaries, form a Union Conference. Union Conferences, which administer Adventist colleges and universities, together comprise a division, and divisions (such as the North American Division [NAD], composed of Canada and the United States) together form the General Conference.

The General Conference is, according to both the writings of Ellen White and contemporary SDA literature, the recipient of divine guidance, and consequently is "the highest authority, under God," on earth (Teel 1980:26). Responsible for administration of the "world church" between meetings of the General Conference, the General Conference Executive Committee—which formulates SDA policy, conducts business transactions, fills General Conference vacancies, reviews recommendations from lower committees, and resolves doctrinal conflict—is composed of over three hundred members who are elected by delegates from around the world every five years at General Conference meetings. Although only fifteen members of the executive committee are needed for a quorum at committee meetings, larger meetings of the committee are held biannually—each spring and autumn.

At the primary meeting of the executive committee (held annually in October), committee members elect officers, adopt an annual budget, decide policies, and make doctrinal and constitutional changes. In addition, the General Conference maintains several departments—including church ministries, publishing, risk management, world radio, family ministries, global mission, communication, health and temperance, education, children's ministries, auditing, public affairs, and religious liberty—which oversee areas of special interest to Adventists. All departments (each of which is advisory, not administrative) have a director, several associate and assistant directors, and an advisory board of governors and trustees (Houck 1987:38). The General Conference also administers specific Adventist offices and programs including ADRA (Adventist Disaster and Relief Agency), the Adventist Media Center, Adventist Health Systems, Layman's Services and Industries, the Office of Human Relations (which oversees issues and policies concerning racial minorities), Risk Management Services (insurance), the Biblical Research Institute, the Geoscience Research Institute, and the Ellen G. White Estate, Inc. (Bull and Lockhart 1989:97–98).

Conference and committee officers are elected every five years at General Conference meetings by delegates-at-large (all members of the General Conference Executive Committee, four delegates chosen by each division, and one additional delegate per division for each two hundred thousand members) and regular delegates (the president of each union, one delegate-at-large, one delegate for each mission or conference in the union's territory, and one additional delegate for every five thousand members) (Bull and Lockhart 1989:98–99).

Delegates select and appoint a nominating committee (only official delegates may be chosen), which in turn selects its own chairperson.[2] Five to ten names are accepted by the committee's chair for the position of General Conference president, the names are discussed, and a secret ballot is taken. Though there is rarely a clear majority, the two or three names that receive the most support are selected and brought for another vote (the other names being discarded). The person receiving the most votes is selected as the General Conference president, and his name is put before the delegates for a confirming voice vote.[3] The delegates as a whole thus do not have a choice *between* candidates, only to accept or reject the choice of the nominating committee. The newly elected president is then made a member of the nominating committee, which goes on to select a secretary, a treasurer, general vice-presidents, division presidents, departmental secretaries, and division officers (see Kwiram 1975).[4]

In addition to the NAD (843,689 members), the General Conference oversees the following divisions: Africa/India Ocean (1,123,569), Eastern Africa (1,525,041), Euro-Africa (444,063), Euro-Asia (112,102), Inter-American (1,642,339), Northern Asia Pacific (157,742), South American (1,386,666), South Pacific (288,623), Southern Asia (231,821), Southern Asia Pacific (938,174), and Trans-European (91,983) (*SDA Yearbook* 1997).[5] Each division contains several Union Conferences, which legally own and control all SDA institutions within their geographical limits, and each union, in turn, oversees its own Local Conferences. In the NAD, each Local Conference consists of one or more states or provinces, and the boundaries of the conferences are determined by geographical features.[6] Local Conferences, like the General Conference, administer departments, including a communication department (coordinates public relations), a trust department (manages estates, wills, and financial gifts), a youth department (oversees conference youth camps and programs), a publishing department, an education department (manages conference primary and secondary schools), and a health and temperance department. Also like the General Conference, Local Conferences have executive committees which manage operations between (in the case of Local Conferences, triennial) leadership meetings. Local Conferences employ pastors, Bible workers, evangelists, administrators, and teachers; "issue and renew licenses, credentials and certificates"; assign pastors to congregations; and sponsor annual camp meetings (Houck 1987:43).

At the most local level of Adventist organization, conferences are subdivided into one or more congregations, which are overseen by pastors. Adventist pastors are normally ordained following formal training at Andrews University Seminary,[7] an internship, and examination of individual beliefs, attitudes, religious experience, and general ability and fitness to serve as an ordained minister. Following ordination pastors may baptize, perform marriages, and conduct the congregation's quarterly communion service (see below).[8] Ordination, according to Adventist teaching, is recognition of a call by the religious body as a group, and should be preceded by a call from God.

The pastor is assisted in meeting his/her responsibilities by lay leaders, elected annually by the congregation. Local lay worship involves elders, who may lead public worship; deacons and deaconesses, who serve the congregation by assisting members in need ("the poor and sick") and by providing assistance during baptism and communion services; Sabbath school superintendents, who manage the Sabbath school; the personal ministries leader, who encourages outreach and witnessing activities; the community services leader, who directs health and welfare programs aimed at meeting local needs; and the church board, which conducts the congregation's business matters.

Formal Adventist Worship

Adventist meetings, particularly Sabbath school meetings, allow an optimal degree of individual participation and interpretation (see Bull 1988:152; Bull and Lockhart 1989:83). Sabbath worship includes Sabbath school (meetings of age groups with a teacher/discussion leader) and worship service (a meeting of the congregation in the "sanctuary" [main chapel]).[9] Adult Sabbath school classes vary greatly between and even within (in larger congregations in which there are several Sabbath school classes) congregations. Some emphasize passive listening (offering a prepared lesson, or even videotape for viewing), but most provide a format for discussion of points raised by the lesson quarterly, with the Sabbath school teacher serving as facilitator. Adult Sabbath school classes also vary greatly in content—although quarterlies[10] are uniform throughout—with some classes adhering carefully to accepted ("traditional," "conservative") SDA teachings, and others allowing and even encouraging questioning of doctrine and examination of the parameters of Adventist teachings (especially in congregations associated with an Adventist college or university). Sabbath school lessons (which would often be more appropriately titled discussions) evolve each Sabbath in response to the needs of class members, the composition of the class, and participants' interests, although the parameters of discussion are determined by shared belief, theology, and doctrine.

Sabbath worship service, which follows Sabbath school, begins with one or more congregational hymns, and involves congregational prayer, at least one offering, additional congregational singing (or special musical performance), and a sermon or Bible study. Once each quarter, congregations hold a communion service. Prior to communion, the congregation's men and women separate and divide into pairs and perform, in the classrooms of the home church, a foot-washing ritual; men wash the feet of, and have their feet washed by, another man, and women wash the feet of, and have their feet washed by, another woman, using prearranged bowls of water and towels. Sometimes referred to as a "little baptism," foot washing is to be accompanied by a confession of sin to fellow believers, and allows participants to humble themselves in preparation for communion.[11] After foot washing, Adventists return to the Sanctuary where they remain seated as unleavened bread (wheat crackers) and grape juice (both prepared by the deaconesses prior to the service) are blessed through an extemporaneous prayer offered by the congregation's pastor or an ordained elder and passed to the congregation by the deacons. The Adventist communion, a symbolic act to encourage remembrance of Christ's death, is open—all who believe themselves worthy may participate (Lindén 1978:123).

In addition to Sabbath meetings, Adventists participate in a number of worship services and activities throughout the week. Adventists, especially older SDAs, gather midweek for a prayer meeting in which an elder or pastor leads worshipers in singing, studying, praying, and sharing personal testimony. Adventists also sometimes choose to meet in "small groups" in the home of an individual member one evening each week to study a text or topic of particular interest to the group's participants. Each summer (in a tradition dating, within Adventism, back to the Millerite movement), Adventists gather with others from their Local Conferences to attend a series of worship meetings lasting between seven and ten days at camp meeting. Speakers offer instruction on a range of topics (including, for example, health, financial planning, parenting, Bible study, and personal evangelism) and conference members participate in enthusiastic religious singing, prayer, and worship intended to inspire religious revival. In addition, each autumn Adventists hold a Week of Prayer which commences with Sabbath morning worship and continues through the week with nightly meetings at the church or in private homes, as well as personal daily study of special *Review* devotionals. The Week of Prayer concludes the following Sabbath with the annual sacrifice offering, during which members are encouraged to donate between one day and one week's wages to the SDA world budget.

Informal Adventist Worship

Despite a lengthy list of formal worship meetings, the worship most emphasized by individual Adventists is informal. Personal and family devotionals, Adventists reiterate consistently, are to take place daily, and although the structure and content of individual and family worship differ widely, most Adventists agree that both should occur at least once daily and should involve some combination of prayer, Bible study, meditation, and possibly (in family worship) song. The goal of family and (especially) individual devotions, is to create "a personal relationship with Christ" and to improve one's "walk with Jesus." This being the case, personal worship may include Scripture or other religious reading, enjoying nature, taking a walk, or listening to a religious broadcast. In addition to daily worship, Adventist families often gather in prayer, song, and Scripture reading on Friday evening to "welcome the Sabbath" (vespers) and participate in a special family worship on Sabbath afternoon or evening.

Conversion

Since the "door to salvation" was opened around 1850, Adventism has gradually come to encourage evangelical efforts both nationally and throughout the world. Ellen White wrote in the *Great Controversy* that although sharing Adventism with nonbelievers may cause one to become the target of ridicule, Adventists have the responsibility to share news of the soon coming advent and to call nonbelievers to repentance (White 1913 [1890]:458–60). Contemporary Adventists participate in evangelical work by "witnessing" to the non-Adventists with whom they come into contact in daily activities as well as by participating in more involved, structured missionary work. Adventists are reminded in sermons and publications that it is their responsibility to witness: "Jesus prophesied that the gospel would be *preached;* the Lord calls us to be his *witnesses*" (D. 1985:13–14; emphasis in original). Adventists are told that witnessing activities "require one to speak up boldly" and are necessary to salvation.[12] Witnessing activities are frequently informal and spontaneous and may involve simply expressing belief in Christ's love to a co-worker, sharing a book with an acquaintance, or living in a manner that illuminates the effect of the gospel on one individual life.[13]

In addition to witnessing, Adventists engage in missionary activities which have "tended to replace local patterns of leadership roles and organization with standard [movement-wide] structures" (Pearson 1990:6). Adventists send missionaries around the world to perform a variety of services in combination with evangelical work. Adventist missionaries offer language training and medical, dental, and health services as they teach potential converts about Adventism. Students also often participate in missionary labors, taking a year away from university or college—again, attempting to meet some practical need of local peoples but in an evangelical context.

In the United States and Europe, Adventists, especially in urban areas, rent public halls or theaters in which to hold evangelical series. Widely advertised, the series generally commence with lectures focusing on secular topics and progress toward more obviously Adventist presentations until an altar call is made. Adventists also hold health seminars (most predominantly meetings to help people quit smoking, but also, for example, dental hygiene lessons or nutrition information presentations) in local churches or health clinics, and use the interaction therein to engage in evangelical work (although some Adventists currently voice concern that such services have lost their evangelical component).[14]

While Adventists offer evangelical series in rented halls and theaters and attempt to attract converts in health seminars, a primary tool for socialization of SDA offspring leading to baptism is the SDA school system. Eighty percent of children from SDA homes who eventually choose to be baptized attended (though not always for the full duration) SDA primary schools. One 1950 study found that 100 percent of Adventist offspring who attended Adventist schools for the entirety of their education—primary school through college or university—were baptized as Adventists (although 12 percent of study participants later withdrew from Adventism) (Bull and Lockhart 1989:117–18). Indeed, the Adventist peer group, a product of SDA educational facilities, plays an important role in the conversion experiences of Adventists who attend SDA schools. One pastor interviewed, for example, noted that many of the young candidates from Adventist families that he interviewed for baptism knew little or nothing about theological explanations of such pivotal SDA doctrines as the sanctuary or the Seventh-day Sabbath prior to specific study of such doctrines in preparation for baptism. He stated that: "The youth [from Adventist families] often choose to be baptized originally because their friends are being baptized. This is not to deny the sincerity of their faith or to demean their religious experience—all candidates study and are prepared for baptism—but the initial choice to be baptized, that often is a result (consciously or not) of the fact that a young person's friends, his peer group at school, is choosing to be baptized. As well, of course, as the fact that his parents and his extended support network are usually hopeful that he will be baptized."

Indeed, Adventist offspring are prepared in the nuclear family setting for Adventist life. Adventists dedicate their children as infants "to God in prayer" as a scheduled part of Sabbath worship service in order to entrust offspring to the "service and knowledge of God" and to commit themselves publicly to raising their children "in righteousness." Depending on the religiosity of a young person's parents, the SDA youth may participate in a lifestyle (health, apparel, recreational activities, worship activities, religious belief) which, although similar to that of her peers (if she attends SDA schools), is distinct (to varying degrees) from that advocated in secular society. In this way Adventist offspring learn not only Adventist belief but the Adventist way of life, and prepare to participate as adults in Adventism.

Prior to baptism by immersion, the candidate is expected to make a confession of faith and to participate in a catechumenical course. Prior to baptism, she is presented to the congregation and is voted into church membership effective upon baptism. Candidates are baptized in a baptismal font in the front of the sanctuary before all those attending worship service. Adventists believe that baptism, which is necessary for salvation, cleanses the sins of the believer, and symbolizes her death to the world and her new birth in Christ.

Adventist Finances

Adventism is organized as a financial cooperative in which moneys are controlled centrally, by the General Conference, and distributed in a manner that allows financially less stable segments to be subsidized by those with greater revenues.[15] Adventism's most important source of revenue—tithing—grew from the practice of "systematic benevolence" established among adventists in the 1850s. Prior to that time adventists participated in voluntary giving, which quickly proved an insufficient means of financial support. In 1855 James White called for systematic giving, and though his request did not receive widespread support, in 1859 systematic benevolence, which requested specific donations based on the age and the sex of the donor,[16] was instituted (Strayer 1986).[17]

Systematic benevolence also proved inadequate, and in the 1860s and 1870s Adventist leaders, especially James and Ellen White, advocated and eventually instituted tithing, a donation system which continues to provide Adventism's major source of funding. Adventists were told, in the 1860s and 1870s, that one-tenth of their earnings belonged to God and should be returned to him (Strayer 1986:52). Though payment of tithes is not required in contemporary Adventism for membership, Adventists continue to be taught that 10 percent of their earnings belong to God (Houck 1987:38). Furthermore, Adventism has evolved an understanding of tithing which distinguishes full payment of tithe as precipitating financial reward.[18] One informant said that as a result of tithe payment she had been "blessed with a beautiful home" and other possessions: "I have been amazed at the blessings God has granted us. If you tithe, you are blessed. We obey out of loyalty, but also, God promised blessings to those who obey."[19]

After tithing, offerings and Ingathering supply Adventism's largest sources of revenue. In addition to the regular mission offering collected in Sabbath school (which supports the World Mission fund), Adventists collect non-tithe donations through Thirteenth Sabbath offerings, Sabbath school investment offerings, and birthday/thank offerings. The Thirteenth Sabbath offering, held on the last Sabbath of the quarter (the thirteenth Sabbath), is preceded by a media presentation, often emotionally evocative, outlining a specific need and requesting that members give generously to support a particular project such as the construction of a girls' dormitory in Guyana or a nursing facility in New Guinea. One-quarter of the funds collected through the Thirteenth Sabbath offering are contributed to the special project portrayed; the remainder go to the general World Mission budget. Funds contributed to Individual Investment offerings are raised as individual Adventists invest funds in entrepreneurial endeavors and then contribute their revenues to the Investment offering.[20] Birthday/thank offerings are collected each month in Sabbath school; members are encouraged to contribute if they have a birthday during the month or simply to express gratitude for their blessings.

Unlike moneys gathered through offerings, outlined above, in Ingathering Adventists solicit moneys from the general public. Adventists go door to door collecting funds for the Adventist Development and Relief Agency (ADRA), and although the literature distributed during Ingathering features graphic images of undernourished children, Ingathering funds, in addition to supporting ADRA, are used to support Adventism as a whole. (According to Donald F. Gilbert [1990], between 1 percent and 1.5 percent of Ingathering funds go to ADRA.)[21]

Adventist Institution Building

In part, Adventism's extensive complex of fund-raising techniques has evolved as a necessary support mechanism for the dramatic development and growth of Adventist institutions. Adventism, with a vast network of publishing facilities, an international system of hospitals and other health facilities, and the second largest parochial school system in the world, "is an alternative social system that meets the needs of its members from the cradle to the grave" (Bull and Lockhart 1989:96). Adventist evangelism, as envisioned by Ellen White and General Conference leaders, incorporated a combination not only of preaching but of the distribution of tracts and literature, physical healing, and institutionalized, religiously focused education (Vandevere 1986). Adventist evangelism thus required institution building, which in turn necessitated a steady, reliable source of funding.[22]

Education

Although Adventism arose as a movement dedicated to proclaiming and preparing for Christ's soon coming, as time continued Adventists of necessity were forced to consider temporal needs: "Eventually the pioneers, while hoping and praying for Jesus' soon return, had to face the issue of whether or not to educate their own children" (Watts 1992:59). Having only recently "come out of Babylon," the idea of creating separate Adventist schools appealed to early SDAs not only as offering a tool for the socialization of children but as providing an "opportunity to establish educational reforms that to them more fully reflected God's will" (Vandevere 1986:66). Though attempts to develop schools prior to the 1870s were unsuccessful, Goodloe H. Bell opened the first officially recognized SDA school on June 3, 1872, with seventy-two Adventist students, in Battle Creek, Michigan. The school, following Ellen White's counsels on education, stressed the maintenance of a balance between physical, mental, and spiritual development, and taught trades and agriculture in addition to providing an academic curriculum.

The implementation of Adventist educational reforms continued with the construction of elementary and secondary schools as well as colleges and universities,[23] until currently, participation in a separate educational system is an expected (or at least desired) component of the Adventist experience.[24] Adventist schools, colleges, and universities socialize young Adventists, train future SDA employees, and employ academic Adventists; Adventist parents plan and make financial sacrifices in order to ensure their ability to pay the tuition necessary to allow their children to attend SDA schools; and members contribute to the Adventist educational system through offerings, estate gifts, prayers for SDA students and teachers, and private donations of time and money.[25] Altogether, Adventists operate 4,522 primary schools, 900 secondary schools, 81 tertiary programs, and 30 worker training institutions (phone call to General Conference Department of Archives and Statistics 1997).

Health Care

The Adventist health care system originated with the construction of the Battle Creek Sanitarium following a disappointing encounter by James and Ellen White with secular health care. The sanitarium, built at the Whites' (especially Ellen's) urging and constructed quickly (over a period of several months), "was not considered as a denial" of Adventists' belief in the imminent advent (Damsteegt 1977:240). Instead, due to the failing health of Adventist leaders (including James White), the sanitarium was seen by many as a way of restoring the health of the movement's leadership and membership, and thereby invigorating the movement and hastening the advent.

The Adventist Health System (AHS) burgeoned after the destruction of the Battle Creek Sanitarium by fire; the Adventist health message was incorporated with evangelical efforts after that time, and foreign missionaries were encouraged by Ellen White to be "medical missionaries," capable of healing body as well as spirit. Consequently, Adventists used their growing educational system to train health care workers, and Adventist hospitals arose to assist in training physicians and nurses, to employ Adventist medical workers, to provide treatment facilities for Adventists, and to provide medical care (ideally accompanied by evangelical efforts) to secular society. The AHS, which grew as a result of the Adventist desire to avoid secular influences in health care treatment, is now a leading national health care corporation, with an annual budget of over two billion dollars (Pearson 1990:29). Extensive development of health care facilities, unlike the rapid construction of the original Battle Creek Sanitarium, provides "evidence that the expectation of the soon coming savior lost some of its urgency" for modern Adventists (Damsteegt 1977:241). With fifty-three hospitals and medical centers and twenty-eight nursing homes and retirement centers, the AHS is one of the largest health care providers in North America (see Bull and Lockhart 1989).

Publication and Media Services

In addition to extensive health care and educational institutions, Adventists maintain publication facilities, including the Review and Herald Publishing Association (Maryland), and the Pacific Press Publishing Association (Idaho), which together publish almost fifty periodicals and print books for distribution in Adventist Book Centers (ABCs) internationally. With the introduction of radio and television, Adventists have also embraced electronic evangelism with the Adventist Radio Network (approximately one dozen radio stations based at Adventist schools and colleges) and the Adventist Media Center (California), which produces the *Voice of Prophecy* (radio), and *Breath of Life, Faith for Today,* and *It Is Written* (television).

Tensions of Institutionalization

Although Adventists believe in and hope for the soon coming of Christ, they spend millions of dollars building and operating temporal institutions and structures of worship. Early adventists who perceived these concomitant goals as incompatible and argued that resources dedicated to institution building detracted from preparation for the advent were told by Ellen White to "let no one conclude that, because the end is near, there is no need of special effort to build up the various institutions as the cause shall demand" (in Branson 1976:23). Instead, Ellen White explained, institution building could further the work necessary to prepare for Christ's coming: "Schools must be established, that the young may be educated. . . . Institutions for the treatment of the sick must be established. . . . Since the Lord is soon to come, act decidedly and determinedly to increase the facilities, that a great work may be done in a short time" (ibid.). "By the mid-1880s" Adventists were simultaneously "creating a considerably isolated subculture and attempting to penetrate the larger society through evangelism" (Vandevere 1986:67). The effort to train Adventist physicians in Adventist facilities so that they could later serve as medical evangelists, the attempt to train colporteurs (literature evangelists) in distinct sectarian institutions for future work in the world—in short, the attempt to socialize and train Adventist youth in separate institutional settings for future evangelical work largely within those same (health, educational, publishing, media) institutions—led to a pronounced tension between the sectarian tendency to isolation and a tendency toward increased concern with secular society (ibid.; see chapter 4).

This tension is implicit in the goals explicated for Adventist institutions, which are not only to serve the needs of individual Adventists but to make a favorable impression on non-Adventists and thereby forward evangelical work. Ellen White claimed that "our sanitariums are to be established for one object—the proclamation of truth for this time. And they are to be so conducted that a decided impression in favor of the truth will be made on the minds of those who come to them for treatment" (in Douglass 1979:144). She wrote further that Adventists "are not only to publish the theory of the truth, but to present a practical illustration of it in character and in life. Our publishing institutions are to stand before the world as an embodiment of Christian principles" (ibid.). "In other words, personally *and institutionally,* Adventism's highest priority is to reveal to the world . . . the glory of God's character, and thus to vindicate his government" (ibid.; emphasis added).

Adventism, in its attempt to build unique institutions conducive to sectarian separation and then to use those institutions to evangelize the world, became poised between two disparate ends. Further, the means (institution building) adopted in the attempt to reach Adventism's desired end (successful evangelism) seemingly denied the movement's explicit raison d'être (the parousia): "For a movement which still formally commits itself to a belief in the imminent end of things . . . extensive this-worldly involvement, particularly in institutions and activities which are directed to the preservation and improvement of mortal existence, would seem to pose something of a paradox" (Theobald 1985:110).

The paradox of Adventist institution building, though it continues to pose a conflict for SDAs, appears to be in the process of being resolved in favor of meeting temporal rather than adventual goals. Although Adventists insist that the two are not exclusive (temporal work, again, is said to hasten the advent) and although Adventists continue to use (especially publishing and educational) institutions to teach about Christ's coming, Adventist institutionalism has simultaneously created space and justification for Adventist separation from secular society and at the same time lessened Adventist distinction from the world. First, Adventist institution building requires a "reservoir of highly qualified workers to operate . . . medical, educational and publishing institutions" (Pearson 1990:87). Although Adventist institutions are to be firmly entrenched in SDA doctrine, including emphasis upon the impending advent, widespread entry into education, medicine, and publishing "entail[s] . . . a shift from an other-worldly preoccupation with the second coming to a concern with the preservation and enhancement of life on earth" (Theobald 1985:114). But Adventists, who share unique rules of diet, dress, and behavior—who are, according to Butler, "a kind of ethnic group"—create networks of social relationships within Adventist institutions and the communities that grow up around those institutions (Butler 1992:xxix).[26] While the seventh-day Sabbath and other religious prescriptions make social interaction with those outside Adventism difficult, development of SDA institutions creates communities in which Adventists can easily associate with others who share a common belief system (Bull 1988:155). Thus, although the SDA tendency to live in "'Adventist Ghettos' may in fact be an attempt to seek the support of a 'counter culture' in maintaining a view of the world that is at odds with radical secularism" (Guy 1972:27), "in the late twentieth century, Adventists have, with the changing social trends, become less distinctive in their lifestyle," even though they are "more isolated in historical and geographical terms" (Bull and Lockhart 1989:91). As Adventists participate in the educational preparation necessary to work in SDA institutions, they are exposed (even in SDA colleges and universities) to secular ideas (especially since the 1960s, when Adventist educators increasingly began to enroll in secular graduate programs; see chapter 4). Consequently, while many Adventists live and work in communities that have a large proportion of Seventh-day Adventists,[27] the Adventist lifestyle has become increasingly concentrated on meeting temporal needs, and has become less obviously distinguishable from that of non-Adventists.

The tensions, both within Adventism as a whole and at the level of individual members, necessitate varying degrees of conflict. Adventists are to be in the world but not of the world, and they attempt to meet this objective by simultaneously withdrawing from secular society into Adventist communities and creating a massive complex of institutions, buildings, and facilities to meet temporal and religious needs, and at the same time, on an individual level, Adventists hope for Christ's soon coming and accumulate temporal education, occupations, and wealth. The tensions which result from these various conflicts have led to specific crises in Adventism.

Notes

1. During approximately the same time period, Adventist membership grew from thirty-five hundred to about eighty thousand (Schwarz 1986).

2. The divisions are represented on the nominating committee based on their proportion of world membership.

3. Because women cannot be ordained, no woman has ever served as the General Conference president.

4. Although selection of SDA leadership is regularly described as "representative" and labeled "democratic" in Adventist publications and by Adventist leadership (Task Force Report 1982), *Spectrum* (a publication by and for SDA intellectuals; see chapter 4) contends that lay people have "virtually no impact on the selection of church leadership" (Kwiram 1975:20) because "very few lay persons and even fewer women are represented in the delegation" (ibid.:18). Further, the NAD has a disproportionately high number of delegates present at General Conference meetings, both because meetings are held within the NAD and because the NAD is the wealthiest division and can afford to send delegates to General Conference gatherings. Lay Adventists and pastors often reconcile this lack of equal representation by explaining, as one Adventist pastor did to the author, that "the church is a theocracy, not a democracy"; thus, God is at the head of Seventh-day Adventism guiding the General Conference in its actions, and equal representation is consequently not crucial. Not all Adventists share this opinion, as some groups of SDAs, especially African Americans, Adventists from developing countries, and women in the NAD, have begun to insist that they be equally represented in the process of leadership selection (see Branson 1972).

5. The General Conference also oversees two large unions—the Southern Africa Union (69,955) and the China Union (199,823).

6. If Local Conferences are not financially self-sufficient they are labeled "missions" or "sections."

7. Practical experience is often determined to be an adequate substitute for this requirement.

8. Some who are not ordained (including Adventist women serving as associates in pastoral care, and elders) also perform these duties.

9. Sabbath school classes include Cradle Roll (infants and toddlers), the Kindergarten, the Primary, the Juniors, the Earliteens, Youth, and Adults.

10. Lesson quarterlies are distributed regularly, beginning in January, and provide daily study texts for Sabbath school preparation.

11. Foot washing, incorporated into Adventist worship before the movement was officially organized, is avoided by some contemporary Adventists who "deliberately absent themselves from the service each quarter because they find it distasteful and repulsive" (Venden 1984b:30).

12. "The Bible even assigns us a certain responsibility for the blood of lost sinners if we fail to warn them. We must confess Jesus before others in order to be recognized by Him" [D. 1985:14].

13. While completing fieldwork, I was frequently the object of members' witnessing activities. Interview participants regularly used the opportunity provided by the interview to speak with an "outsider" to express belief in the tenets of Adventist doctrine.

14. A majority of new converts to Adventism are in marginal positions both socially and economically. In addition, the overwhelming majority of SDA converts are previously Protestant (73 percent), though some have no religious affiliation (19 percent), and some (6 percent) are previously Catholic. The average age of a convert to Adventism is thirty-five, she is most often (59 percent) a woman, and has, on average, an eleventh-grade education. Fifty-four percent of converts have an annual income below $15,000; 19 percent are professionals; 16 percent, students; 11 percent, skilled laborers; 19 percent, homemakers; and 11 percent, unskilled laborers (see Bull and Lockhart 1989). A relatively high proportion (13 percent) of those who choose to embrace Adventism are Hispanic (Hispanics comprise only 3 percent of the general population in the United States) and have at least some Christian background (95 percent of converts) (Pearson 1990:31).

15. Ten percent of moneys collected at the Local Conference level are donated to the Union Conference and Union Conferences, in turn, give 10 percent of the moneys they collect to the General Conference. The General Conference uses its funds to administer SDA institutions (colleges, universities, hospitals) and redistributes funds to divisions that lack adequate financial support.

16. Men between the ages of eighteen and sixty were to donate between five and twenty-five cents each week, and women in the same age category were to donate between two and ten cents each week. Adventists were also to donate between one and five dollars annually for each $100 of property they owned.

17. Ellen White's *Testimonies* supported systematic benevolence and cautioned that those who failed to give would meet with financial failure (Lindén 1978:117).

18. In one 1935 *Review* feature, for example, Adventists provided examples of how

specific needs had been met as the direct result of tithe payment. Interestingly, the feature was a regular addition to the *Review* for the duration of the Great Depression.

19. As Schwartz pointed out in 1970, a historical Adventist belief in the investigative judgment prior to the advent, accompanied by a concomitant belief that those who live righteously will be tangibly "blessed by God," has also contributed to an Adventist association between righteousness and attainment of a middle-class lifestyle. Adventists, who generally regard as desirable the careful management of financial resources, associate those characteristics typically identified with an American, middle-class lifestyle with personal, spiritual refinement. Schwartz found that Adventists, with a collective emphasis on meeting temporal needs (institution building) and a devotion to attaining the symbols of status associated with a middle-class lifestyle (homes, automobiles, jeweled watches) had an ambiguous conviction of Christ's soon coming (although this ambiguity was found to be at least partially reconciled by a conviction that present temporal work hastens the parousia)(Schwartz 1970; see also Pearson 1990:89).

20. Individual Investment projects net more than four million dollars each year (Houck 1987:13).

21. Funds from Ingathering and offerings totaled over $150 million in 1993.

22. Institutionalization commenced outside of North America in Europe during the 1870s, in Australia, Africa, and the West Indies in the 1880s, and in China, India, Japan, and Latin America in the 1890s.

23. In an attempt to implement White's educational ideas (to train Adventist workers to fill positions in newly developing SDA institutions), and to make education more widely available to members' children, additional Adventist schools, including Battle Creek College (later Andrews University), were built in the 1880s. The curriculum offered by Battle Creek College was not originally unlike that offered at secular colleges of the time. Ellen and James White, displeased by the lack of peculiar Adventist identity embodied in Battle Creek College, insisted on reforms.

24. In part as a result of Adventist emphasis on participation in higher education, Adventist membership is highly correlated with upward social mobility: "There is a good deal of evidence to confirm the view that Adventists value material success, are upwardly mobile, and are disproportionately represented in the professional and skilled occupations" (Pearson 1990:86). Forty percent of Adventist men and 33 percent of Adventist women have earned college diplomas, over half have at least some postsecondary education, and the number of Adventists without a high school diploma is half that of the general population. Moreover, Black and Hispanic Adventist men are slightly more likely than Caucasian Adventist men to complete college (see Sahlin 1989). Consequently, Adventists, although they often are employed by SDA institutions whose salaries are lower than those paid for comparable positions in non-SDA facilities and institutions, earn relatively high wages. Even Adventist women, who, like women generally, earn less than their male counterparts, are disproportionately represented in

skilled and professional occupations. Seventy-five percent of Adventist women who are not retired are employed for wages; 66 percent of these women work full-time. Only twenty percent of Adventist women identify themselves as homemakers (ibid.:21).

25. While participating in Adventist activities, for example, I had the opportunity to assist in painting the exterior of a primary school with other local Adventists in preparation for the upcoming school year.

26. Although Ellen White warned Adventists against the tendency to congregate in isolated communities, "The principal means of achieving a measure of insulation from the modern world, . . . is through the establishment of Adventist communities. A large number, though not a majority, of members live in communities clustering around medical or educational institutions" (Pearson 1990:27).

27. Communities comprised of a proportionately large number of Adventists offer services and products desired by Adventists which are not always easily available in relatively small communities (as many of these communities are). In one fieldwork community, for example, groceries and restaurants provided residents (a large number of whom attended or were employed by an Adventist liberal arts college) with a wide variety of food items appropriate to the Adventist diet (but not widely available in most rural communities at the time). The local McDonalds sold a vegi-burger, for example, that other outlets in nearby towns did not offer. Business also closed on Saturday but were open on Sunday.

4

Contemporary Crises in Adventism

Early Adventists (1844–60) were outsiders not only to American secular society but to mainline Protestant tradition: "They were the come-outers of the come-outers, a remnant of the remnant" (Teel 1984:25). With the introduction of systematic benevolence (1859), formal organization (1860s), a written statement of "fundamental beliefs" (1870s), and institution building (1870s–present), Adventism began to move toward a changed, less hostile, though still ambivalent response to secular society. It would be an oversimplification to portray Adventism's progressive response to the world as one of continually increasing accommodation. Rather, Adventism has fluctuated between attempts to align itself with mainline Protestantism and efforts to emphasize Adventist distinction and thereby dissociate from those outside of the movement. In the last three decades, crises within the movement have profoundly influenced Adventism's response to the world.

Secular Graduate Education and the Formation of the AAF

Adventism has, since the 1960s, undergone a number of internal crises, the most important instigator of which was increased Adventist participation in higher education (especially in secular graduate programs). Between 1930 and 1960, NAD Adventist participation in college and graduate level education increased by 400 percent (Reynolds 1986).[1] This increase was precipitated by articles in the *Adventist Review* encouraging Adventist youth to attend secular graduate programs in order to better prepare themselves for a variety of occupations and in order to allow greater opportunity to "witness" to nonbelievers in secular educational facilities (see Reynolds 1955). Adventist leaders recognized the likelihood that secular graduate education would introduce Adventist students to critical thought and methodology and cautioned those participating in secular graduate education to guard against "religious liberalism" and the danger of accepting "rationalism" and rejecting inspiration

(Ellen White) as the way to truth (Nichol 1960).[2] Despite these warnings, Adventist graduate students trained in secular universities were often dissatisfied with the traditional Adventist aversion to critical questioning. "Probing, open to change, skeptical of tradition, imbued with the values and culture of higher education, this new breed of 'progressive' Adventist intellectual soon began to reevaluate Adventist tradition.[3] A conflict with church leaders, who represented the Adventist mainstream, was predictable" (Lugenbeal 1984:23).[4]

To Adventists educated in secular graduate programs, "many pastoral sermons and many denominational journal articles seemed unreasoned, if not unreasonable, shallow if not irrelevant, and illogical if not downright anti-intellectual" (Osborn 1978:43). In decades of antiwar protests, the Black Power Movement, and the modern feminist movement, young, educated Adventists began to probe fundamental tenets of Adventism. Believing that Adventism had failed to adequately address contemporary ethical issues (including questions of race and gender), these Adventist intellectuals began to meet informally to discuss social, political, and religious problems (in Ann Arbor, Michigan; Cambridge, Massachusetts; and San Francisco, California) and eventually formed the Association of Adventist Forums (AAF).[5] As the Cambridge area group grew, members recognized the need for a publication by and for Adventists but not sponsored (or controlled) by the General Conference. On October 25, 1967, the California Division of the NAD approved the AAF (originally as an association for Adventists enrolled in secular graduate programs, though later expanded to include all academic Adventists) and simultaneously approved the publication of the group's journal.[6] *Spectrum,* a periodical published by Adventists but not officially controlled by Adventist leadership, was "to encourage thoughtful persons of Seventh-day Adventist orientation to examine and freely discuss ideas and issues relevant to the Church in all its aspects" and "to be instrumental in the exchange of ideas among Adventist scholars among themselves and [in] their communication to the Adventist Church as a whole" (Osborn 1978:48).

The formation of the AAF and the publication of *Spectrum* provided Adventist academics their first opportunity to participate in free, (relatively) uncensored, critical academic, intellectual, and theological exchange. Adventist scholars, most often employed by Adventist institutions of higher education, had not previously experienced academic freedom as it is popularly defined by secular scholars. Instead, Adventists were told that academic freedom was the freedom to interact with students, colleagues, and Adventist leadership insofar as their academic work "fit" into the context of Adventist belief.[7] If academic work did not "move students" toward the goal of personal salvation as defined within the context of Adventist belief and practice, scholars were told that they should seek other pursuits (see Beach 1970). *Spectrum* offered a new aperture for scholarly endeavors, uncensored (at least overtly) by those who would dismantle efforts to pursue controversial areas of investigation. The AAF and *Spectrum* "gave Adventist academics the opportunity to turn their scholarly expertise on the Adventist tradition, sometimes to devastating effect" (Bull and Lockhart 1986:36). Adventist scholars, trained in the secular academic tradition of critical interpretation, did not set out to challenge fundamental Adventist beliefs, only to explore those beliefs from an academic perspective. In interpreting closely held religious beliefs and traditions through critical eyes, however, Adventist academics saw those beliefs and traditions from the perspective of one who must consider not divine but historical explanation and context. Thus, the emphasis on education promoted by Ellen White in part to isolate Adventists from the world served eventually to introduce Adventists to intellectual debate and critical questioning (see Butler 1989:45).

"Spirit of Prophecy" or Plagiarism? The Ellen White Debate

The maturation of an increasingly intellectual body of believers in the NAD renewed interest, during the 1970s, in a protracted and divisive debate about Ellen White's use of secondary source materials in her writings. The debate over the meaning and practical implications of the "spirit of prophecy" began, in Adventism, in the early 1900s, when at the specially called 1919 Bible Conference for teachers and ministers (the minutes of which were concealed from the Adventist laity until they were discovered and published in *Spectrum* in the 1970s) prominent Adventist leaders, including A. G. Daniels, struggled with serious doubts about Ellen White and the spirit of prophecy (Butler 1992:lix).[8] Dudley M. Canright, a former Adventist pastor, accused Ellen White, at the 1919 meetings, of copying extensively from other authors in her writings without crediting them (Anderson 1977).[9] Nonetheless, books published (and widely distributed) about White during the 1930s, 1940s, and 1950s, defended her and promoted a view of inspiration that precluded the sort of questioning in which the 1919 Bible Conference engaged.[10] "By the 1950s, the problems [questions about White's use of other authors in her writings] seemed to have been swept into the dustbin of history, and the church appeared to be firmly united and settled in its view of Ellen White's spiritual gift" (McAdams 1978:39).

A spate of articles in *Spectrum* in the early 1970s called for and offered examination of Ellen White's writings in historical context. Beginning in 1971,

White's "literary borrowing" was also brought under scrutiny (McAdams 1978). Whereas early discussion (in the early 1900s) and controversy regarding White's inspiration and literary borrowing were carried on within the confines of SDA leadership, the debates of the 1970s were prominently published in *Spectrum* and widely discussed throughout the NAD (McAdams 1984:2). The 1970s debate over White's inspiration also differed from earlier controversy in that later Adventists engaged in the debate were not critical of Adventism or Adventist leadership per se but were attempting to reconcile questions posed by simultaneous participation in academic and religious communities (McAdams 1978:28): "The Ellen White scholars of the 1970s began their research as committed Adventists who fully accepted the authenticity of Ellen White's spiritual gift. They were not seeking to 'tear down' Ellen White or to undermine confidence in the 'spirit of prophecy'" (ibid.:39). Instead they conducted research because they were aware of discrepancies and "statements that appeared inaccurate" (ibid.).

William S. Peterson was the first to question White's use of source materials, especially her use of sources that were "anti-Catholic and anti-democratic," and concluded that White had "borrowed" materials from other writers, and further, that "she used them carelessly, sometimes misreading them, other times exaggerating them, and occasionally leaving out crucial facts" (McAdams 1978:29). Roy Branson and Harold Weiss followed Peterson, suggesting that in order to understand Ellen White's writings, Adventists needed to: (1) research her relationship to other writers; (2) understand the historical context in which she wrote; and (3) carefully examine the development of White's writings through her lifetime, and with reference to Adventism's development (Branson and Weiss, 1970).

Although the call for critical, historical analysis of White's writings was not without detractors (Paul Bradley, in response to Branson and Weiss, insisted that White *could* be understood correctly without extensive scholarly examination [1971]),[11] controversy over White's use of source materials continued. A 1972 article by Ronald Graybill (then research assistant at the White Estate) concluded that not only had White used secondary source materials without crediting the authors from whom she borrowed but that she had adopted Uriah Smith's interpretations of those materials instead of consulting the original works.[12] Donald R. McAdams discovered, while viewing an original rough draft of Ellen White's writings, a "strong correlation" between White's writings and those of nineteenth-century Protestant historians. In 1976, Ronald Numbers fanned the flames of the White controversy with his publication of *Prophetess of Health,* a book which placed Ellen White in the context of the nineteenth-

century health reform movement and attempted to demonstrate that her counsels on health reform originated not in divine revelation but in historical context. White's health reforms, he argued, were not original but were borrowed
from her nineteenth-century contemporaries in the national health reform
movement.[13] Numbers argued further that some of White's health reforms, for
which she claimed divine revelation, had proven scientifically untenable, and
others, such as dress reform, had changed over time (see McAdams 1978:31;
Numbers 1992).

Adventist leadership, which had not responded strongly to the controversy
surrounding White's writings in the early 1970s, launched an immense effort
to rebut charges of plagiarism following the publication of *Prophetess of Health.*
The staff of the Ellen G. White Estate (which had access to Numbers's manuscript prior to publication, and had requested revisions before the book went
to press but was not satisfied with the revisions Numbers made) published *A
Critique of the Book "Prophetess of Health,"* which was sent without charge to
all history and theology teachers at Adventist colleges and universities (Land
1977). The fifty-eight-page transcript acknowledged that Ellen White used
historical sources to articulate things she saw in visions and admitted the possibility of factual error in White's writings, but insisted that White used other
authors only to better explain that which had been divinely revealed to her
(McAdams 1978:36).

General Conference leaders also candidly criticized *Spectrum.* One member
of the General Conference stated that "I was under the impression that when
Spectrum started it had as its objective the strengthening of the unity of the
church. I believe that it is veering away from that purpose" (Osborn 1978:31).
When *Spectrum* editors printed a review of Numbers's book suggesting that
Ellen White may have been emotionally disturbed (Fawn Brodie's "Ellen
White's Emotional Life: A Psychological Profile of Ellen White" [1976]), Gen-
eral Conference leaders threatened to "close down" *Spectrum* (Butler 1992:1).
Instead, the General Conference set up a committee to examine charges that
Ellen White had plagiarized other authors. The committee found that Ellen
White *had* borrowed extensively (without giving credit) from other authors
and concluded that Adventists' notions of the inerrancy of White's writings
were therefore unsound. The committee recommended that "the church
should undertake a major program of education regarding the way(s) in which
Ellen White's books were produced" (Hackleman 1978:9).

The education campaign sponsored by Adventist leaders set as its explicit
goal to uncover truth: "We want to know all that can be known [regarding
charges of plagiarism against White] because truth has a way of invigorating

the believer" (Wilson 1980:8). Acknowledging that Ellen White "used sources more extensively than we have heretofore been aware of or recognized" (ibid.), the committee noted that "it is evident that individual members of the church need to understand more clearly the doctrine of inspiration and just how God reveals himself to his people," but deemphasized controversy arising as a result of plagiarism allegations: "In spite of what some would have you believe there is no internal upheaval or major crisis in the Adventist church. This is God's church. . . . There is no reason to become alarmed[,] unnerved or panicky" (ibid.). Instead, Adventist leaders used Adventist publications (editorials and articles) to revise understanding of White's inspiration—Ellen G. White, they contended, had been visually, not verbally, inspired. Thus, although she saw major events, "minor details and incidental references not basic to the account . . . could be ascertained from sacred writings [of others], some from common sources of knowledge, such as reliable historians" (McAdams 1978:36). In their attempt to prepare the Adventist laity to respond to charges of plagiarism, Adventist leaders postulated that: (1) "originality is not a test of inspiration"; (2) God inspires people, not words; (3) the "Holy Spirit" guides the selection of materials used to convey things seen in vision; (4) a prophet may use existing material without being dependent on that material; and (5) that the similarities between White's writings and those of other authors must not blind readers to the differences between the works (Wilson 1980). One White apologist noted that Adventism had taken an official position supporting "thought" (not verbal) inspiration as early as 1883, and concluded that this understanding could allow contemporary Adventists to make verbal corrections of White's writings "without in any measure" changing White's message (Olson 1981:86–87). White's defenders generally recognized that "it is a fact that Ellen White did use the works of others to some extent while engaged in her writings," but urged members to recognize that such borrowing did not provide "evidence of intent to deceive on her part" (ibid.:64).

While the efforts of SDA leadership to educate members in order to prevent widespread defection in the face of charges of White's "literary borrowing" were largely successful among Adventist laity, the questions introduced into the movement, and their resonance, particularly among academic Adventists, continue to threaten Adventism's unity of belief—at least in regard to Ellen White's authority in the movement: "The subject of this debate may seem a minor one, but the issues involved—the validity of historical criticism and the relationship of its findings to an understanding of Ellen White—were large. . . . [The findings] threatened the authoritative role Ellen White had come to play in the church" (Land 1986b:220). Jonathan Butler and Ronald

Numbers wrote in their entry on Seventh-day Adventism in *The Encyclopedia of Religion* (1987) that Adventism was "torn" by the discoveries of the 1970s and 1980s concerning White's use of other authors as well as the factual errors contained in her writings, and that these discoveries "forced a rethinking of White's role in the community" (Butler and Numbers 1987:26). It is clear that White's formal authority as an inerrant leader underwent at least a subtle shift in response to questions surrounding her unacknowledged use of other authors (ibid.). Clearly, within the pages of *Spectrum,* Adventists' perception of Ellen White has been revised. While it is unclear "to what degree this historical revolution has spread from the academic elite to the rank and file," modern Adventists do seem hesitant to equate faith in Ellen White with faith in Adventism to the extent that they did in the past (Butler 1992:lx). Official Adventist publications now speak of White's "confirmatory authority" and stress that her writings are not to be placed above the Bible.

Ellen White, who counseled Adventists on attire, diet, recreational activities, sex, family, divorce, marriage, health habits, use of jewelry and cosmetics, worship, and other behaviors, is irreconcilably linked with those beliefs and practices that define Adventism. This being the case, "to consider her words as possibly derived from someone else and not necessarily the final authority introduces an element of chaos into the very heart of Adventism that makes all of us [SDAs] uneasy" (McAdams 1978:40). Consequently, critical examination of White's role as an inspired leader (and subsequent threat to that role) led Adventist leadership to reaffirm, in various ways, not only White's position as divine messenger but those beliefs and behaviors, introduced by White, which offer Adventism its distinct (sectarian) identity.[14]

Rethinking the Heavenly Sanctuary: The Ford Controversy

The Ford controversy involved a movementwide effort to reconsider the doctrine of the heavenly sanctuary and, more specifically, to deliberate the means to salvation. While on sabbatical at Pacific Union College in October of 1978, Desmond Ford, invited to speak to the AAF, presented a lecture which challenged the traditional Adventist understanding of the sanctuary doctrine. Specifically, Ford argued that belief in a literal heavenly sanctuary was unbiblical, that belief in Christ's confinement to the Holy Place until 1844 was unbiblical, and that the Adventist understanding of a pre-advent judgment was erroneous. Further, Ford implicitly and explicitly raised questions regarding the nature of Ellen White's inspiration (see Land 1986b). Ford's audience, at the time reeling under accusations of plagiarism directed at White in *Spectrum,* was not pleased with Ford's presentation: "Some interpreted his remarks as a challenge to the church. There was a strong reaction which led the Pacific Union Conference and Drs. Cassell and Madgwick—president and academic dean of Pacific Union College—to take the initiative in bringing the problem to the General Conference" (Cottrell 1980:4).

Ford was given a six-month leave of absence to prepare a full statement of his position. Assisted by an ad hoc guidance committee, Ford spent months researching and clarifying his position; a document of almost one thousand pages was the result of his efforts. On completion of his work, Ford was asked to defend his position statement at Glacierview (an SDA youth camp facility in Colorado), in a meeting of 116 Adventist delegates representing a cross section of international Adventist leadership.[15]

Delegates pored over and debated Ford's paper, which they had not been allowed adequate time to study prior to the weeklong series of meetings. Most significantly, for Glacierview delegates, Ford denied the reality, and even the necessity, of the "second phase" of Christ's ministry in the heavenly sanctuary; Christ's atonement, Ford asserted, had been completed in the crucifixion and the ascension. Presenting the sanctuary as a metaphorical concept, Ford challenged the Adventist understanding of the year/day principle and the basic tenet of original Adventist theology—the commencement of the cleansing of the heavenly sanctuary in 1844 with Christ's entrance into the Most Holy Place (see also Brimsmead 1980).

Adventist leadership, already facing questions surrounding the nature of Ellen White's inspiration, was unwilling to submit to the reexamination of "fundamental" beliefs that Ford's statement necessitated. Adventist leaders instead attempted simultaneously to allow Ford a hearing at which to present his position and to silence him. Neal Wilson, a General Conference leader, prior to the conference, asserted that "at no time has this church endeavored to control minds. It gives considerable latitude for opinions," but at the same time he reiterated that "this [freedom] carries with it an enormous sacred responsibility. It does not give latitude to create doubts, to undermine faith, or to muffle the message of this church. We cannot afford to confuse others' minds with our personal opinions" (Wilson in Cottrell 1980:11).[16]

Concerned that Ford was creating divisiveness and doubt in Adventism, General Conference leaders hoped to heal rifts among membership by rescinding his credentials and, in so doing, allowing Adventists to become less polarized with regard to the doctrinal questions Ford posed. Adventist scholars and intellectuals attending Glacierview, on the other hand, hoped to heal the divisiveness surrounding Ford's teachings by allowing him to retain his SDA membership *and* his divergent opinions. Many conference delegates, especially those associated with institutions of higher education, shared at least some of Ford's doctrinal concerns (see Adams 1981:4), and felt "personally involved in the issue because censure of Dr. Ford on the exegetical points inevitably [implied] censure of them also" (Cottrell 1980:21). Adventist leaders, in the face of opposition from Adventist intellectuals and sensing a threat to basic SDA doctrine, presented Ford, in a closed (Friday morning) meeting, with a statement with which he could agree (and retain his credentials), or disagree (and loose his credentials). Ford initially agreed to the statement, but when he was later presented with a typewritten copy of the statement to sign, he found it to be significantly altered and refused to agree to its revised contents. At the close of the Glacierview meetings, Ford was informed that he would receive six months' severance pay. Although he continued to communicate and negotiate with General Conference leaders for several months following the Glacierview meetings, the General Conference Executive Advisory Committee eventually informed Dr. Ford that he could voluntarily surrender his credentials or they would be withdrawn.

The revocation of Ford's ministerial credentials, rather than healing divisions created by divergent opinions surrounding the heavenly sanctuary (and ultimately the way to salvation), instigated further divisiveness. Adventist pastors, academics, and laity alike protested Ford's dismissal: many pastors publicly disagreed with the General Conference's decision to dismiss Ford; congregations formed in which Ford's views were openly advocated; and an independent periodical, *Evangelica,* emerged (at Andrews University, Michigan) to defend Ford's position. The General Conference moved quickly to quiet dissent.[17] The student publishers of *Evangelica* were threatened with expulsion and eventually toned down the magazine's content; approximately two dozen pastors were "forced from their pulpits by one means or another, most of them in areas where Ford's influence was strongest" (see Londis 1981:17); a number of "Gospel Fellowship" congregations arose (primarily in northern California) that expressed support for Ford, claimed to reject the "legalism" of Adventism, and left Seventh-day Adventism en masse.[18]

The overwhelming response of General Conference leaders not only to Ford's initial challenge of specific Adventist teachings but to subsequent expressions of support by Adventist pastors and laity for Ford's positions demonstrated the pivotal role that the beliefs Ford questioned played in the SDA paradigm of faith, the depth of crisis that would result from their loss, and Adventism's sectarian resistance to challenges which would threaten its distinctiveness. The doctrine of the sanctuary has been questioned at various times in Adventism's history, but SDA leadership consistently affirmed the truth and the centrality of the doctrine in the construction of SDA identity: "It would be extremely difficult to conclude that so central a historic affirmation is no longer tenable, because such a conclusion might well result in a traumatic crisis of identity for the whole community [of Adventists] as well as for individual members" (Guy 1980:7).

Nonetheless, in the decade following Glacierview and its aftermath, Adventists have continued to struggle with their interpretation of the heavenly sanctuary. Adventism has moved (though almost imperceptibly) away from a literal perception of the heavenly sanctuary, with its two tangible, distinct apartments, to discussion of Christ commencing the "second phase" or the "final phase" of his heavenly ministry in 1844. Accompanying this subtle rethinking of the heavenly sanctuary is a more explicit, and currently far more controversial, debate concerning salvation. For Adventists, the heavenly sanctuary, wherein the investigative judgment is taking place, is irrevocably linked to salvation. If the heavenly sanctuary is a tangible, literal place, then the judgment therein, as Adventists have traditionally understood it, is now underway and will be completed prior to the parousia. If, however, Adventists are somehow mistaken in their interpretation of the heavenly sanctuary (not completely mistaken, necessarily, but in some way misunderstanding its purpose) then the investigative judgment, which many Adventists associate with salvation based on adherence to SDA "standards," may also be mistaken. Stated simply, a strict traditional interpretation of the heavenly sanctuary and its investigative judgment portend salvation of those whose "works" (actions) are worthy, while a more "liberal" interpretation of the sanctuary deemphasizes the *investigative* aspect of the judgment, and instead emphasizes salvation by grace. Though Ford was the initial symbol of the controversy surrounding this theological quagmire, the debate surrounding the relative necessity of works *(sanctification)* and grace *(justification)* for salvation currently presents Adventism with its most pressing crisis.[19]

Justification and Sanctification: Exclusive or Equally Necessary Roads to Salvation?

The justification/sanctification debate currently being waged within Adventism is not primarily a public contest but a private struggle. Though the issues involved may seem insignificant to the outsider, it is in this debate that the strains toward denominationalism and sectarianism most overtly find expression. Because sanctification is equated, by advocates, with correct behavior (adherence to "standards"), salvation based upon sanctification requires attention to those beliefs and associated behaviors which distinguish Adventism. Justification, on the other hand, emphasizes "grace" for salvation and thus places less importance on maintaining sectarian distinction. This being the case, the sanctification/justification debate provides the sociologist an arena for examination of sectarian/denominationalism tension. Still, the debate stems from uncertainty regarding personal salvation and is waged in intensely private ways. Although proponents on either side of the controversy do not hesitate to promulgate their positions—publish books, present sermons, produce videos—ultimately individual Adventists attempt to resolve the crisis in their own lives in order to relieve personal insecurity regarding salvation.

The justification/sanctification controversy, which is by no means unique to Seventh-day Adventism, first surfaced publicly in Adventism at the 1888 meeting of the General Conference. Although Ellen White originally began to voice dissatisfaction with "legalism" in the 1880s, it was not until Ellet J. Waggoner and Alonzo T. Jones, editors of the *Signs of the Times*,[20] presented the doctrine of "righteousness by faith" in a series of lectures to the General Conference that the issue came to a head.[21] Although Ellen White responded positively to Jones and Waggoner's message (stating, in part, that "the Lord in his great mercy sent a precious message to his people through Elders Waggoner and Jones" [in Olson 1966:35]), the General Conference as a whole was far less receptive.[22] General Conference leaders perceived the doctrine of justification presented by Jones and Waggoner as a threat to those beliefs and practices which served to distinguish Adventism. "Righteousness by faith" was defeated at the 1888 meeting of the General Conference "for a variety of complex reasons but primarily because leading figures in the movement believed that such a move would represent a shift away from . . . the fundamentals of Adventism: the law and prophecy" (Theobald 1985:118).[23] Opponents of Jones and Waggoner "regarded themselves as *savers* of [Adventism], reasoning that by devaluing the role of the moral law, it would ultimately . . . compromise the Sabbath truth and would sound the death knell of Seventh-day Adventism" (ibid.). Ellen White, disappointed in the General Conference's rejection of justification (see Olson 1966:39), continued to advocate salvation through "righteousness by faith," but her plea was seen as an "attack on the very fundamentals of Adventism" (Theobald 1985:118).

With Ellen White's death in 1915, proponents of "righteousness by faith" lost their most prominent advocate (although White's writings and sermons were widely published) and the struggle to define the way to salvation became less clearly associated with specific personalities, though the debate did not cease.

In 1920, W. W. Prescott published *Doctrine of Christ*, a book which insisted that Adventist theology focused too exclusively on the prophecies of Daniel and Revelation, to the extent that it failed to create a holistic, congruent faith, and then aspired to construct a more integrated theology, incorporating the notion of "righteousness by faith." More significantly, in 1957, a group of Adventist academics, pastors, teachers, and leaders published *Questions on Doctrine*, a highly controversial work which attempted to place Adventism within the parameters of mainstream Protestantism by deemphasizing distinct SDA beliefs—especially the widespread applicability of Ellen White's writings and sanctification. Written in a question/answer format, *Questions* was published in response to Protestant criticism (and apparent misrepresentation) of SDA belief. Because the book sought to demonstrate Adventism's common ground with mainline Protestantism, it offended many Adventists, particularly those most interested in maintaining Adventism's distinct identity.

As in the 1888 debate regarding justification/sanctification, throughout the twentieth century those Adventists who promoted sanctification as the way to salvation did so (and *do* so) based on the premise that to "follow the law" (to adhere to SDA behavioral ideals) is to defend and promulgate unique (sectarian) characteristics of Adventism (dress, diet, attire, etc.). Thus, renewed emphasis on sanctification following Ford's 1981 ouster was explicitly expressed in public appeals for Adventists to adhere more closely to SDA standards and thereby to participate in creating and maintaining a more clear delineation between Adventism and the world (see below). While the sanctification/justification controversy within Adventism had continued since (and even before) the 1888 General Conference session, the contemporary debate, commencing with Ford's dismissal (but extending back to the 1957 publication of *Questions on Doctrine*), is of particular interest as it marks the simultaneous attempts by various groups within a movement to, on the one hand, diminish distinction and create an accommodating position toward the world, and, on the other, to demand distinction (heightened sectarian character) in order to better distinguish the movement from the world.

Proponents of justification believe that salvation may be achieved as one assumes a new *status* as a believer, while those who advocate sanctification insist that salvation requires one to achieve a new *life* as a believer. Proponents of each include the other as a lesser but essential necessity for salvation and the sanctification/justification debate, therefore, is not a dispute of the *exclusive*, but the *primary*, means to salvation. Those who promote justification argue that Christ's character was unique, that the human character, unlike Christ's, is typified by depravity and sin, and that although one may (and should) model one's character after Christ, humanity cannot attain perfection and therefore must be "saved by grace." Adventists who promote sanctification, on the other hand, insist that "man's redeemed nature" is similar to Christ's perfect nature, that it is possible for humans to overcome sin as Christ did (Guy 1980:9). Justification emphasizes the "gift" of salvation, thus providing "assurance" of salvation to believers and the "joy of experienced forgiveness," while sanctification necessitates continued conscious striving for perfection, for adherence to "the law" (the Decalogue, SDA standards)(ibid.).

Adventist belief ebbs and flows along the continuum between these two poles. When Adventism's distinct sectarian singularity is perceived to be threatened (as when Ford challenged fundamental SDA doctrines in the late 1970s and early 1980s) Adventist leadership accentuates sanctification—living in a manner which clearly demarcates Adventists from the world (see also chapter 3). Thus, Robert H. Pierson, in his attempt to explain the delay of Christ's coming, focused his attention on the conduct of Adventists, calling repeatedly for "revival and reformation" throughout the movement, and the attendant need for increased evangelism. Following Pierson's appeal, Herbert Douglass (perhaps the most active and best-known advocate of sanctification) used the *Review and Herald* to formulate a theology of sanctification (see Land 1986b:216). Arguing that Christ, like humans, had a sinful nature, Douglass contended that as Christ had overcome sin to become perfect, so too must Adventists be perfect, and that in so doing, Adventists will initiate the advent. Douglass asserted that: "The last generation of Adventists will demonstrate the all-sufficiency of grace and power of God as Jesus did in His day. They will confirm . . . that men . . . can overcome all sin in this life" (ibid.). In advocating sanctification, Douglass "restored traditional Adventist thinking . . . which had faded from view at about the time that *Questions on Doctrine* had appeared" (ibid.).

By the end of the 1970s, the justification/sanctification debate had established clearly demarcated camps, with Pierson and Douglass (promoting sanctification) serving as officially recognized Adventist leaders, and Robert D. Brimsmead and Ford (associated with justification) making up an opposition which was increasingly portrayed not only as being outside of Adventist tradition but as apostate and therefore aligned with the world.[24] At about the same time that Ford's challenge to the heavenly sanctuary, the investigative judgment, and ultimately, sanctification, was pushed further toward the periphery of Adventism, Douglass was embraced in Adventist periodicals and Sabbath school study guides.[25]

Adventist perfection, then—adherence to SDA standards of belief and practice—was associated with both SDA distinction from the world ("God desires that the perfection of His character shall appear. . . . We are to be distinguished from the world because God has placed His seal upon us" [White in Douglass 1979:144–45]) and, concurrently, with Adventist evangelical efforts (which, as discussed above, may result in an increased proportion of new members, diminishing ability to maintain distinction). Thus, rather than resolve Adventist ambiguity toward salvation, Douglass revitalized the sectarian struggle between hostility toward the world (manifested in insulation and isolation from the world) and evangelism (which, according to Wilson, often results in some degree of accommodation to the world [1975:38]).[26]

Individual Adventists, caught within this struggle for preeminence, were constantly confronted with disputes about "legalism" and "grace," but by the late 1970s and early 1980s, sanctification seemed to have achieved the endorsement of Adventist leadership. Schwartz, writing about Adventism in the 1970s, concluded that, to Adventists, "everyone is a sinner and must overcome his inborn spiritual defects through continuous effort to reach standards of conduct required by law" (Schwartz 1970:102). Schwartz saw Adventists engaging in "a lifelong struggle . . . to create the most favorable record possible" before the investigative judgment was complete (ibid.), so that one achieved salvation "through a gradual process of behavioral reform and improvement" (ibid.:104). One *Review* writer defended the SDA emphasis on adherence to standards of behavior: "To insist on obedience to God's law is not legalism. We must not quail before the charge that we are legalists" (Bradford 1980:12).

Nonetheless Adventist academics and intellectuals used *Spectrum* not only to discuss the Glacierview controversy but to offer alternatives to the prominent "sanctification" emphasis in Adventist publications. As early as 1970, one writer proclaimed "righteousness by faith," "The first milestone. . . . left for Adventists to pass before victory is complete": "Far too many of our members still depend too much on the law and too little on the merits of Jesus" (Rock 1970:21). Jack Provonsha distinguished between strict obedience to law without consideration of mitigating factors as "legalism," and recommended that instead of merely adhering to SDA standards without question, Adventists should attempt to determine ethical conduct in the context of specific situations ("situationism") (Provonsha 1969). Dick Jewett, in 1978, wrote that one cannot earn salvation by doing good works, but that those who surrender themselves to God can and should be assured of salvation (26–27).

By the mid-1980s, Adventism began cautiously to attempt to achieve a more balanced understanding of the relative importance of justification and sanctification. In 1980, Richard Rice noted that "salvation has probably received more attention from Adventists than any other doctrine in recent years," and that "the discussion of these issues has become so heated that some are fearful of its effects on the unity of the church" (Rice 1978:62). General Conference president Neal Wilson called in 1980 for a moratorium "on public presentations dealing with 'the fine points and the controversial aspects of the theology of righteousness by faith'" (in ibid.). Adventists, poised between proponents of justification and sanctification, had difficulty abandoning a matter of such import for personal understanding of (and, consequently, possible ability to attain) salvation. Furthermore, despite Adventist leadership's apparent endorsement of sanctification, justification "appealed to a large number of Adventists because it offered an assurance of salvation that they felt the traditional emphasis on sanctification had not allowed" (Land 1986b:218).

Despite periodic published espousal of sanctification (see, for example, Fowler 1990:120–31), Adventism is currently endeavoring to present a more equal emphasis on justification and sanctification. In the 1993 Week of Prayer *Review* discussion articles, the General Conference president presented the official reconciliation of justification and sanctification: people are sinful. Humanity in and of itself is irredeemable, so that, like in pulling back the layers of an onion, if a person attempts to rid herself of sin by completing "good" acts or avoiding "bad" acts, she is eventually left with nothing. Instead of earning salvation by doing good and avoiding sin, the individual must accept Christ into her life and develop a close, personal relationship with him (see below). From this relationship springs a desire to "live righteously" and a compulsion to "follow God's law." Thus Adventism has embraced an admixture of justification and sanctification which, while portraying different steps to correct action than did sanctification alone, ultimately has as its outcome adherence to SDA standards of behavior.

It would be an oversimplification to portray Adventism's current position as merely restated sanctification, however, and it would be equally inaccurate to portray Seventh-day Adventists as united in their understanding or acceptance of this position. Adventists disagree widely about the best (or only) way to achieve salvation, with some SDAs clinging to sanctification and the necessity of perfection and others pushing for full endorsement of justification. Although most Adventists fall between these two extremes, informants expressed a great deal of ambivalence about the certainty of personal salvation. Though most agreed that the idea of justification relieved a previous sense of the imminent possibility of damnation (see Callahan 1993), justification, as informants portrayed it, continues to be assessed by right action, by adherence to SDA standards of conduct. Informants pointed out repeatedly that only through "a personal relationship with Christ" ("a close walk with Jesus") can one hope to develop the type of character that will be saved. Further, Adventists with whom I spoke and attended worship services were overwhelmingly dedicated to achieving this "close walk" through personal, congregational, and small group study, worship, and prayer. Despite this commitment, Adventists continue to express a great deal of uncertainty about the possibility of personal salvation. One Adventist man attending a prayer meeting (in a not uncommon display of this uncertainty) expressed his appreciation to "God for allowing me this gift of salvation. It is a free gift and all we have to do is accept it. I accept salvation!" Then, less than ten minutes later, cried openly and expressed regret for "the things I did when I was young. I don't know if God can accept me; I just don't know. Because of the sins of my life I don't know if God will accept me."

Although Adventist debate surrounding justification/sanctification may seem mundane, trivial, or inconsequential to those outside of the movement, to committed Adventists, for whom judgment is currently underway, and for whom Christ's coming is "soon," assurance of salvation is no small matter. Instead, it is a topic which dominates conversations, publications, and worship services. Adventism's current fusion of justification and sanctification hints at the notion of grace as it is presented in mainline Protestantism, but maintains Adventism's sectarian distinction, finding evidence of a relationship with Christ in adherence to health counsels, recommended attire, dietary guidelines, correct Sabbath worship, and other Adventist standards. Thus, this balance of "works" and "grace" continues to encourage Adventist "works" as evidence of the acceptance of "grace," but has attempted to reshape motivation for works from fear of personal damnation to love for a personal Savior.

In the World/Of the World: Crises and Denominationalism

During the 1970s the Seventh-day Adventist church reeled under a number of internal blows to its official teachings that resulted in great confusion and consternation for many of its members.
—Lian 1987:55

Tension in Adventism, most pronounced during the 1970s and early 1980s, emanated from the division between Adventism's administrative branch, which sought loyalty and unity, and Adventism's educational branch, which "challenges blind acceptance" (Brunt 1989:9).[27] Instead of merely reaffirming belief or providing opportunity for witnessing activities, secular graduate education introduced young Adventist scholars in the 1960s and thereafter to critical methodology, which they, in turn, carried with them to their academic positions at SDA colleges and universities. In the context of this questioning of beliefs and practices that served to distinguish Adventism from the world, and in the context of broader social unrest, Adventism was perceived by Adventist leadership as being under attack. Almost immediately, "a corps of men arose to defend what many Adventists term 'traditional Adventism'" (Lian 1987:55). Herbert Douglass, Kevin Paulson, Lewis Walton, Kenneth Wood, Robert Pierson, and others lashed out at secularizing tendencies within Adventism: "As these men view[ed] it, the Adventist church must never deviate from its historical beliefs. The truths proclaimed by the pioneers must not be compromised or de-emphasized, but must always act as the guiding light for Adventists everywhere and at all times" (ibid.).

In their defense of fundamental distinguishing (sectarian) tenets of SDA belief and practice, Adventist leadership specifically identified the tension (the crises) within Adventism as being associated with secularization of the movement. Adventist leadership explicitly identified Adventism as a sect and commented on the "dangers Adventism face[d] as it gradually move[d] from sectarianism" (Pierson 1978:26). Pierson pointed to the "subtle forces" moving Adventism away from its distinct sectarian identity and toward the world, including a declining concern with SDA standards of behavior, a lessening of faith in literal creationism, escalating questions about and mistrust of revelation (Ellen White), and an abating interest in maintaining the peculiarities that set Adventists apart from the world. Specifically appealing to Adventist institutions of higher education, General Conference president Pierson called on academics to halt what he identified as a tendency toward secularization: "More [Adventist] schools, universities and seminaries are established. These go to the world for accreditation and tend to become secularized" (ibid.). Most significantly, Pierson urged Adventists to avoid accommodation with the world. He noted that as a sect becomes secularized: "attention is given to contemporary culture. . . . The group [comes to enjoy] complete acceptance by the world. The sect has become a church! . . . Brethren and sisters, this must never happen to [Seventh-day Adventism]! This will not happen to the Seventh-day Adventist church!" (ibid.:33). "It is not just another church—it is God's church!" (in Teel 1980:2).

There is evidence that Adventism, notwithstanding Pierson's warnings (and more importantly, Adventist leadership's resolute opposition to questions raised by Ford, Numbers, and *Spectrum* authors),[28] has moved toward a more accommodating response to the world. Lindén wrote in 1978 that "the story of Adventism illustrates how a radical sect gradually changes to denominational-like status" (259). Lowell Tarling agreed, observing that Adventism's response to the world changed dramatically in the late 1950s (accompanying the publication of *Questions on Doctrine*) as was evidenced by the fact that breakaway groups increasingly didn't feel the need (nor were they forced) to sever membership ties. Beginning in 1965, Seventh-day Adventists commenced an ongoing, annual dialogue with the World Council of Churches' Faith and Order Commission, demonstrating a previously absent tendency to ecumenicalism. Almost a decade later, in 1976, Adventist publishers of *Ministry* began to distribute their periodical to all North American Christian ministers on a regular basis. By the 1980s and early 1990s, Adventist presses increasingly published books on theology which acknowledged and openly discussed non-Adventist theologians and theologies. Employment of a professional, full-time ministry, massive institutionalization, widespread participation in graduate and professional education, extensive centralized control of local congregations, and the publication and wide distribution of large numbers of periodicals led one Adventist historian to conclude that by the late 1980s, "the social alienation that had characterized [Adventism's] origins, though still alive, was no longer as all inclusive and dominant in Adventist faith and practice as it had been" (Land 1986b:230).

The Seventh-day Adventist laity is not unaware of the shift toward a more accommodating response to the world that is apparent in some aspects of Adventist development. Ralph Martin noticed in 1990 that in the past, members "wore our Adventism like a uniform . . . and understood our unique vocabulary. And though we sometimes squabbled among ourselves, we stood united against the outside world" (7). Informants were quick to note that their Adventist parents and grandparents had maintained very clear and distinct identities as SDAs ("their relationship to the church came even before their relationship to God") and had believed that that identity was essential for salvation ("older Adventists believed that you must be an Adventist in order to be saved"). At the same time, informants expressed concern that contemporary Adventism not be *too* distinct: "You don't want to be weird or looked on as trying to be better than everyone else, trying to be something that no one else is. We need to fit in and not move so fast that we leave everybody else to say, 'Oh, those people are just out to lunch,' and not ever listen. We have to move along with everybody else even if we feel like we're more enlightened and have good ideas. We still need to be with everybody else." One Adventist student associated this more accommodating response to the world specifically with younger Adventists ("in the church I came from, the older people were very set in their ways, but younger people were bringing in a lot of new ideas"), but though there is a strong generational component in the tension in Adventism between sectarian and secularizing influence it would be a vast overgeneralization to associate Adventism's shift away from sectarian distinction solely with the maturation of a younger generation. Several retired and older informants expressed support for secularizing tendencies within the movement ("I think our viewpoints are liberalizing. I think in many ways [we are more] ready to accept new ideas, new concepts and new interpretations that move us away from the traditional interpretations").

It would be perhaps even more misleading to discuss Adventism's changing response to the world without also noting that Adventism has by no means undergone a gradual and continuous evolution toward denominationalism. Rather, Adventism has at times encouraged accommodation to various aspects of secular society, and at times resisted secularizing influences. "From a theological point of view,"

> there is little evidence to support the widely held contention that Adventists have moved from the margins of society toward the mainstream. Adventist theology has developed in parallel with that of the mainstream. It was at its most distinctive during a period of great diversity; it became fundamentalist in an era of fundamentalism [1920s, 1930s]; and it softened with the rise of evangelicalism [1940s, 1950s]. Throughout this process, Adventist theology has served as a barrier between the church and its opponents. The nature of the competition has changed—from rival sects to liberal Christianity to secular humanism—and Adventist theology has changed accordingly. But the changes have served to maintain the distance between Adventism and the most threatening ideological formations of the day. (Bull and Lockhart 1989:91)

Thus, contemporary Adventists, who perceive a greater threat in secularism than in mainline Protestantism, define themselves in opposition less to Lutherans or Baptists or Methodists (as did post–Great Disappointment Adventists) than to "unbelievers." But to understate Adventism's distinction, even from mainline Protestantism, would also be to lose sight of Adventism's struggle to retain its identity. Caught in a vast network of relationships, individual Adventists attempt to be "in the world but not of it." Adventism, historically, has altered its theology based upon perceived (and changing) threats to belief, and Adventism has fluctuated in its desire (and ability) to retain distinction from the world. But in the face of threatened loss of sectarian identity, Adventist leadership resolutely clings to the idea of the necessity of adherence to SDA standards for salvation and in so doing consistently reaffirms Adventism's commitment to beliefs and practices which serve to distinguish it as a religious body. Adventist advocates of the "liberal" interpretation of justification (grace alone, completely without accompanying works, is sufficient for salvation) currently pose the greatest prospect for transformation from Adventism's traditional (sectarian) identity, but they appear contained, at least for the time being, by Adventist leaders' interpretation of the simultaneous necessity of sanctification and justification, resulting in "a new life in Christ" (i.e., adherence to SDA standards).

Adventism defines itself not "against individual denominations in the mainstream but against the mainstream as a united body of tradition" (Bull and Lockhart 1989:165). "The world," for Adventists, is comprised of those who are not Adventists (one SDA man explained to me that "when I say 'worldly' I mean non-Adventist"); it is a place that has rejected Christ; it is "equivalent to evil" (Vick 1976:39). Although Adventists acknowledge that some outside of Adventism will attain salvation, there is a general recognition among members that Seventh-day Adventism alone has access to the entirety of God's revealed truth and that it is much easier to achieve salvation within Adventism than outside its boundaries, without the assistance of its teachings. Adventism, despite its tensions, its crises, its struggles, retains its sectarian identity: "An Adventist's religious affiliation is still the single most significant fact about him" (Pearson 1990:32).[29]

Consequently, Adventism, while retaining its sectarian identity, has vacillated in its response to the world. Though variously more or less accommodating, "there has always been a combination of ideas sufficient to differentiate those who hold them [Adventists] from the rest of American society and to maintain a sense of distance between [Adventism] and the world" (Bull and Lockhart 1989:165). Even Bryan Wilson, the thrust of whose work is to demonstrate the denominationalizing tendency of sects, wrote that "In the modern world it appears to be more and more difficult than ever to be in but not of the world. Seventh-day Adventists appear to be continuing to wage that struggle—and not without success" (Wilson in Pearson 1990:31).

Notes

1. In the same period, SDA participation in secondary and elementary school education also increased dramatically (442 percent and 1,987 percent respectively).

2. "The graduate student . . . is presumed to be at least tinged with iconoclasm and to exude more than a faint odor of skepticism regarding long-held beliefs of every kind. He is supposed to . . . do creative thinking, to be honored as much for his doubts as for his beliefs" (Nichol 1960:4).

3. Timothy Crosby wrote in 1976, "In the last decade or so, we [Adventists] seem to have lost a good deal of our reticence about putting conflicting opinions into print" (62).

4. Bull and Lockhart found that theologians were more likely to express conservative positions with regard to SDA belief and less likely (half as often) to be influenced by secular thinkers if educated in the Adventist educational system (Bull and Lockhart 1986:33).

5. Alvin L. Kwiram wrote in 1976 that intellectuals had had difficulty in the last decade being "at home" in Adventism "because they feel that the church fails the test of relevancy in many of its practices, and all too often, refuses to speak at all when ethical issues are at stake" (37).

6. The General Conference originally desired veto (editorial) power over *Spectrum* articles but compromised with the AAF to provide a list from which five of twenty editorial consultants were to be chosen (Osborn 1978:48).

7. "The academician has every right to probe and search for truth, but he is beyond his depth when he announces that the conclusions he has reached contradict the plain, clear statements of those whom God has used to convey revelation to us" (V. 1980:18).

8. Daniels was president of the General Conference at the 1919 meetings but was replaced in 1922, at least in part as a consequence of the misgivings he voiced about Ellen White's prophetic gift in 1919.

9. For discussion of Ellen White's contemporaries' criticisms of her literary borrowing see Graybill (1983:208–14).

10. Some examples of this defense-through-publishing include *In Defense of the Faith: The Truth about Seventh-day Adventists: A Reply to Canright,* by W. H. Branson (1933); *The Testimony of Jesus: A Review of the Work and Teachings of Mrs. Ellen Gould White,* by F. M. Wilcox (1934); and *Ellen G. White and Her Critics,* by Francis D. Nichol (1951).

11. Bradley noted that White was fallible, as Branson and Weiss claimed, and that "God alone" was infallible. "But," he insisted, "she received revelations from the Holy Spirit who is infallible, and her messages written in human language reflect as accurately as human language can the mind and will of an infallible God" (Bradley 1971:59).

12. Smith, a longtime editor of the *Review and Herald,* was an important early Adventist leader and friend of the Whites.

13. At about the same time as Numbers's publication of *Prophetess of Health,* Walter Rea, an Adventist pastor in California whose early books had been widely distributed throughout Adventism, was interviewed by the *Los Angeles Times* about his discovery of White's apparent use of other writers. As a result of the publicity surrounding the interview (in which Rea referred to White as a "plagiarist"), Rea was fired from his pastoral position. He later wrote and published *The White Lie,* a book which perpetuated the White controversy but is not generally considered an example of good scholarship (see Spectrum Editors 1979).

14. Although formal discussion of White's unacknowledged use of secondary source materials has disappeared from at least Adventist-sponsored periodicals, the questions raised by the controversy continue to shape academic work (by those within and with-

out the movement) and, with less consistency, the practical applications and interpretations of White's writings by Adventists at all levels—from pastors, to authors, to professors, to Sabbath school teachers.

15. Participants (including fifty-six administrators, forty-six Bible scholars, six graduate students, six pastors, five editors, nine [of ten] world division presidents and six former members of the Committee on Problems in the Book of Daniel) spent mornings in small group study, afternoons reporting findings, and evenings reviewing the day's discussion.

16. Following these and other remarks to Ford, "some of the scholars [assembled among the delegates] began to wonder if their presence at Glacierview had been intended to provide support for a decision concerning Ford that had already been determined" (Cottrell 1980:10).

17. Branson wrote in 1981, "Right now the greatest threat to the Adventist church in North America is not doctrinal error, but fatigue. We are so exhausted from fighting each other we have little energy to undertake bold new tasks—or ignite the enthusiasm for the next generation" (3).

18. In response to Adventist leadership's continued discomfort with and discouragement of the expression of divergent views, seventeen teachers from Adventist colleges and universities met in Atlanta in 1981 to draft the Atlanta Affirmation which reiterated faith in and commitment to the fundamental beliefs of Adventism, but also expressed the need for continued learning, questioning, and dialogue in an "open" academic environment, expressed regret over firings and forced resignations that followed Ford's dismissal and the consequent polarization of Adventism, and called for "healing" in Adventism. Despite this and other calls for reconciliation, General Conference leaders continued to explicitly threaten dissenters with revocation of credentials. Adventism's Policy on Discipline, for example, was revised in 1982 to indicate that "discipline may also be administered in the case of a minister who openly expresses significant dissidence regarding the fundamental beliefs of the Seventh-day Adventist Church" (Spectrum Editors 1982:20). The revised policy elucidated that "continued and unrepentant dissidence may eventually be seen by the church to be apostasy" (ibid.:20–21).

19. "There is pluralism—a diversity of views, a diversity of understanding and formulation even on so central a matter as . . . personal salvation" (Guy 1977:29). "The experience of salvation is one aspect of Adventist theology which exhibits a notable lack of consensus" (Rice 1978:65).

20. The *Signs of the Times* was an early Adventist periodical.

21. Jones and Waggoner had previously used positions as West Coast editors of the *Signs of the Times* to expound similar views and had been chastised by General Conference leaders and by Ellen White for doing so.

22. According to Emmett K. Vandevere, there was, in early Adventism (1860s–early 1900s) a strong tendency toward "legalism" (sanctification), though Ellen White attempted to discourage this emphasis (1986).

23. George I. Butler, president of the General Conference, though unable to attend the meetings, sent a letter to delegates urging them to "stand by the old landmarks" (Pease 1983:6), to continue to advocate salvation by adherence to "the law," and, in so doing, to continue to give predominance to SDA "standards."

24. Quoting Ellen White, Douglass created an extensive and influential theology of perfection. Insisting that Adventists could and must achieve flawlessness, Douglass encouraged members to "overcome all sin"; he argued that Adventists who were "less faithful" and failed to develop their talents would not be "lifted up at the last day" (Douglass 1979:147, 110). Adventists, he declared, might easily be "good church members" but not work actively enough for good. Douglass overtly associated the lack of perfection among Adventists with the delay of Christ's coming: "Christ is watching with longing desire for the manifestation of Himself in His church. When the character of Christ shall be perfectly reproduced in His people, then He will come to claim them as His own" (ibid.:165).

25. In 1977 Douglass's "Jesus, the Model Man" was published as a Sabbath school lesson.

26. Wilson notes that "The swift conversion of people who are but little socialized to the values and norms of a movement cannot but lead to the dilution of the movement's goals and lifestyle. Since the characterization of a sect depends upon the members being recognizable as sectarians before they are described by their occupation, ethnicity, education, etc. this process is a clear intimation of incipient denominationalism" (1975:38).

27. Because Adventists limit participation in secular society, in part, by restricting or avoiding secular television, living and working, when possible, among other SDAs, avoiding theaters, even limiting fiction reading, Adventist participation in secular graduate education serves as a primary junction between Adventists and secular society. Currently, SDAs do interact with "the world," but NAD Adventists are often employed by SDA institutions, live in Adventist ghettos, shop in SDA-owned groceries and book centers (ABCs), and socialize widely with other Adventists.

28. In response to charges of plagiarism on the part of Ellen White by *Spectrum* authors, Neal Wilson publicly disassociated Adventism from *Spectrum,* charging that *Spectrum*'s "material is perceived as planting seeds of criticism, polarization, negative questioning, undermining confidence in church organization and lessening the respect for the legitimacy and authority of church leadership" (1983:26).

29. In addition, Adventist theology predicts that immediately prior to the parousia, righteous Adventists will be united against all of the wicked who will seek to destroy God's people. Satan will lead the masses in their attack on believers, and though Christ will come and the righteous will prevail, Adventists recognize that in the not-too-distant future they will literally "battle . . . the world": "In anticipation of this final separation, Adventists have maintained . . . distance between themselves and the rest of the world" (Pearson 1990:32).

Part 2

Gender and Adventism's Changing Response
to the World

5

Definition of Sectarian Identity and Delineation of Gender in the *Adventist Review*

As Adventism struggles to mediate its relationship with the world, it simultaneously wages an internal battle for definition of identity. In addition to demarcating theology in order to locate and preserve singularity, Adventism, like other sectarian movements, finds definition in a shared understanding of appropriate behavior, and moreover (and often more subtly) in definition of appropriate gender behavior. Although modern sectarians overwhelmingly perceive their movements' historical delimitation of gender and appropriate gender specific behaviors as being more restrictive (particularly for women) than are current sect norms and expectations, in fact, a more careful analysis of Adventist literature reveals a far more complex relationship between the sect's response to the world and its understanding and advocation of gender norms. In order to consider this relationship in the context of Adventist historical change, this chapter will first adumbrate Adventism's response to the world as it has been recorded in the sect's primary periodical, the *Second Advent Review and Herald of the Sabbath* (currently the *Adventist Review*), and will then explore in some detail gender behavioral expectations as they have been advocated for Adventist women and men both historically and contemporarily in the *Adventist Review*.[1]

The *Advent Review and Herald of the Sabbath*

Initiated in 1850 by James White in response to Ellen White's prompting, the *Review* became, in the first years of its distribution, the primary link between scattered sabbatarian believers. From a small paper written, printed, and distributed by one man for the "remnant," the *Review* became, with successful Adventist evangelical efforts and the introduction of a systematic system of monetary support (tithing), a regularly published, widely distributed periodical serving as the primary vehicle for establishment and promulgation of Adventist theology and doctrine. While not claiming to be the official organ of Seventh-day Adventism (except, interestingly, between 1973 and 1979; a time of crisis in Adventism [see chapter 4]), the *Adventist Review* remains the "'unofficial' voice of the church" (Kenneth Wood in Graybill 1981:19). Responsible for publication of articles on doctrine, Adventist news and information, Week of Prayer reflection/discussion series, and a number of other matters of importance to Adventists, the *Review* is and has been unquestionably the primary source of religious information and guidance published for Adventists.

Response to the World as Depicted in the *Adventist Review*

Adventism's portrayal of, and proposed response to, the world has changed dramatically in the *Review*'s one and one-half century history. Early copies of the periodical identified the world as the seat of corruption and encouraged separation from secular society: "[Adventism] . . . lays its first foundation in the renunciation of the world, as a state of false Gods and false enjoyments, which feed the vanity and corruption of our nature, fill our hearts with foolish wicked passions, and keep us separate from God" (Smith 1858:73). Separation from the world appears to have been a crucial component of Adventist identity between 1848 and the late 1860s, but due to the lack of legal organization in adventism at the time, the world appears to have been defined as consisting not so much of those outside of a particular, well-defined group but of those who rejected the truths that adventists were in the process of uncovering and (to a limited extent)[2] sharing.[3] Ellen White wrote in 1868 that Adventists should "agree with others in theory and in practice, if we can do so, and at the same time be in harmony with the law of God, and with the laws of our being" (278). Prior to Adventist organization, then, the movement's definition of the world was not strictly constructed with reference to group membership but to shared belief and practice; the world was identified as evil, nonetheless, and adventists were to remain separate from it.

Through the 1870s, the Adventist response to the world remained adamant, but began to distinguish the world as more specifically non-Adventist. One anonymous 1873 article noted that "the religion of the day is entirely unlike the religion of the Bible": "In Bible times religion separated people from the world. . . . The heart cannot be fired up with the love of God and the love of the world at the same time. . . . We need earnestly to inquire for the old paths of experimental religion, and to walk therein. We want radical Christianity" ("Modern Religion" 1873:194). This emphasis continued through the 1880s and 1890s. In 1884 Ellen White insisted that Adventists must reject the world or reject God: "The Lord himself has established a separating wall between the things of the world and the things which he has chosen out of the world and sanctified for himself" (17). Though Adventists might attempt to destroy this distinction, she wrote, "God has made this separation, and he will have it exist" (ibid.). The following year, Ellen White asked Adventists to consider whether they were "separating in spirit and practice from the world." While she observed "how hard it is to come out and be separate from worldly habits and customs," she declared that such separation was essential as "eternal interests are involved" (White 1885:65). Other Adventists agreed with White's assessment: "Few things more accurately determine our moral standing in the sight of God than the manner in which we relate ourselves to the world. . . . If from choice we seek the society of the world, it indicates that the love of God is leaking out of our hearts" (Stone 1886:227). In 1887 another *Review* author called separation from the world "imperative" and portrayed association with the world as posing danger to Adventists: "We must remember that we are in an enemy's land, and that he who is a friend to the world is an enemy of God" (Peebles 1887:274).

Ellen White, the *Review*'s most vocal proponent of separation from the world, insisted in the 1890s that there should be "no union between the church and the world" (1895a:129): "By union with the world, the character of God's people becomes tarnished" (1892:529); "Through union with the world the church would become corrupt" (1895a:129); "The world is the chief enemy of religion" (ibid.). White maintained that "those who are not wholly on the side of Christ are to a large degree controlled by the maxims and customs of the world" and then forbade "fellowship with the world" (1894b:753). Even in Adventist evangelical endeavors White argued that SDA missionaries "cannot conform to the world" because "the world is not God's way" (1894a:721).

The *Review* demonstrated a marked decline in insistence upon separation from the world following the turn of the century. Writing in 1910, Ellen White reiterated that a "great gulf [was] fixed" between Adventists and the world but warned that SDAs should "beware of indulging in a spirit of bigotry [and] intolerance" toward the world; such an attitude of animosity, she cautioned, might deter Adventist evangelical labors (3). Adventists were to continue to avoid worldly associations and activities, but Adventist missionary efforts necessitated increased interaction with, and at least a more overtly tolerant response toward, the world.

In the 1920s, *Review* articles continued to criticize alliance and intimacy with the world, but began to do so with reference to specific examples of Adventist interaction and association with secular society. In one fictitious *Review* illustration, a non-Adventist interested in Adventist literature visited SDA homes accompanied by an Adventist woman. The potential convert was bemused by the lack of distinction from the world she found therein. She told her guide, "You needn't tell me that the people we visited today believe that Jesus is coming soon. If they did they would not be living in such houses as we have seen. . . . They are living, acting and dressing like the world" (Farnsworth 1920b:20). The story's author went on to discourage "imitating the customs and practices" of the "wicked world" (ibid.:21). By the 1930s, however, the *Review* insisted that it was the "direction" of a person's life at the time of the advent, rather than her "place" (religious affiliation), that determined salvation, and that not only Adventists would be saved (N. 1935).[4]

This decreased emphasis on separation from the world continued through the 1940s and accelerated rapidly during the 1950s. While *Review* articles of the 1940s continued to emphasize Adventism's unique beliefs, authors concluded that "we can agree on many points with those in other churches, in so far as they have derived their teaching from the unadulterated word of God" (L. 1940:6–7). The 1950s, which saw an explosion of Adventist evangelism (including televangelism efforts), initiated a period of Adventist accommodation to the world.[5] One 1955 author, identifying Adventists with non-Adventist Christians, asked, "are Christians to have no intercourse with people of the world? Are they to cut loose from all their friends who aren't Christians? . . . Are they never to mingle with people of the world?" The respond was that though Adventists were not to marry "unbelievers," they should interact, as Christians, with non-Adventists as such interaction would provide opportunities to "witness" to unbelievers (Dickson 1955). Though the world was still identified as "the enemy," accommodation to the world was viewed as being acceptable to the extent that conversion efforts necessitated such accommodation and worldly interaction (Wentland 1950).

In the 1960s, Adventists basked in the success of their burgeoning worldwide evangelical campaign. Recognizing Adventism's accession of cultural norms in its efforts not only to further missionary labors but to demonstrate maturity as a Protestant religious organization (with the publication of *Questions on Doctrine* in 1957), *Review* authors defended Adventism: "Magazines, newspapers, books, as well as radio and TV feature the work of Adventists and usually commend it. . . . A few [Adventists] express the fear that this more respected position of Adventists is an indication that the church has drifted toward the world . . . that we are no longer the distinct, peculiar people we once were. [Adventists must not be] misled to believe that every change and adjustment in our work is worldliness" (Figuhr 1960:3). Another author, asking "How liberal are we?" concluded that although Adventists should refrain from joining the ecumenical movement, "it does not follow that we should ever permit ourselves to conclude that other religious groups are in some way really outside the fold of God, that they are insincere in their religious worship" (Nichol 1965:12–13).

In response to Adventism's tendency toward accommodation throughout the 1950s and 1960s, and more especially in response to perceived threats to the movement's distinct doctrine and, therefore, identity (posed by Desmond Ford [the sanctuary doctrine] and *Spectrum* authors [accusations of plagiarism by Ellen White]) in the 1970s, *Review* authors drew back from their previously more accommodating position and attempted to draw attention to the "dangers" of secularization. One author specifically distinguished between the characteristics of a church and those of a sect, identified Adventism as a sect (a religious body which endeavors to "'stand apart' from the world"), and called Adventism's then recent progression from sectlike status to churchlike status "tragic" (W. 1970:13). The author pointed to Adventists' failure to accept and live according to the "commands and standards of the Bible" as one indication of creeping Adventist "liberalism," and called for a renewed emphasis in Adventist teaching on "standards" (and thereby a return to distinct Adventist sectarian behaviors) "to sharpen the line between [Adventism] and the world" (ibid.). In 1975, W. J. Hackett warned that Adventism was in danger of becoming secular: "Have we [SDAs] slidden from the primitive gospel that characterized the religion of our fathers? Is there a religious tide of worldliness creeping into our ranks? . . . Are we mixing too thoroughly religion and secularism?" (4). Because Adventists were "taking a new look at righteousness by faith . . . [and] our stand on revelation—inspiration," Hackett warned, they were in danger of "drifting away from the great landmarks of our faith" (ibid.). Another author wondered "why . . . so many Christians—even some Adventists—become so much like the world?" and called for increased Adventist separation from secular society (Dakar 1975:6).

Despite the *Review*'s backlash against "creeping secularism" in the 1970s, by the mid-1980s and 1990s, the periodical began once again to forge a path toward increased accommodation. Adventists, one author explained in the early 1980s, did have "the truth," but Adventist doctrine alone was not truth. Instead, he asserted that "truth" was a broad category that encompassed the Bible. Therefore, "Adventist doctrine is what the Bible teaches and in that sense is truth," but Adventists are not alone in their possession of truth (Ashbaugh 1980:14). Another author advocated Adventist "distinction" while concurrently recognizing that Adventism could not remain entirely separate from the world if members were to witness effectively (Bietz 1985:7). Paul A. Gordon took this argument to its logical conclusion in 1993, noting that "the message we [SDAs] bear is not ours, it is God's, and we must find an acceptable way to warn people without creating unwarranted conflict" (14).

Preservation of Identity through Gender Prescriptions in the *Adventist Review*

In the context of this changing response to the world, Adventism has defined belief in a manner which emphasizes distinction in times of strong sectarian response to the world (separation) and deemphasizes distinct identity in times of accommodation. At the same time, Adventism has used gender norms, ideals, and expectations to preserve distinct identity when separation from the world was valued and sought, and has advocated gender norms, behaviors, and expectations not out of keeping with those of the wider society when some accommodation to the world was concomitantly emphasized. This tendency is apparent upon examination of gender archetypes and standards as advocated historically in the *Review*.

While nineteenth-century North American women were expected to be exclusively responsible for the care of children, the nurturance of husband, and the maintenance of the home, Adventist women were, in addition to being presented with this ideal, deemed to have an important participatory role *in Adventism.*[6] B. F. Robbins pointed in 1859 to the active participation of women in Adventism as one peculiarity that served to distinguish Adventism from other religious movements: "I know that most of us have been gathered into the message of the third angel from [other] churches where we received our religious training . . . and . . . in some of [those churches] the prejudice against women's efforts and labors in the church have crushed her usefulness. This kind of training has in many of you caused timidity, and discouragement, and the neglect of the use of gifts designed to edify the church and glorify God"[7] (Robbins 1859:21–22). Another author appealed to Adventist women to engage actively in religious work, arguing that biblical sanction against women's full religious participation was destructive and had been misconstrued: "Biblical passages have been construed as an objection to women's speaking in public; and thousands of females that have submitted their hearts to God . . . have been deprived of the privilege of speaking out their feelings in the public congregation, to the almost entire loss of enjoyment, by false construction put upon these paragraphs, notwithstanding the great amount of evidence that can be brought to prove that all who are made partakers of such love have a right to speak forth his praises" (Welcome 1860:109). Interpreting Pauline injunctions against women speaking in meetings as simply an appropriate response to an overwhelming number of questions posed to early Christian teachers which would have been "better answered at home," S. C. Welcome concluded that "the prohibition of the apostle" had nothing to do with women's participation in "preaching, prophesying, exhorting or praying in public," each of which Welcome encouraged women to do (ibid.).

> The mind of the female . . . has equal access to the fountain of light and life. And experience has proved that many females have possessed the natural qualifications for speaking in public, the range of thought, the faculty of communicating their ideas in appropriate language, the sympathy with suffering humanity, a deep and lively sense of gratitude to God, and of the beauty of holiness, a zeal for the honor of God, and the happiness of his rational creatures—all these are found among the female part of the human family, as frequently and as eminently as among men. (ibid.:110)

"Where is the authority for saying that females should not receive a gift of the Holy Spirit in the last days?" asked Welcome: "Verily God hath promised it"; "We are informed on the authority of divine revelation that male and female are one in Christ Jesus; that in the relation in which they both stand to him, the distinction is completely broken down as between Jew and Gentile, bound and free" (ibid.). "Then let no stumbling block be thrown in their way, but let them fill the place that God wants them to fill" (ibid.). Other *Review* authors agreed that scriptural exhortations forbidding women's full religious participation were culturally and historically specific and therefore not applicable within Adventism: "When women are forbidden to speak, the spirit of the gospel is violated" ("Shall Women Speak" 1871:99).

One obvious explanation for the *Review* debate concerning the role of women in Adventism in the mid- to late 1800s was to determine, and to convince Adventists of, Ellen White's place in the movement. In part, discussions regarding gender specific expectations for women, particularly in regard to their proper role in worship services and movement leadership, were undertaken to defend and promulgate Ellen White's authority.[8] Andrews (1879), for example, agreed with Welcome that Pauline exhortations were historically specific and not meant to have general application, and he presented numerous examples of biblical women who served in public positions of church leadership as illustrations of the positions that women should assume in Adventism. George C. Tenney concurred that Paul's injunction was no longer applicable and accused those who cited it in order to prevent women from fully participating in the movement of "look[ing] no further than these texts and giv[ing] them sweeping application" (1892:26). Contending that "God has given to women an important part in connection with this work throughout its entire history," Tenney noted that in biblical times women "wrought righteousness, exercised omnipotent power of faith, braved dangers, and witnessed for the truth as effectively as those of the other sex" (ibid.). Citing "the work of the gospel" as removing "distinctions among men in race, nationality, sex or condition," Tenney concluded that "women who labor acceptably in the gospel are included among those of whom the savior says, 'Whosoever therefore shall confess me before men, him will I confess also before my father who is in heaven'" (ibid.). James White, Ellen White's most ardent and consistent defender, agreed in his *Review* articles that Paul's mandate pertaining to women "certainly . . . does not mean that women should take no part in those religious services where [Paul] would have both men and women take part in prayer and prophesying, or teaching the word of God to the people." James White also cited numerous examples of biblical women who served in important positions of religious leadership and told *Review* readers that "The Christian age was ushered in with glory. Both men and women enjoyed the inspiration of the hallowed hour and were teachers of the people. . . . And the dispensation which was ushered in with glory, honored with the labors of holy women, will close with the same honors" (1897:74).

While the *Review* did not hesitate to defend and encourage women's active participation in worship services and in evangelical efforts, after 1880 the periodical portrayed such endeavors as occurring within the context of a woman's position as wife and mother and including, rather than replacing, the responsibilities of those positions.[9] Instead of overtly challenging Victorian prescriptions for women, early Adventism, as depicted in the *Review,* added a dimension of religious responsibility and authority to Victorian expectations. Adventist women, like non-Adventist women in nineteenth-century North America, were presented with a delimited "sphere": "[Woman] has a sphere, and she cannot with propriety go out of it. She cannot go out of the circle which nature and propriety have drawn about her. Neither can man go out of his and invade hers" (Bowers 1881:373). Women's place, as outlined in *Review* articles, consisted of "homemaking" (cleaning, making the family "comfortable," and completing other housework) and, more significantly, of caring for, and teaching religious principles to, children. Adventists were told in 1895 that mothers had the primary responsibility for raising their children to become dedicated Adventists: "Every word spoken by maternal lips, every act in mother's life . . . every expression on her face will influence for good or evil [the child]" (Caro 1895a:7); "There is no other work that can equal this [mothering]. The impressions now made upon their developing minds will remain with them all through life" (W. Bland 1895:551). Adventists were informed further that there was a "great responsibility resting upon parents, but more especially upon mothers, who are or should be the constant companions of the little ones" (F. Bland 1895:454). Ellen White, writing in the *Review* in 1891, cautioned women that "If you ignore you duty as a wife and a mother, and hold out your hands for the Lord to put another class of work into them, be sure that he will not contradict himself; he points you to the duty that you have to do at home. If you have the idea that some work greater and holier than this has been instructed to you, you are under a deception" (545).

Notwithstanding admonitions of *Review* authors encouraging women to undertake and fulfill gender responsibilities consistent with cultural ideals, Adventists, recognizing the imminence of the advent, called upon all members to participate in the work necessary to hasten Christ's coming: "Sisters . . . everywhere, you can help prepare the way for blessing. You can be messengers for the Lord. . . . Awake! arise! and let your brightness shine. . . . Hasten the coming of him for whom the ages have waited" (Morton 1885:484). As a sectarian movement defining itself in opposition to the world, Adventism was able at once to acknowledge and even perpetuate gender restrictions placed upon women by its sociohistorical context and to allow women participation, position, influence, and authority unavailable to them in the wider society. Declaring that "only in Jesus Christ is there neither male nor female" (Armory 1890:517), *Review* authors continued their attack on Pauline prohibitions against women's public participation in religious service (Pauline sanctions "by no means intimated that when a woman received any particular influence from God to enable her to teach, she was not to obey that influence; on the contrary, she was to obey it" [Bowers 1881:373]) and called upon women to "pray, testify, and exhort and expound the word" publicly (ibid.:372). Authors were quick to note historical religious contributions of women: "In the work of God women have ever acted an important part. . . . In these days when the great plan of salvation is well-nigh accomplished, and the years of time are almost ended, we find a similar spirit, and noble, brave, God-fearing women everywhere are taking hold of the work of warning the world" (Morton 1885:484). In addition to being cautioned regarding the importance of their homemaking/mothering responsibilities, Adventist women were reminded that "mind, voice, and every jot of ability are only loaned as talents, given by God to be used in his work" (H. 1899b:357): "The work which the Lord has given us to do must go on. Each woman must carry on her part of it, regardless of any other, or lose the greatest opportunity that has been accorded women in any generation" (H. 1899a:21).[10] Thus, while the *Review* (1860s–1900) acknowledged societal prescriptions regarding women's "appropriate" responsibilities, the periodical's authors simultaneously advocated that women actively participate in the work of preparing for Christ's soon coming; that they contribute to the functioning, spiritual leadership, teaching, and evangelism of Adventism.[11]

Adventist men were also challenged by *Review* authors to assume a masculine identity which, while not contradicting the ideals of the wider society, included dimensions not widely encouraged in popular definitions of men's roles. In 1875, an anonymous *Review* writer lamented that "hundreds of men . . . have no time to get acquainted with their children" and claimed that men would benefit from increased interaction with their offspring ("Rights of Home" 1875:19). The *Review* portrayed the "Christian family" as comprised of a mother and father who each had a "solemn responsibility" to contribute to the welfare and growth of other family members (Gros 1891; see also Bull and Lockhart 1989:184). Fathers were expected, according to the ideal presented in the *Review,* to be loving, committed, empathetic, and forgiving ("Rights of Home" 1875:19): "A wise father will make himself one with his children" (Caro 1895b:822). Fathers were encouraged to "leave worldly cares" outside of the domestic sphere and to concentrate instead on "committing children to God."

In addition to asking them to participate more actively in fathering, *Review* writers encouraged men to develop and maintain an "equal partnership" with their spouses. One author, writing in 1895, observed that women, even if not employed for wages, worked as hard as wage-earners, and that it was therefore "fair to regard [marriage] as an equal partnership in which both partners have an equal right to share the profits" (Inter Ocean 1895:678). Adventists were told that men and women should become a "perfect blending of two imperfect parts into one perfect whole" upon marriage, and that "this union is not complete while one [partner] holds the purse strings" (T. 1895c:437). They were cautioned further that women and men (in marriage) should participate together in decision-making (Sel. 1890), and that failure to share authority and leadership in the home would invoke eternal consequences: "A serious account at the bar of infinite justice awaits that man who solemnly promises to love and cherish as his own flesh a trusting wife; then subjects her to bondage—to life-long servitude without other reward than the bare necessities of living" (T. 1895c:437). Moreover, men were expected to complete housekeeping responsibilities: "If our homes are to prove a 'success,' each child, as well as father and mother, must be taught to hold himself or herself responsible for the smooth running of the domestic machinery" (Reed 1888:64). Men were told to be "the man *of* the house": "In his home the threshold is not the boundary line of [the man's] care. He invites his wife to participate in the management of his work. He, on his part, is always ready to do all in his power to divide burdens evenly. He builds the fires and brings the water. He will prepare vegetables, lay a table, sweep a floor or cook a meal" (T. 1895a:261). Though younger SDAs were not given (nor are they currently given) particular attention in the pages of the *Review,* sporadic articles addressing gender norms for young people were consistent with the ideals outlined above for Adventist women and men. One author remarked in the mid-1890s that "it is a mistake to teach boys the false idea that 'woman's work' is something beneath them. . . . Rather let them learn to wash clothes and dishes. Teach them plain cookery and housekeeping" (ibid.). "The sensible young woman," on the other hand, was "self-reliant": "She is not merely a doll to be petted. . . . Though she may be blessed with a father able and willing to care for her every want, she cultivates her capabilities, she seeks to prepare herself for possibilities, and, though she may not need to, she qualifies herself to feed and clothe herself, so that if left alone, she can stand upon her own two feet, dependent upon no human being" ("Sensible Girl" 1889:501). Holding self-reliance and financial independence as ideals for women as well as men, contributors to the *Review* did not hesitate to encourage young Adventist women to learn skills that would allow them future independence. One author elucidated in 1879 that girls should be taught to sharpen knives, complete home maintenance, harness horses, whittle, nail nails, and so on, so that they would never be forced to rely upon men: "Learn to help yourselves[, girls], even if sometimes you trench upon 'boys'' work" ("Lesson for Girls" 1879:91). This sentiment was asserted even more adamantly in 1893: "The curse of our modern society is that our young women are taught . . . to get somebody to take care of them. Instead . . . the first lesson should be how, under God, they may take care of themselves. . . . The simple fact is that the majority of them [girls/women] have to take care of themselves. . . . It is inhumane and cruel for any father or mother to pass their daughters [to] womanhood, having given them no faculty for earning a livelihood" ("Our Daughters" 1893:133).[12]

In spite of the *Review*'s penchant (between the 1850s and the early 1900s) for a less restrictive interpretation of gender standards and expectations, Adventists, following Ellen White's counsel, strongly opposed the nineteenth-century feminist movement. Employing popular nineteenth-century antisuffragist rhetoric, *Review* contributors identified the suffrage movement as threatening women's unique and ideal qualities (the ability to nurture, patience, and other "mothering" characteristics) and as pulling women "down" to the "level of men" (Banks 1981:95; T. 1895b; T. 1895d; Yonge 1880).

Haven and Heartless World: Distinguishing Gender Spheres

Beginning in the 1890s, and more especially following 1900, the *Review* began to promote ideals of the Cult of True Womanhood and the Cult of Domesticity. The Cult of True Womanhood, which had been embraced by mainline Protestantism in the 1830s and 1840s, drew from the Enlightenment to identify strict distinctions between men (who were considered within this construct to be rational, intellectual, and physically strong) and women (who were thought to be irrational, physically weak, innately maternal, gentle, kind, loving, and moral), and to inculcate "appropriate" gender specific behaviors based upon these perceived gender differences (see Welter 1976). The Cult of Domesticity, in turn, embraced divisions defined by the Cult of True Womanhood and associated them with specific and separate spheres. A woman's domain ("sphere") was in the home, fulfilling domestic responsibilities, while the man's realm was in commerce, business, or some form of wage labor (Banks 1981:85). Subsequently, the world outside the home (the man's world) was conceived as a harsh, competitive, and hostile environment, participation in which led to the moral degradation of men's characters, which, consequently, needed to be nourished, replenished, and morally improved in the home (woman's sphere) which was, in contrast, portrayed as a "haven."

The shift in Adventism toward acceptance and promotion of the Cult of Domesticity, while subtly present in 1890s *Review* articles dictating women's child care and housekeeping responsibilities, became more overtly apparent after the turn of the century (see Daily 1985). Judd, as early as 1891, called "the ideal home" "a little heaven on earth in which to prepare for the heaven above" (357), and by the mid-1890s authors more readily portrayed "the home" as an idyllic setting in which correct moral behavior was rooted (T. 1894a). Before the early 1900s, however, *Review* authors, unlike their non-Adventist contemporaries, did not specifically associate the "home as haven" with restrictive, gender specific behavior norms and expectations for women. A. R. Wilcox, in 1894, promoted the home as "a place of refuge for the adult *man or woman*" (emphasis added): "They flee to home [for] protection, and gain from intercourse with congenial friends the strength and courage to go forth with renewed determination to conquer in the battle of life" (628).

While prior to the 1900s the *Review* discussed women of biblical times with reference to their religious authority and leadership capacity, by the turn of the century articles outlined a much more limited interpretation of Bible women, stressing foremost that biblical women were housekeepers, and, by implication, that housework ought to be the primary responsibility of

Adventist women in the early 1900s. The *Review,* which began in the mid-1890s to carry a "Home" section—targeting women with housekeeping and parenting suggestions—by 1900 began occasionally to define strictly separated masculine and feminine spheres. One 1900 article, for example, portrayed "homemaking" not only as something that women should do but as women's sole "vocation." Adopting the language of the Cult of Domesticity, the author depicted "man, with his strength of body and soul to battle the world, . . . and woman with her no less God-given power to put inspiration into his work, and to make a place of rest and refreshing for him when the day's conflict is over" (Stanley 1900:391). Another author departed from the ideal of partnership present in earlier *Review* articles to construct a more singular interpretation of women's (and by implication, men's) responsibilities: "The virtuous wife and mother seems to be the central figure of the home. She is industrious. She interests herself in all that is of interest to her loved ones. She becomes a safe counselor for both her husband and for her children" ("Her Husband Also" 1905:13).

This revised understanding of gender expectations applied not only to mature Adventists but also to young SDAs, most specifically to Adventist girls. By 1910, young Adventist women were advised in the *Review* to be "selfless" and to assist and encourage others. Gone were admonitions of self-reliance and independence. Instead, SDA girls were warned against "ambition": "Little by little, some intellectual ambition will draw us away from our true place in life if we are not careful, and will make cold, unloved and unhelpful women of us, instead of the joyous, unselfish ones we might have been. Ambition is all right, but let us give it its just proportion; let us use our talents, but keep them forever subordinate to simple human duties of life" (Morrison 1910:12).

Although these changed gender expectations did not go unnoticed or unopposed, by 1915 the *Review* began increasingly to emphasize women's work in the home. (Luella B. Priddy protested the narrowing scope of women's responsibilities in 1910, for example, adamantly and specifically calling for women's participation in Adventist labors: "There are many kinds of work in which women can successfully engage, and the spirit of prophecy tells us that their work is needed" [11].)[13] After 1900, however, women's evangelical efforts were to be concentrated in the home (Graham 1915) and moreover, "women's work" was defined expressly as nonwage labor (homemaking): "There are many new professions open to women today, but in none of them can she shine brighter, or serve God and humanity better, than in the old profession of homemaking" (Lewis 1915:14). Women were encouraged to be efficient and effective homemakers and mothers and warned that their failure as mothers or homemakers would have long-lasting repercussions: "An incompetent . . . ill-trained . . . mother is a curse unto the third or fourth generation of those who love her and fall under her influence" (Moore 1915:12).

This trend continued in the 1920s and 1930s as the Cult of Domesticity was increasingly perpetuated in the pages of the *Review*. The work of Adventist women was defined in the context of the wife/homemaker role to the exclusion of a variety of activities and endeavors in which earlier Adventist women had been encouraged to participate. Adventist women were told that they were "needed in the world's great work," but that they could "not find time to work outside the four walls of home." The work that Adventist men and women were to do, then, became rigorously distinguished. While men were to engage in evangelical and wage labor efforts that required participation in the world, women's work was defined more exclusively as meeting the needs of husband and children within the home. It was the woman's work in the home, according to the *Review* (in keeping with the home as haven paradigm), that provided men with the sustenance and moral character to succeed in wage labor. One fictitious 1925 *Review* character married a "brilliant" husband and, lacking skills (except the ability to "keep house") or education, "she planned the delicate, dainty, healthful meals, and kept the home clean." Her efforts "invited the tired husband to rest, to litter [the house] with books and papers. . . . And the quiet wife, who had time to love him, to share his hopes, listen to his plans, and make his life supremely happy, was an element in his success which counted more largely than even the husband knew" (Sunday School Lesson 1925:14). Women were described, beginning especially in the 1920s, as caring for and teaching children from infancy (Stoner 1925b). Although *Review* authors acknowledged that some SDA women lamented that "other women are doing things and getting paid for it," the *Review* countered that "when these home duties become sacred privileges, there will come a feeling of peace and satisfaction that cannot be exchanged for dollars and cents" (Stoner 1925a:10). Furthermore, the *Review* asserted that a homemaker's/mother's "power is the great force that moves the world" and that women, by properly completing their responsibilities in the domestic sphere, "might cure half our national evils of divorce, extravagance, . . . marital unhappiness, [and] inefficient parenthood. They will never do it in the office, but it might be done in the kitchen" (ibid.).[14] Women's domestic labor was represented as being responsible for the success or failure of men ("With such a wife at the hearthstone, it is easy to understand why husband and sons live clean, noble lives") and was delimited in such a way as to be portrayed in opposition to intellectual, financial, or educational endeavors. Women's domestic work was "a far finer thing than the writing of any novel, or the painting of any picture," and so on. Thus, while between 1850 and 1900 gender expectations for Adventist women did not preclude extra-domestic activities, later the Adventist ideal for women was defined strictly within the bounds of homemaking and motherhood, and these responsibilities were more directly associated with the success/failure of men in particular and of society generally. ("The home that is not in harmony with the laws of purity, justice, high ideals, and obedience is sending out a poisoning stream that will leave its blight everywhere" [Harter 1925:16].)

Again, this evolution of gender norms and expectations was not without its detractors (see Tyrell 1930:6). By the 1930s, however, even those *Review* authors advocating extra-domestic activities for SDA women did so primarily within the parameters of emerging homemaking expectations. Women's evangelical labors were to be concentrated in the home (ibid.; Williams 1930:18) and "busy homemakers" were encouraged to take SDA higher education courses at home via correspondence (Olsen 1930:15). While women (wives/mothers) were instructed to set aside wage labor participation and to make the home a "haven"—a reprieve from the world—father was told to assume "his rightful position as head of his household" and to provide for the fiscal well-being of his nuclear family (Shinn 1930:13–14). Whereas nineteenth-century Adventist women had been depicted as independent, competent, and intelligent workers (especially prior to 1880) whose responsibilities included, but were not limited to, domestic work, the woman portrayed in the *Review* of the 1920s and 1930s appeared to have little knowledge, experience, or ambition outside of the domestic sphere.

As Adventist women increasingly were encouraged to assume responsibility for domestic labor, SDA men were admonished to seize headship of the family. Most significantly, husbands and fathers were told to provide financially for their families and to be the moral and spiritual leader of the household (see Farnsworth 1920a:20). Men were admonished that "a father has no right to be so absorbed in business that he has no time" to talk and interact with his children (ibid.) and boys were encouraged occasionally during the 1920s to "assist" their mothers with household work ("Father in the Home" 1925). Nonetheless, the home was, for men in the *Review* of the 1920s and 1930s, a place "where a weary father comes at night and lays aside all care" (Newville 1925:11).

Reprieve, 1940–45

The *Review*'s newly embraced emphasis on separate, gendered spheres of responsibility (home, women; world, men) was briefly amended between 1940 and late 1945 to include women's participation in wage labor and, concurrently, to reemphasize the importance of women's participation in public religious work. As women in secular society were invited, during World War II, to contribute to the paid labor force in occupations and positions normally reserved for men, Adventist women also left the domestic domain long enough to be employed "regular hours" in addition to "keeping house" (Mallory 1940).[15] Although the ideal Adventist woman was still a wife and mother who was a "true helpmeet" to her husband, was "selfless," and who completed the family's cooking, cleaning, and "mending," she was not overly involved in nor dependent upon her children's lives (Andross 1940). One *Review* article, for example, depicted a woman pursuing interests independent of her homemaking responsibilities: "For the first time since I've been their mother, I'm studying something for myself! I have just discovered that my children's interests have been absorbing so much of my attention that I have almost no interest apart from them" (Mallory 1945:15). Other articles sought to justify women's participation in public religious endeavors: "We are sure that Paul never intended that his words, which were directed to a specific situation, should be used to prevent any woman, simply because she was a woman, from taking any active part in public church services. . . . We believe that it is altogether reasonable for us to hold that there are other women, besides those strictly called prophets [Ellen White] who have been called of God to do a public work, and who have received a special training for that public work in schools set apart by God" (Nichol 1940:9, 15).

Though not all women depicted in the *Review* during the years of World War II chose to participate in wage labor, and though the *Review* continued to portray women as being responsible for household work, as secular society insisted that women's contribution to the workforce, especially in occupations usually reserved for men, was essential to the war effort, *Review* authors, instead of discouraging SDA women from participating in wage labor, encouraged Adventist women in extradomestic enterprises.

Retrenchment, 1950–70

The *Review*'s penchant, between 1940 and late 1945, for defining women's responsibilities as including, but not being limited to, housekeeping and mothering, was reversed immediately and completely following the end of the war. As secular employers laid off female employees to make room for male workers returning from military service, and as the secular media encouraged, and attempted to legitimate, women's forced retreat from "male" (higher wage) occupations, *Review* writers resumed a definition of appropriate gender behavior that precluded (even more strictly and overtly than it had prior to 1940) women's participation in the paid labor force and delimited women's responsibilities as involving solely mothering and homemaking.[16] Furthermore, *Review* writers did not hesitate to blame employed wives, and especially mothers, for perceived social ills. Immediately after the war, one author noted a rise in juvenile delinquency and attributed the problem to employed women: "With too many mothers working, the atmosphere of security and stability that a child needs so much has departed from many homes. . . . The lure of easy money has taken many mothers away from their homes, and their children are left to shift for themselves" (Lloyd 1945:11). Claiming that women were employed for wages because "there has been so much emphasis on earning more money, on a higher standard of living," *Review* writers criticized women who "farmed out" their children (placed them in child care) and accused them, in so doing, of contributing to the "breakup of the home" (Bietz 1955:12). Lamenting that "there was a time when women felt that the highest possible vocation that they could fulfill was in the home and in motherhood" (ibid.), the *Review* presented a bleak picture of children left alone, "crying" for "good mothers—mothers who make home and loved ones their first duty" (Oswald 1955c:12).

By the 1950s, *Review* authors uniformly portrayed women as wives, mothers, and homemakers, and held them specifically (and apparently exclusively) responsible for their children's welfare. Women were told repeatedly that wage labor participation would interfere with, perhaps even circumvent, the well-being of their offspring: "What a fearful thing it is for a mother to yield to the temptation to earn a high salary while others look after her children. 'Others' can never give the child the motherly interest and care the child deserves and requires" (Lloyd 1950:14). Women (wives/mothers) were portrayed by *Review* authors of the 1950s and 1960s as being responsible for their own children's success and, on a more general level, for the moral success or failure of society: "The man who has had a good mother will never wholly lose his faith in God and humanity. That faith will keep him from drifting down the river of sin to the awful falls of perdition. . . . A good mother is better than all the policemen in the state. She is the one best able to nip trouble in the bud. The good mother prevents unfortunate tendencies in children from growing into serious problems" (ibid.). "The power of woman in shaping the destinies of men and of nations has always been greater than that of man. We have always expected women to live purer and better lives than men. As long as women are what they should be, even if men go wrong, there is hope for the future;

but when women go wrong there is nothing to hope for. The world will then go from bad to worse, until, as in Noah's day, conditions will become hopeless" (Kress 1950:15).

Whereas early (1840s–80s) Adventist women were encouraged to pursue activities and interests outside of the domestic sphere, the *Review,* throughout the 1950s and 1960s, presented Adventist women with ideals of womanhood which failed to extend beyond the borders of domesticity. One fictitious female character in a 1950 *Review,* when asked what she had accomplished during the day, replied that "I had the sweetest consciousness of helping those about me as best I could, and keeping the home running smoothly. This is the privilege and duty of the mother in the home. Had I failed in any phase of my part of the program, it would have brought disappointment and inconvenience and perhaps discouragement to those dear ones depending on me" (Odom 1950:14). No longer did the *Review* present possibilities for women's foreign evangelical work or attempt to endorse public religious endeavors by women. Adventist women were instead informed (in an article on child-rearing) how to "prepare" "homemakers and breadwinners" (Moore 1950:13), and told that while worldly failures might be rectified, failure in the home (the woman's/ wife's/mother's domain) was of "eternal significance" (Oswald 1955d:12). Women were, the *Review* of the 1950s reiterated consistently, "important to God's work": "God created woman to be a helpmeet" and as such, women were to sacrifice, thereby contributing to the success of others (Johnson 1955:12). "Many a man enjoys a fame that is really due to his self-sacrificing mother. People applaud the president, the governor, [etc.], but the real secret of their success is in that unknown, unappreciated, unheralded mother" (ibid.). Thus, women's value was made dependent upon personal sacrifice and the achievement of others: "The greatest heroes in the world are the mothers. No one else makes such sacrifices or endures anything like the suffering that she uncomplainingly endures for her children" (ibid.). *Review* authors of the 1950s propounded a feminine gender ideal that precluded personal aspiration, ambition, or purpose outside of the domestic context. Women were told to find fulfillment as wives and mothers to the exclusion of other pursuits.

The redefinition, and ultimate limitation, of woman's sphere was accompanied, in the *Review* of the 1950s, by a reformulation of appropriate gendered behavior for men. As noted above, men were increasingly held responsible for the financial provision of the biological, nuclear family. In addition, the Adventist man of the 1950s, unlike his earlier counterpart (1840s–early 1900s), was not presented with an ideal of participatory parenting and spousal partnership so much as with an ideal of singular strength and individual leadership: "God in his infinite wisdom planted deep in [the husband's/father's] heart the sturdy qualities of leadership, valor, bravery, fortitude, and courage. He endowed him with a strong body, steady nerves, and a powerful mind" (Oswald 1955a:12). Adventist men were told that "a desire to protect and a zeal to provide are a father's true nature. . . . In the sweat of his brow he works untiringly, that he may provide well for those in his care" (ibid.; see also "Memories of a Father" 1965). Instead of being encouraged to participate in parenting or housekeeping, the Adventist husband/father of the 1950s was told that when he saw "the burdens and cares that fall upon his companion's shoulders as wife and mother and homemaker" he could help to relieve those burdens by "understanding" and refraining from complaining when "things have not gone smoothly at home" (Oswald 1955b:12).

The *Review*'s clear division and separation of ideal gender behaviors, not unlike that advocated in secular society at the time, effectively idealized gender norms and distinguished activities, pursuits, and interests into purportedly dichotomous gender spheres. Women, idealized primarily as mothers and caregivers, were to heal, comfort, sustain, and remain unapplauded; men, portrayed as strong, intelligent leaders, were to protect the family from external threats and to provide financially for family members: "Father is the 'houseband,' keeping things firm and strong on all sides. He takes the blows of life's hardships. Mother is the hub—the center of the home. She works faithfully from within to keep it firm and strong" (Oswald 1955b:12). Although the "[Mother's] beautiful place in life is as important as father's strength and leadership," her fundamental responsibility was to provide for his comfort and well-being, thus allowing him the emotional resources necessary to confront the harsh and hostile world (Oswald 1955c:12): "In the darkest hours, when burdens like mountains weigh him down, when adversities have left him almost exhausted in the midst of fierce struggles that try every fiber of his manhood, she speaks courage" and "comforts him"; "Good mothers are the healers and soothers of human woes" (ibid.).

Thus limited to the domestic sphere, Adventist women were informed that wage labor inherently impaired their ability to complete gender appropriate responsibilities and "robbed" their families of "time and energy that rightfully belonged to them" (West 1955a:12). *Review* readers were presented with a bleak picture of the hypothetical home of an employed mother, in which "A lonely child arrives home from school. Regardless of how lovely the furniture, if the mother is not there, if she is away working, he stands on the threshold in dismay. His whole being longs for the loving welcome that should await him. The emptiness of the house chills his very soul, and he shrinks from entering"

(Bradley 1955:12). This predicament, according to *Review* authors, presented hazards for children (primarily "juvenile delinquency") and families: "The late entrance of a weary, nervous, and often irritable mother does not restore much. It may even chill [the child(ren)] more. The father's arrival to greet a tired companion and an unhappy youngster, in a disorderly home, does nothing to remedy the situation. Tense nerves are like clouds in a thunder storm" (ibid.).[17]

Adventist women, in the *Review* of the 1950s and 1960s, were in this way held responsible not only for the perceived ultimate failure or success of their children but for incidental happenings and circumstantial occurrences, for every component of their children's lives and personalities. In one 1960 article on mental illness, a *Review* author cited research by a secular psychologist indicating that "mothers can control the development" of their "unborn children," and therefore that mothers (or prospective mothers) can cause a child to be an "ill-adjusted, neurotic" or a "happy, healthy, sweet-tempered individual" (C. 1960:3). The *Review* insisted that a mother's influence also contributed fundamentally to the development of her offspring as they grew older: "Teenagers," for example, "as much as, or more than, younger children, need their mothers full time!" (Lunday 1960:12). Quoting Ellen White to support this interpretation of motherhood, the *Review* located a mother's ability or inability to fulfill her gender specific duties ("your God-given duty at home" [ibid.]) in wage labor participation or nonparticipation. Parents were warned repeatedly that if they "would save their young people, they must make the home life so pleasant, so attractive and charming, that they [children] will not want to leave it for outside attraction" (Oswald 1955e:12). Women who participated in wage labor were accused of sacrificing "the child's good character or [the] child's eternal life" for material possessions: "Mothers give various excuses for their away-from-home job, but if each of these is studied and analyzed it will be seen that in most cases the real reason is selfishness, thoughtlessness on the person's part, or placing too high a value on earthly possessions" (Lunday 1960:12).[18]

Within this construct of carefully delimited gender appropriate spheres, girls were no longer explicitly encouraged to learn skills that would render them independent. Rather, "since girls are the future homemakers," it was proclaimed their "right" "to know how to perform that work [cleaning, washing, laundering, sewing, preparing food] acceptably when the time comes" (F. Rebok 1955:13). Labeled "vitally important," the work of keeping house and caring for children was offered to young women as a consuming and ultimately independently fulfilling vocation. Interestingly, girls were portrayed as being slow to recognize the inherent value of learning and completing household tasks, and others (often men) regularly deemed it necessary to remind girls of the merit and desirability of their admittedly unrecognized contributions. (In one example, a pastor, upon hearing a young girl describe her child-care responsibilities as "nothing important," recites to the girl stories in which women help men and boys to overcome temptation. As he is leaving, the girl exclaims how glad she is that "you came here today to teach me this lesson" [Robinson 1960:13].)

Although the *Review* had not hesitated, in the 1950s and 1960s, to embrace and even embellish the popular *secular* understanding of gender appropriate behaviors and spheres of influence, when, in the late 1960s and early 1970s, the feminist movement (labeled "the Women's Liberation Movement" in the *Review*) began to assert that these delineations were limiting and unfair, the *Review* hesitated to explore or endorse criticisms raised. Instead, as SDA mothers of young children increasingly began to leave the domestic realm in order to participate in wage labor (see Pearson 1990), the *Review* variously resorted to reiterating previous claims regarding men's and women's roles and later, hesitantly, began to explore those claims more critically. In one 1970 attempt to reassert the periodical's 1950s/1960s position regarding women's appropriate role, an author asserted that Eve's "downfall" "was her desire to rise to a 'higher sphere' than her present status afforded her" (Otis 1970:9). The author concluded that the same was "true of women today! How true!" (ibid.). In his critique of "modern Eves" the author singled out employed mothers for criticism: "Many mothers today are spending their energies striving to reach that 'higher sphere' all the while neglecting the important task at hand, that of rearing their families. We do not have to look far to see mothers who, while trying to satisfy their own personal ambition and hunger for unnecessary praise, are leaving their families to suffer for the want of a real mother" (ibid.). Another writer used the *Review* to insist that the archetypal Adventist woman was a proficient homemaker and wife who had few desires beyond meeting her husband's needs: "A man should look for a wife who has no desire for a college education and/or career. She should be a good, old-fashioned girl from 'down on the farm' who realizes her responsibilities to her children and husband" ("Homemaker's Exchange" 1970b:12).

Debating Gender, 1970s

Other Adventist authors used the *Review* as a format through which to initiate (diffidently, at first) discussion and criticism of blatant gender stereotypes. Betty Holbrook asserted that women might seek employment "out of necessity, . . . out of boredom when the children are grown, . . . [or] for the challenge it brings" (1970:9). Though she failed to assail the assumption that housework was primarily women's responsibility, Holbrook did aver that when women were employed "the family can be put to work too": "It's good for them, teaches them how to work, how to be thoughtful to others, and gives the family a chance to work together at projects. . . . [Family members] may grumble in the process, but someday they will be more than grateful to you" (ibid.). In addition, Holbrook contested the notion that self-sacrifice by women was inherently beneficial; women, she wrote, "must provide for quiet hours [for themselves] . . . [and] for sufficient sleep and health" (ibid.).[19] In another example, in a series of *Review* articles "especially for men," Roland R. Hegstad introduced Adventists to a number of contemporary feminist critiques. Condemning the objectification of women and the inherent limitations of gender-role stereotyping, Hegstad encouraged Adventist men to accept women as unique individuals and to communicate openly with their wives (1970a). In a later article, Hegstad asseverated that Adventists had blamed "youth's rebelliousness" on "false causes" like "working mothers" rather than accepting individual and social responsibility for children's behavior and harshly reprimanded (hiring and wage) gender discrimination in SDA employment practices. He concluded that "women's lib is on the march. The 'good old days' of male dominance are giving way to the delightful days of the emancipated female" (Hegstad 1970c:12).

Notwithstanding Hegstad's conclusion, the *Review* of the 1970s saw a committed, almost nostalgic, insistence upon adherence to gender specific behaviors and roles as they had been delineated in the periodical in the 1950s and 1960s. While *Review* authors at times addressed such topics as the use of sexist language in Adventist publications and worship services (W. 1975) and Adventist-sponsored child care for employed parents (Kuzma 1975b), most authors agreed that any challenge to gender norms as they had been defined in the *Review* during the two previous decades was inherently a secular threat to Adventism's distinct identity.[20] Although the gender standards advocated in the *Review* throughout the 1950s and 1960s were compatible with popular secular expectations of those decades, when those expectations were challenged, the *challenge* was identified as secular and as threatening norms considered necessary to the perpetuation of distinct Adventist belief and practice. *Review* editors explicitly identified feminism as a secular threat to Adventism's distinct identity: "It is important for us to avoid unnecessary offense to any group. But let us not become so relevant that we become irrelevant. In our efforts to do justice to the feminist movement or any other contemporary movement, let us not do injustice to the word of God" (W. 1970:14).

Assuming that feminism posed a secular threat to Adventist gender ideals, *Review* authors reiterated the gender paradigm perpetuated in the *Review* of the 1950s and 1960s. Authors insisted that "both the Bible and the spirit of prophecy [Ellen White] state that a woman's greatest work is that of home-maker" (Bietz 1975:13). Calling any deviation from a mother's commitment to keeping house and caring for family members "unfortunate," *Review* authors charged women with the responsibility of "lift[ing] men to new heights of morality and spiritual achievement" (ibid.). "Woman was born," one author contended, "to soothe a troubled child, to speak to him of Jesus, to make a home where laughter falls like sunshine through the rooms. She's there to light the candles, to read poetry, to gentle all the awkwardness of childhood and the aggressiveness of manhood, to introduce her loved ones to beauty in all its varied forms" (Strong 1975:15). Employed mothers were deemed, in the *Review*, unable to fulfill these "God-given duties" (ibid.) and, further, accused of harm-ing their children irreparably (Doherty 1975:15), presently, and eternally (Newman 1975).

In contrast to the "selfless" mother who chose to stay at home with her chil-dren, the employed mother was "selfish," compelled to pursue wage employ-ment in order to satisfy personal desires (Strong 1975). Employed women were portrayed as participating in wage labor in order to purchase superfluous material items ("We should consider . . . carefully before taking a job as a tele-phone operator so that our sons can drive Hondas and our living rooms sport a color TV" [ibid.:16]), to "feel fulfilled," or to "broaden their horizons" (Doherty 1975:14). Employed women were depicted as uncaring and materi-alistic: "Too often the chief reason why women feel it necessary to work out-side the home, leaving the family without a warm center and letting the chil-dren fend for themselves, is that the family is materialistic" (W. 1980:3). At the same time, women who were employed in order to "'find themselves,' or . . . search [for] an identity" "put their own interests and goals above those of everyone else in the family" (ibid.). These sentiments led one author to conclude that employed women did "need liberating, not from the menial tasks of housekeeping, but from selfishness" (Strong 1975:16), and another to sur-mise that "it seems that some of us have gone a little too far in our liberation" (Doherty 1975:14).

Rethinking Gender, 1980–94

In the face of vehement opposition by a majority of *Review* writers in the 1970s to any rethinking of gender norms and expectations as they had been outlined in the *Review* of the 1950s and 1960s, the *Review* began, by the 1980s and 1990s (especially in the mid- to late 1980s and 1990s) to reconsider its previous strict definition and separation of gender appropriate behaviors and spheres. While women in the *Review* continued to be couched exclusively as homemakers, husbands began to be encouraged to concern themselves with their spouses' well-being and to express love for their wives in "daily acts of kindness"; specifically, husbands were to encourage their wives' spiritual growth (Stutzman 1980:12) and to participate more actively in parenting (Lowe 1980). Although one author admonished men to "just keep on bringing home the dollars" (Bakker 1980:14), another urged fathers to "show affection! Kiss your children! Boys need love just as much as girls!" (Brannaka 1980:11).

Within the context of rethinking (though subtly) masculinity in the *Review,* Adventist authors took the opportunity to discuss the husband/wife relationship and to portray it with a renewed emphasis on equality and mutuality. Women, the *Review* asserted, should submit to their husbands, but the "wife's submission [was] not one of bondage, but one of mutual effort toward a beautiful goal" (Vernon 1985:13). A woman was not to "lose her identity or dignity to her husband." Rather, "she [was to] contribute her individuality [to the relationship] as he [did] his to make a new creation" (ibid.). This ideal of partnership (benevolent patriarchy), which implicitly incorporated submission and dominance but did so in the context of attempting to recognize a standard of equality and mutuality being advocated by the feminist movement, left men in a position of leadership in the nuclear family, but redefined that position as one of "tireless effort, selfless ministry, and sacrificial love" (ibid.). The ideal of benevolent patriarchy introduced a new understanding of masculinity to the Adventist marriage relationship; the husband was to "be willing to share" with his spouse "the duty of ministry" in the family. Instead of independently leading, protecting, and providing for the family, the Adventist man was now to share with his partner the "burdens of marriage" (ibid.). Within this renewed relational context, husbands were to "never stop working" for their partner's "growth, uplifting and welfare" (ibid.).

As Adventists began to rethink masculinity and to reconsider ideals for marital relations, *Review* authors also began to explore alternative role expectations for women. One 1985 article, for example, considered possible positive implications of women's participation in wage labor. Noting that women might choose to work for wages for financial or personal reasons, the author asserted that "the problems a family faces when mother goes to work can either destroy *or reinforce* the qualities that make a house a home" and added that all family members should contribute to completing "household chores" in order to ensure the latter outcome (Todd 1985a:11; emphasis added). Offering practical tips for provision of child care, division of household labor, and financial and career planning, the author concluded that "[for women] working has its rewards and problems. But you, your family, and your relationship to God can survive and even thrive while you work" (ibid.).[21]

The shift in the *Review* toward more inclusive definitions of gender appropriate activities and roles did not go uncontested; initially some of the periodical's authors resisted any reformulation of gender ideals, particularly as applied to women. One week following Sharen Todd's assertion that women's participation in wage labor might benefit not only employed women but their families as well, Arnold Wallenkampf used the *Review* to reassert an understanding of gender appropriate activity consistent with that promulgated in the *Review* most vociferously in the 1950s and 1960s (and, in response to the secular feminist movement, in the 1970s). Completion of housework, Wallenkampf insisted, was directly related to children's salvation: "Cooking, cleaning, washing and mending are not ends in themselves, but a means to the end of rearing a healthy family to be pure, honest, and courageous men and women who will one day walk the gold-paved streets of New Jerusalem because their mothers built into them characters fit for heavenly society" (1985:7). A woman's role as mother, which according to Wallenkampf was directly related to the eternal destiny of her child(ren), was more important than any participation in wage labor, and was the most appropriate life choice for women: "Some women may have been teachers, nurses, office workers, or musicians before they married and became mothers. Now they feel they are not using those skills; but rearing a family provides ample scope for all their skills and talents. The mother becomes the child's most effective teacher, sharing with her children the secrets of successful living, imparting knowledge that will open to them the pearly gates. . . . Her work is more important than that of any profession" (ibid.). Despite such a reassertion of idealized womanhood, *Review* authors were working, by the mid-1980s, to promote an understanding of gender norms and behavior more consistent with those presented in the *Review* of 1850–80 than 1950–80. One 1985 article noted that "homemaking is more than physical, material work; it is an emotional, spiritual responsibility" and encouraged all family members—men, women, and children—to participate in "sharing values, listening well, communicating intimately, accepting another's feelings, [and] offering respect" (Johnston 1985:11). Although women were still encouraged to provide, and portrayed as participating in, child care, no longer were they held solely responsible for the child's present well-being or eternal destiny. Adventists were told that "if the wife *decides* to stay home while the husband earns the income, the couple needs to examine the emotional needs unique to their roles and needs to plan for them" (ibid.; emphasis added). Adventist husbands were admonished "to recognize *openly* [their spouses'] job as equally important" (ibid.:12; emphasis original) and SDA women were told that they had "every right to expect [their spouse] to aid in [their] individual development" (Vernon 1985:13). Adventists were told to be supportive of those women who participated in wage labor ("we need not create unjustified guilt" [ibid.]) and were increasingly cautioned to work toward gender parity in primary and secondary relationships.[22] This reemphasis on gender norms in a manner allowing for less strictly divided gender appropriate spheres and behaviors was presented as being not inconsistent with early Adventist gender expectations: "Adventist history is replete with women who made major contributions, some in quiet ways behind the scenes, but many in positions of leadership. Thus each modern family has to *decide for itself* [concerning appropriate gender roles and activities] considering its needs, goals, responsibilities and convictions of God's leading" (Johnston 1985:12; emphasis original). By the early 1990s, *Review* writers embraced a revised and less rigid understanding of gender behaviors, responsibilities, and spheres. "If the traditional concept of the husband as sole breadwinner is disappearing," the *Review* argued by 1990, "then it is time that the traditional concept of the woman as exclusive caretaker of the home disappear with it. And we'll all be better for it" (Moore 1990:18).

As *Review* authors of the 1980s and 1990s challenged gender ideals as they had been promulgated in the periodical in prior decades, the *Review* simultaneously began to grapple with the issue of women's public participation in Adventist leadership and worship, an issue with which *Review* editors had struggled over a century previously. Roger L. Dudley (like James White) asserted that Pauline prohibitions against women's active participation in religious worship were culturally and historically specific and not relevant to contemporary Adventism (1985). Other authors noted that among Adventists "a consensus is developing that we have no prohibition in scripture or in Ellen White's writings against the ordination of women to the gospel ministry" (Adams 1990b:4) and that "if Adventists take the Bible seriously, if we take Ellen White seriously, only one course lies ahead: equality, equity and justice for women. Our attitudes, behaviors, policies, and practice must come into line" (Johnsson 1990:4).

Significantly, *Review* authors from the mid-1980s through the 1990s proposed an ideal of religious participation not dissimilar from that advocated by early *Review* contributors (1850s–80s). But whereas Andrews, Robbins, Tenney, Welcome, White, and others insisted that women participate in religious leadership and worship *because Adventism was unlike the world* and had a pressing responsibility to share the message of the advent, *Review* authors of the 1980s and 1990s called upon Adventists to work toward gender equity *in order not to alienate the world.* Dudley, for example, regarded Adventism's unequal treatment of women as a hindrance to the group's relationship with secular society and mainline Protestantism generally, and to Adventism's evangelical efforts specifically: "What does failure to treat all people as equal, the practice of separating races and genders in Christian activities, say to our watching world? Today a church that does not foster human dignity and equality will not be perceived as morally responsible" (Dudley 1985:7). When an opponent of women's ordination wrote, in a letter to the editor, that Adventists must "not let current trends pollute our church" by agreeing to ordain women and, more broadly, that to fully incorporate women into the ministry of Adventism was nothing but a bow to "current trends," editors responded by observing the effect that such an obviously misogynist sentiment might have on Adventism's public image: "If such thinking is allowed to prevail in our church we can easily become the laughingstock of intelligent people" (Adams 1990b:4).

Though Adventist proponents of gender equity consistently argued that "Scripture demands" more equitable treatment of men and women and quoted the writings of Ellen White at length to support their contentions, calls for equality based on sex were almost exclusively identified, in Adventism, with accommodation to the world. Gender ideals adopted by the movement (as expressed in the *Review*), concomitantly with secular definitions of, and limitations on, gender specific realms of activity, were not perceived as having arisen in tandem (particularly during the 1950s and 1960s) with increased Adventist accommodation stemming from a broad and dramatic increase in evangelical efforts. Thus, interestingly, during a period of accommodation (1900s–1960s; particularly the 1950s) NAD Adventists accepted gender norms *consistent* with those of the wider society *only to cling to those norms as a vestige of unique Adventist identity during a period of sectarian retrenchment* (1970s). Current Adventist debate surrounding appropriate gender norms accepts these presuppositions, and attempts to fully incorporate women are therefore largely perceived as being an example of capitulation to secular society, more specifically to secular feminism.

Notes

1. This work will concentrate on gender norms advocated for women primarily because Adventist women, like women generally, have been considered gendered be-

ings, while Adventist men, like men in the wider society, have often (though not always) been regarded as normative, and have therefore been discussed less specifically in regard to gender norms and ideals.

2. Though adventists did not at this time participate in widespread evangelical work, they did experience some unexpected (and, in many cases, uninvited) evangelical success, particularly among other former Millerites.

3. This is evidenced in part by the fact that adventists did not clearly associate Seventh-day Baptists (who accepted the doctrine of the seventh-day Sabbath) with "the world."

4. In 1935 the official Seventh-day Adventist statement of belief was changed to reflect this new belief that all people (not only Adventists) could attain salvation. Fundamental belief number nine was changed from reading "immortality and eternal life come only through the gospel" to asserting that "immortality is bestowed upon the righteous at the second coming of Christ" (see *SDA Yearbook,* 1931 and 1935 editions).

5. One 1950 *Review,* typical of the *Reviews* of the decade, contained a high proportion of articles discussing evangelical labors, including: "Religious Liberty and the Earth's Closing Work," "Christ and His Service Are Forever Mine," "A New Day in Southern Asia," "The Time Has Come to Give God Your Best," "Advances on a 3,000 Mile Front," "Progress of the Message in the Dominican Republic," "The Radio Reaches Hearts," "Ringing Doorbells for God," and "Pictures of Progress" (*Review and Herald* 127, no. 7).

6. Even nineteenth-century feminists who worked for more equitable treatment of women in society perceived their goals "in terms of women's traditional role" (Banks 1981:98). Therefore, Adventist women who were actively engaged in movement work but perceived that work in the context of a traditional understanding of their role in society were as "radical" as many early feminists in the sense that they defined women as having important work outside of their traditional sphere as well as within it.

7. The Women's Missionary Movement arose in North America in the early nineteenth century, dedicating itself to evangelical work by women throughout the world. By 1882 the sixteen major Women's Missionary Societies had raised six million dollars and had sponsored 694 single women missionaries. By 1900 the societies were supporting 856 single women missionaries, 389 missionaries' wives, ninety-six doctors, and numerous educational, medical, and welfare institutions (Pearson 1990:137). Adventism lacked a counterpart to the Women's Missionary Societies, probably because Adventism was slow to begin evangelical work outside of North America.

8. Bull and Lockhart argue that women's role in Adventism was not specifically differentiated until the 1880s, because the dominant issue in Adventism regarding women was whether Ellen White should prophesy in front of men.

9. Prior to 1880, Adventist women's roles as wives and homemakers were not emphasized in the sect (see Bull and Lockhart 1989) although mainline Protestantism had embraced the Cult of Domesticity by the 1830s–40s.

10. Moreover, women were encouraged to participate in evangelical efforts as such work would specifically help *women*. Bessie M. Bee, for example, urged women to participate in missionary work in order, in part, to discourage such cultural practices as female infanticide and foot-binding in China (1899).

11. Ellen White encouraged women's full religious participation further, though less obviously, by advocating dress reform as more convenient, healthy, and comfortable than contemporary Victorian dress, which included, among other impediments, the corset and large, cumbersome hoops (see White 1868; Numbers 1992). Other *Review* authors also encouraged women to dress in a manner more conducive to freedom of movement (see Tabor 1894).

12. *Review* writers also lamented the deplorable conditions and low wages that women working in urban areas were forced to endure and called on politicians to change those conditions (Clarke 1871).

13. Priddy specifically related women's responsibilities in Adventism and the world to the soon coming advent: "God designs that women as well as men shall have a part in carrying the third angel's message to the world. The day in which we live is no ordinary time. The last great conflict with the powers of darkness is being waged, a battle whose issues are victory or death to every soul. It is the climax of all the ages" (Priddy 1910:11).

14. The text from which this passage was taken portrays a dissatisfied Adventist homemaker lamenting her lost career: "Mrs. Carr goes down everyday to her office work. I would so enjoy that sort of work. I want to earn money and have it all my own—have a bank account, like Mrs. Carr, and be independent. I am so tired of washing dishes and pots that they may be made dirty again, cooking all to be eaten . . . making garments to be worn out. I gave up my teaching when I married—for what? Why should a woman of brains spend her life doing what a woman with little or no brains can do, especially if she pays the woman who does her manual duties?" (Stoner 1925a:10)

15. According to Hymowitz and Weissman, "six million women took paying jobs during [World War II]. The proportion of women in the labor force during the war increased from 25 to 36 percent. Two million of these women went to work in offices—half for the federal government. . . . An even greater number of women went to work in the factories. Heavy industry alone created nearly two million jobs for women during the war" (1980:312).

16. "Two months after VJ Day 800,000 workers, most of them women, lost their jobs in the aircraft industry. Lay-offs of women in the auto and electrical industries were equally high. Such companies as IBM and Detroit Edison resurrected their prewar policy against hiring married women. By the end of 1946 two million women had been fired from heavy industry" (Hymowitz and Weissman 1980:314). Nonetheless, women in secular society did not leave the paid workforce, they simply left higher paying "men's" work: "More women were in the work force in 1952 than during the war" but they were segregated into "female only" jobs—as bookkeepers, file clerks, secretaries,

seamstresses, operators, teachers, etc. (ibid.:315). Adventist women, also, often did not leave the paid workforce but did lose access to positions of leadership and authority with SDA institutions (see chapter 8).

17. Although women's (mothers') participation in wage labor, according to the *Review*, destroyed the family, "there are circumstances that make it necessary for mothers to work, and there are widows who must support their families. In such cases we ask the Lord to help us counteract the resulting evils" (Bradley 1955:12).

18. The *Review* of the 1950s and 1960s seemed to assume that only a biological mother was capable of providing her child necessary affection: "No thinking mother would consent to leave her child without love and guidance for a paycheck" (Lunday 1960:12).

19. Interestingly, like those who had defined a more narrow ideal for women and insisted upon self-sacrifice by women, Holbrook quoted Ellen White to substantiate her conclusions.

20. One author asked rhetorically, "can we, who believe that Jesus Christ is the same yesterday, today and forever, who believe that some values are absolute because they are a reflection of God's character, leave our children's value system and character development to chance, and to the baby-sitter? Can we allow secular researchers, who see values as relative . . . to determine our course of action?" (Newman 1975:8).

21. Todd cited the writings of Ellen White extensively in her 1985 article to support her contention that women and their families could benefit as a result of women's participation in wage labor.

22. One *Review* editor wrote a column concerning the division of household labor and confided that "my wife was right, I have not been carrying my fair, equal share of child care" and concluded that "it's time I, and I suppose other husbands in similar situations, change our attitudes and carry our portion of child care" (Widmer 1990:4).

6

The Adventist Family, Gender, and Society

The family is regarded [by Adventists] as the basic social unit.
—Crider and Kistler 1979:44

The Adventist worldview, which presupposes an ongoing and increasingly violent conflict between the forces of good and evil on earth, identifies the home as the place from which good (or evil) emanates; the home is "the place where basic principles are maintained and observed" (Crider and Kistler 1979:45). Preceding other social relationships in importance, the family is ideally, according to Adventists, a place of refuge and acceptance, a place in which to teach and uphold Adventist principles and practices.[1] Because "it is [in the family] that children internalize values and patterns of behavior that enable them to . . . maintain behavior standards that are compatible with Adventist philosophy and faith," Adventists place emphasis on ideals which are thought not only to strengthen biological family relations but to increase the effectiveness of religious socialization within the family (ibid.).

According to informants, the ideal Adventist nuclear family is "emotionally close-knit"; members are nurturing toward and supportive of one another, communicate openly and well, and spend time together engaged in "both secular and religious" activities. Further, according to informants, the ideal SDA family worships together—most explicitly: "the Adventist family should be together to welcome the Sabbath. Friday night vespers is such a good time to get everyone together. It's family time—time for singing, to socialize, to sit together and to be together." In addition to weekly Sabbath and vespers worship, "The Adventist family should . . . have devotions each [day]." Despite acknowledged constraints upon informants, the ideal of daily (and in some cases twice daily) family devotionals is almost ubiquitous among Adventists.[2] Family worship, in a variety of forms, allows Adventists, according to informants, to teach children correct principles and standards of behavior and, more importantly, to assist children in developing a personal relationship with God, each of which contributes to the child's ability to resist evil influences that she encounters as she interacts with the world.

Marriage and Parenting

Adventist ideals of masculinity and femininity emerge, as the above discussion indicates, from a specific understanding of the marital relationship and of familial responsibility. Marriage, like the seventh-day Sabbath, was, according to Adventist belief, God's "original gift" to humanity (Ministerial Association 1988:296–97). Adventists look to the marriage of Adam and Eve in the Genesis account of creation to illustrate the appropriate reasons for, and parameters of, matrimony. Adventists generally agree that men and women were originally created as equal beings, but that with the introduction of sin to the earth, women were reprimanded and rebuked, and admonished to assume a position of submission to their husbands (though *not* to men generally).

Ideally, Adventists agree, marital relationships should be "permanent": "[The] promise by which married couples are bound together . . . is spoken of as a 'covenant,' the term used for the most solemn and binding agreement known. . . . The relationship between husband and wife is to be patterned after God's everlasting covenant with His people, the church. . . . Their covenant to each other is to take on the faithfulness and endurance that characterize God's covenant" (Ministerial Association 1988:297).

In order for the marital commitment to be more easily "permanent," and in order for the religious socialization of children (which is to take place within the family) to occur most effectively, Adventists are expressly and repeatedly instructed to marry only others "within their own communion": "Differences in religious experience lead to differences in lifestyle that can create deep tensions and rifts in marriage" (ibid.:298). Most Adventists (72.7 percent) are married and of those, the majority (75 percent) are married to other Adventists. Endogamy is important to SDAs, 40 percent of whom met their spouses at Adventist educational institutions. Though Adventist endogamy is not as rigorously enforced as it was in the past, marriage to non-Adventists is believed to dilute the member's spiritual commitment and is strongly and regularly discouraged.[3] Adventists are further cautioned not to marry in haste. In one *Review* article, titled "Are You Ready for Marriage?" the author cautions that Adventists should not marry simply to avoid "singleness," that members should not "rush into" marriage, that divorce results from the lack of objective analysis of future compatibility, and that potential marital partners should seriously consider the practical (especially financial and emotional) implications of their possible union (Bennett 1980; see also Engelkemier 1967). In another *Review* article, Adventists are asked to take time to get to know their potential partner well before considering the "serious and dangerous" prospect of marriage (Carr 1965).[4]

Adventists are warned after marriage to assume the same kind of caution in determining whether and/or when to have children. Ellen White attributed much of the suffering of unwilling parents (especially mothers) and unwanted children to the "carelessness of husbands" and asked potential parents to consider carefully whether God would be "glorified or dishonored" by the birth of children into the situation that they could provide them (see Pearson 1990: 59, 60). Though Ellen White never discussed use of contraceptives, by 1928 A. W. Spalding wrote that contraceptive devices were an acceptable method of deterring conception only if the birth of a(n) (additional) child would prove detrimental to the family (ibid.:74). By 1931, however, Adventist physicians in *The Home Physician and Guide to Healthcare* concluded that it was the wife's prerogative to determine how many children would be born in a marital relationship and when, and that though a husband had the right to expect that his spouse would bear children, contraception "may take its place as one of the scientific agencies" for the prevention of unwanted pregnancies (Evans et al. 1931:678). Adventists, who by 1924 had a lower-than-average fertility rate, currently most often choose to have families with between two and four children (if they choose to have children), generally accept and advocate the use of contraceptives, and define marital sex as having the primary function of increasing the intimacy of marriage partners (see chapter 7).[5]

Family Worship

As noted above, the Adventist family serves an important function in providing the primary setting for personal spiritual growth and religious training. When discussing the relative "success" of their families of origin or neolocal families, informants did so with specific reference to family worship (vespers, devotions, prayer, song, etc.) and by assessing the regularity and effectiveness of such worship. Adventist parents said, often without being queried, that they had unfailingly attempted to assist their children in developing "close, personal relationship[s] with Christ," by holding family prayer and worship gatherings: "As our kids were growing up we tried to worship each morning. We'd have prayer together as a family. We got everyone together on Friday night, too, for vespers, which my husband led." While men, as the "spiritual leaders of the home," are urged to lead family worship, women, particularly those who are not employed for wages, or who are employed on a part-time basis, often lead children in daily worship when the husband/father is not present: "When I was home with my children when they were younger, every morning I would try to have worship with them after [my husband] left for work."

Realities of Seventh-day Adventist Family Life

Studies of Adventist families have found that while 33 percent of NAD Adventists identify themselves as "very happy," 45 percent "moderately happy," 12 percent "very or moderately unhappy," Adventists in North America, not unlike the general population, face conflict and difficulty, as well as emotional reward and solace, in the nuclear family setting (Kuzma in Banks 1992:119–20). One 1990 study, for example, found that after "financial difficulty," "not having enough time with family" and "conflict/problems between parents, children" were identified as primary sources of stress by Adventist respondents. Tension associated with a two wage-earner household was ranked seventh (after the above and "adherence to church standards" and "difficulty in meeting job requirements") and "marital problems" were ranked twelfth (ibid.:119). Not surprisingly, Charles Crider and Robert C. Kistler, in their comprehensive 1979 study of Adventist families, found that wage and occupational success were positively correlated with marital happiness among Adventists and that younger Adventists (under age thirty) expressed more concern with problems associated with raising children while older Adventists (age forty-six and over) claimed more freedom from economic concern, less familial conflict and higher self-assessed levels of spirituality and religiosity.

Divorce

Although Adventist leaders have "long been opposed to divorce" (Crider and Kistler 1979:196), Adventist divorce rates have risen dramatically in recent decades as have those in North American society generally. At the first state conference of Adventists, the issue of divorce was raised, discussed, and referred to committee, unresolved. In 1883 the issue was again raised when some wishing to convert were found to have been previously divorced. At that time it was determined that each case involving divorce should be decided individually (see Winslow 1975).[6] Though the 1925 annual meeting of the General Conference passed a resolution "deploring" divorce, no comprehensive policy was adopted by the conference until 1942, when Adventist leaders agreed that in cases involving marital infidelity spouses might divorce, but that the "guilty party" in such cases "forfeits the right" to remarry and, should she remarry, would be disfellowshiped while the second marriage continued. Adventists thus introduced and established the notion of "continual adultery"—the idea that only a person's first marriage was recognized by God unless she had "legitimate" reason for remarrying (e.g., one's spouse committed adultery and then divorced one). Within this construct, if a "guilty" (adulterous) spouse remarried following divorce she was said to be living in a "perpetual state of adultery" and was to be disfellowshiped. To be readmitted to Adventist fellowship, the erring party was required to divorce her second spouse and then to either remain unmarried or to remarry her original spouse (Gardner and Winslow 1986:27; Winslow 1975:6). Although the 1941 divorce policy was reworked in 1950 to specify that the "guilty party" could be readmitted to membership following a second marriage without divorcing his current partner if he "sincerely repented" (Gardner and Winslow 1986:28), Adventism has retained the notion of perpetual adultery. Many who were readmitted to Adventist fellowship as a result of the 1950 policy change still believe "they are living in a state of perpetual adultery" (ibid.).[7]

Adventists have codified the following points in regard to divorce: (1) divorce is necessary in some circumstances; (2) when divorce is necessary, but adultery isn't involved, the divorced parties may not morally remarry; (3) only when adultery is involved may the divorced be morally permitted to remarry; (4) only the "innocent party" has a moral right to remarry following divorce involving marital infidelity; and (5) if a "guilty party" remarries following divorce resulting from marital infidelity, she commits perpetual adultery as long as she remains in the subsequent marital relationship, or until her first spouse dies, remarries, or has sexual intercourse with another individual (see Winslow 1975).[8] According to one Adventist author, "society's courts may release a person from an unhappy marriage, but marriage is more than a legal contract. At marriage, vows were taken in the sight of God as well, and no court in the land can presume to act for God in releasing a couple from such vows" (Kistler 1987:124).

Although divorce is *allowed* in cases involving infidelity, Adventist authors have stressed that "even the unfaithfulness of one's spouse does not necessarily mean that the marriage must end in divorce" (Ministerial Association 1988:302). One author went so far as to assert that when adultery occurs, "compassion compels us to say to the grieved parties: Your marriage has not been broken by the fact of your spouse's adultery; but *you* can break it if you do not have the creative power to deal with your marriage in terms of what it can still be. It is up to you" (Kistler 1987:133; emphasis original).

Despite Adventist leadership's preoccupation with allowing or disallowing divorce based on sexual infidelity, informants expressed less concern with divorce resulting from adultery than with marital problems and divorce resulting from domestic abuse. Three of the four divorced women formally interviewed confided that their marriages had ended as a result of spousal emotional or physical abuse and/or abuse of children, and one married informant stated that "some of the earlier divorces that took place [among Adventists] probably were the result of abuse, but it wasn't acknowledged or talked about." One Adventist author who previously divorced her abusive spouse noted the apparent inconsistency of Adventism's divorce policy, particularly for women: "The crimes of assault/battery and attempted murder are not listed in the *Church Manual* as valid enough grounds for remarriage—only adultery. It would have been so much easier had my husband been cheating on me instead of beating on me. I feel victimized by the unreasonableness and irrationality . . . imposed by [Adventism's divorce policy]" (James 1986:19).

In an attempt to reconcile past silence on domestic abuse, General Conference publications recently began to address domestic violence and its implications in the Adventist family. One 1983 General Conference publication noted that "while the divine ideal for marriage is that of a loving and permanent union that continues until the death of one partner, at times legal separation becomes necessary because of offenses such as physical abuse to spouse or child" (General Conference 1983:10).[9] Informants, though generally unaware of General Conference writings pertaining to divorce in cases involving spousal and/or parental abuse, agreed (with seven exceptions) that "in cases of physical abuse, unless the [abusive] person can be rehabilitated, God doesn't expect people to stay in situations like that. Or if there is sexual abuse [of children], it would be acceptable to divorce." Nonetheless, because the General Conference continues to disallow divorce except in cases involving marital infidelity, informants were careful, while characterizing (especially physical and sexual) abuse as legitimate reasons for divorce, to do so within the parameters of divorce historically accepted by Adventism. One informant "believe[d] that God created families to be a nurturing environment, and if that nurturing environment breaks down, *then God may have another plan for you;* so divorce may be an option" (emphasis added). Another informant agreed:

> God hates divorce. That was never in God's plan. But God understands marriage may need to be dissolved due to sin. If someone marries another person whose heart isn't converted, there can be reason for divorce. A person can be abusive, even if they have a relationship with God. (But a Godly person won't sexually abuse.) If a person beats his wife or is violent explicitly, God didn't want that. In cases involving

[physical] abuse [or] sexual abuse, divorce may be needed. God understands that. He doesn't want people to stay in abusive relationships. He doesn't want you to stay with someone who will lower your self-esteem.

In reconciling and attempting to explain Adventism's position on divorce in relation to domestic abuse, informants relied on personal experiences or knowledge of others' experiences involving abuse, and attempted to place that knowledge within an explanatory framework with which they were familiar. One informant, for example, directly associated her sister's experience of domestic abuse with the criterion commonly accepted by Adventists for divorce—adultery:

> The individual situation is totally, totally unpredictable. The reason why I say that is my relation to my . . . sister who married an abusive man and she lived with him for two years and it was two years of absolute Hell. There was no adultery, but yet the abuse was so overwhelming physically and mentally that he might as well have committed adultery. His sin could be equal to that of an adulterer: you're separating, you're tearing apart, you're destroying a human being when you're abusing them physically and mentally. So I don't want to say . . . you can divorce for this and this and this. Even though the Bible says "only for adultery" . . . I think that those boundaries have broadened simply because adultery is no more considered just a physical attraction to another human being. Adultery, at this point, is adultery in the perspective of the marriage vows you took. [In abusing a spouse] you're going against everything that you vowed that you would do.

Although they responded differently to Adventism's current divorce policy and the practical implementation of that policy, informants unanimously agreed that Adventism's position (especially in the practical implications of the policy) toward divorce has become more "lenient" in recent years. One woman noted that although divorce "is only okay in cases of adultery": "In the last five to eight years the church has become more tolerant—there are even pastors who are divorced. (But they're not remarried.) It's not okay, according to the church, to remarry after divorce. In the past, it was typical that if you divorced, it was well known. If you worked for the church you'd lose your job and pretty much it was expected that you'd be disfellowshiped. Now people are more open-minded. Divorce is more common and people are learning to be more supportive." While other respondents lamented that Adventism had become "too lenient" in allowing divorce, all informants noted an increasing tendency among Adventist laity and leadership to offer acceptance and support to the divorced, despite an unchanged official divorce policy.[10]

Home as Haven and the Evil World:
Determining Gender Roles in the Family

Because the Adventist family structure is deemed an important component in "waging resistance against Satan," in the ideal Adventist family, "mothers should be raising the family to protect kids from the wages of sin." One informant explained that "we live in a sinful environment that requires a mom to be a full time [caregiver/homemaker]." "The father," on the other hand, "should provide financial and psychological support to the family" in order to allow women to serve as homemakers. The modern Adventist understanding of an ultimate division, and ongoing struggle, between good and evil thus gives rise to legitimation of an ideal family structure in which the father is "*gainfully* employed [emphasis original], though he spends time—Sabbath especially—with his family," and "a mother [who] is able to stay home" to complete housekeeping and child care responsibilities. Despite widespread agreement about the necessity of both family worship and gendered division of responsibility within the family for the successful socialization of SDA children, the reality of Advent families is far more complex and diverse than the ideals here adumbrated indicate.

The Ideal Adventist Woman

The ideal Adventist woman, like the ideal Adventist man, should, before all else, develop "a relationship with the Lord." As a number of informants explained, she should "put Christ first, and everything else will fall into place." "An Adventist woman should ideally have a close walk with the Lord"; that relationship, in turn, "would be evident in her life"—primarily manifesting itself in a willingness "to serve and be sensitive to the needs of others." The Adventist woman, as a result of her relationship with Christ, is to "make an effort to help her community as well as her friends"; "she puts Christ first, her family second, and service to the community after that." The ideal Adventist woman should "always try her best to make her husband happy" and "be willing to serve her children." One young Adventist woman explained (somewhat disdainfully), that "the stereotypical Adventist woman is someone who is submissive to spouse [and] is there to serve her children. Basically someone who just stays home all the time and doesn't have a life of her own."[11]

Female informants generally agreed that the ideal Adventist woman did not participate in wage labor, particularly not full-time wage labor, while her children were young. Although women were much more likely to recognize and acknowledge changing employment patterns among Adventist women than were SDA men, they maintained (with some exceptions; $N = 7$), that wage labor was primarily the domain of men (and unmarried women).[12] As one woman explained, "roles have changed; I realize that some have to work outside the home. But I think she [women] should stay home if possible." Only three female informants explicitly expressed disagreement with the ideal of nonparticipation in wage labor and of these, one couched her revised ideal of expectations for women within the context of the ideal outlined above: "My ideal for what an Adventist woman is is someone who knows herself—her strengths and her limitations, and is close enough to the Lord that she is able to go out and minister in whatever capacity she has the talents for, whether it's business, or in the home, or in the community somewhere. Part of that image is still someone who takes care of the home; someone who has enough respect for herself and for her husband that she can take care of the home and make it a pleasant environment." Only one informant described the ideal Adventist woman in a manner inconsistent with the ideal of womanhood outlined above: "[The ideal Adventist woman] does *lots* of things. She's not limited by a stereotype. She does more than just stay at home. She provides for her own emotional and spiritual needs. And she is a person of her own. She can be a [legislative] judge; she can do things. She is well-rounded."

Implications of Gender Ideals for Women: Expectations

Given the comprehensive nature of the Adventist portrayal of women's responsibilities in marriage (see below) and, more especially, in the family, it is not surprising that the expectations of Adventist girls and women are shaped by personal interpretations of those expectations. Female informants, for example, when asked about their hopes and expectations as girls (with few exceptions), presented an image of future goals consistent with ideals of femininity presented to Adventist women and middle-class North American women generally.

Female informants discussed girlhood ambitions shaped by the assumption that Adventist women should be wives, mothers, and, above all, homemakers. One woman summarized the sentiments of most informants, stating, "I grew up thinking that a woman should be a homemaker while the man was working for the money." Adventist women, as girls, based their hopes and visions of the future on this assumption: "My only goal," noted one woman, "was to be a good mother and wife." Others agreed:

When I was a child and people asked me what I wanted to be when I grew up, I always said, "A plain housewife." I wanted to have a home and a loving husband. I wanted to have children and to have a home.

When I was younger I had no desire to do anything but be a housewife; to be in the home, that's what I was raised to be.

When I was in elementary school they would ask what we wanted to be and I would say, "A housewife," . . . because that's what women did.

I didn't think about [what I would do as an adult]. I assumed I would meet an Adventist [man] and be married.

Only one informant presented a clear exception to this general consensus of expectation: "I don't remember restrictions for women. I was told I ought to be a Bible worker. . . . Another teacher told me I should be a lawyer, I never felt restricted until I was an adult."

With the assumption that they would eventually assume roles as wives, homemakers, and mothers, informants who attended college or university did so in order "to have something to lean [fall] back on" in the event of a future spouse's death or disability. The majority of female informants pursued training as nurses or teachers, although some attended secretarial training, five attained graduate degrees, and one attended Andrews University Seminary program for ministerial training.[13] Though almost all informants embarked on higher education with the expectation that skills, training, or education that they sought should be applied primarily in the home ("When I started college," explained one informant, "I wanted to either be a nurse or a Bible worker; though I was mostly looking for a husband"), the overwhelming majority of informants who participated in postsecondary education (including male informants), agreed that such participation dramatically changed self-perception; participation in postsecondary education was identified as increasing self-confidence, improving skills, clarifying ability and personal competence, and widening expectations. One woman explained that: "[Participation in higher education] gave me more self-confidence and it helped me to be in tune enough with myself to realize that I could make choices that would be okay for me even if that same choice would not be a good choice for you. It also helped me to realize that I do have a brain. It helped me to realize that I'm not a lesser being because I'm female."

Although female informants overwhelmingly expected to assume primary roles as mothers/homemakers/wives, the majority of informants described their adult lives as being inconsistent with the personal expectations and ideals of SDA womanhood that they had had as children. When asked if their lives now were consistent with what they had expected them to be as children, respondents replied:

No. My life now is consistent with what I thought it would be with respect to my-self, with who I am, but it is not consistent in what I thought I'd be doing. I didn't think I'd be working in a position of leadership.

No. For one thing, I'm working. For another I have a college degree and I never thought I'd have that. I'm considering going on for a Master's [degree].

I just figured that someday I'd grow up and have a family and I thought about work-ing but it was that I really wanted to be at home with my family and that I really wouldn't be a career woman. I've come to work in the last nine years. Other than that I've had jobs off and on along the way.

When I first went to college I expected to become a homemaker and mother. That was what girls did. After attending school for a while, I decided to teach. I saw women who became role models to me, who were still mothers, but had part-time work and I decided that I wanted that also. After I graduated, I had the opportunity to study for a Master's degree, so I pursued that and that led to further career opportunities.

Only two female informants stated that when young they had expected to participate in wage labor upon reaching adulthood (whereas all male infor-mants had such expectation). One Adventist woman, currently a self-described "stay-at-home mom," explained that "I never did picture myself staying at home with my children, which I do now. I always pictured myself working part-time. . . . I tried to do that and it was too frustrating for me so I quit my job." Another female informant, currently a part-time employee, "never gave much thought to having kids." She explained of the mother/homemaker/wife ideal, "I struggle with it":

My career was my main interest. I struggled with the notion of having kids. I want to be a paid minister. Some have skills in other areas. . . . Some of my roommates in college—their reason for going to college was to find someone to marry. Then there are some like me who struggle with what Ellen White says—[that] the mother's calling is most important. It is a high calling; teaching moral values is important. But it's a father's responsibility too. The mother doing everything can break the home. Work is a part of my identity. I have to work, but I also *like* to work. (Em-phasis original)

Despite the apparent disparity between the Adventist ideal of womanhood and the lived reality of Adventist women, female informants defined wage la-bor participation within the context of the homemaker/mother ideal: "The traditional, stereotypical message is still that you [women] have to be the heart of your home, a little happy homemaker, and cook and clean; some women just don't like [or are unable] to do that." Female informants did not question or criticize the ideal presented to them per se, but continued to define, or to attempt to define, their lives with reference to that ideal.

Ideal Adventist Masculinity

Gender specific expectations for Adventist men, as for SDA women, are achieved, ideally, in the context of a close, personal "relationship with Christ" (see also D. Rebok 1955). The ideal Adventist man is assumed to be both husband and father and is, according to informants, to maintain a balance between authority and leadership of the family, and service and compassion for the family. Although informants emphasized differently various aspects of this ideal, all agreed that some combination of leadership and ministration was necessary to the adequate fulfillment of the masculine role. The appropriate balance, though portrayed by some informants in a manner that accented leadership and by others in a way that highlighted service and compassion, was thought by all to be best achieved by attaining "a closer walk with Christ": "First, he [the ideal SDA man] should have a strong relationship with Christ, the rest will follow"; "The ideal Adventist man is a good Christian. He has a personal relationship with Christ."

From this relationship, developed through regular personal and (in worship services) congregational prayer, Bible study, song and worship, and personal meditation, spring the characteristics of ideal Adventist masculinity. The Adventist man is to be "a person who's committed to his family." Unlike the Adventist woman, the Adventist man's familial responsibility is explicitly expressed in provision of spiritual leadership and temporal needs: "Men are expected to take the formal leadership role in the family." Foremost among the Adventist man's obligations is to serve as "the spiritual leader in the home": "The husband is the head of the house; in worship he leads out." This is not an option, "he must do it." "I think [Ellen White] definitely had the biblical viewpoint that the man was the head of the household. From the religious standpoint, the man is considered the priest—you might say 'the religious leader' of the family."

Spiritual leadership of the family seems, at times, not to be clearly distinguished, by informants, from the other primary component of the masculine ideal—provision of monetary income: "Both in the family and in the world . . . men should be open to God's work. Not just ministries in the church, but ministries in the home. Overseeing things, making sure that their families are provided for, making sure that they are honorable in their business dealings. They should lead family worship. They are the spiritual leaders of the family."

Another woman explained that "to describe the ideal Adventist man I can just describe my husband. He puts God first in his life—the first thing in the morning he prays right away. He is a good provider, committed to his family and his job."

While informants did not hesitate to portray the ideal Adventist man as spiritual leader of, and financial provider for, the family, they defined fulfillment of these ideals as being predicated upon submission to principles of service and compassion. The Adventist man is to be "sensitive, warm, understanding, wise," "kind, compassionate, patient, supportive," "gentle," and "respectful of others." "He's not to dominate."[14] Adventist men and women agreed that the ideal Adventist man fulfills familial responsibilities without becoming "domineering." Men are to lead "unselfishly": "The *ideal* Adventist man is someone who is the provider, the spiritual leader, and also has internalized biblical principles to the point where he is truly beyond the need to be dogmatic [emphasis original]." "To be very concise, [the ideal Adventist man] would be Christ-like. He should be considerate above all, and kind, loving, interested in helping others, not hurting others. He wouldn't be domineering."

In part, ideal Adventist masculinity was defined by the notion of benevolent patriarchy. Adventist husbands were to lead, but that leadership, particularly with reference to one's spouse, was to exemplify benevolence: "The ideal Adventist man is a good spiritual leader. He treats his wife well. As Christ is to the church, so is the husband to the wife. He's not to be overpowering or dictatorial." In addition, despite the explicit SDA ideal of male leadership, Adventist women, in particular, portrayed the marriage relationship as one of partnership and shared responsibility:

[The Adventist man] should be a *leader* in the home, someone the children can look up to. . . . He should be a good worker and reliable in his job—dependable. I do feel that he should be in charge, but not *dogmatically* in charge. Marriage is a partnership, and if it isn't, you're headed for trouble. (Emphasis original)

[An Adventist man] to me is someone that's kind and loving and very understanding. [He] would be willing to study with you and go to church with you, . . . or at least not [try] to force something different upon the other person.

He would be understanding to what my ideas are and give me freedom to [do] what I want to do, and not feeling that he has dictation [control?] over me to tell me that I can't do this or I should do this or whatever. I want him with the family, to share responsibilities of parenting and discipline, to try and reach those conclusions with as much harmony as possible.

Ideals in Tandem: Marital Partnership

The most important (and most discussed) aspect of the Adventist marriage/ family relationship is the husband/wife partnership. As noted above, Adventist women are to "submit" to their husbands. With the rise of feminist criticisms of unequal and unfair female/male relations, Adventists began to redefine (or at least more carefully and explicitly define) the husband/wife relationship. As discussed above, this clarification resulted most specifically in a changed emphasis in ideal Adventist masculinity from control and leadership to empathy and support. Modern Adventists generally assert that a woman is to submit to her husband "as unto the Lord" and that husbands are to "love their wives as Christ loved the church." This relationship, contemporary SDAs allege, does not give "the implication of hopeless servitude": "God has not commanded wives to submit to a relationship of slavery, but to submit to a loving union in which they should reap great benefit" (Vernon 1985:12, 13). Men and women are to be equal in the marital relationship, but men, according to one General Conference publication, are to be "the first among equals" (General Conference 1984:25). Adventist men and women, then, are presented with a precarious model of leadership and submission: Though husbands are to "lead" their wives, they are to do so "as Christ led the church." "Christ did not intimidate the church or violate her free will. He did not burden or enslave her. Instead he became like a servant in order to tenderly care for her, and died to secure her welfare. Human husbands are commanded likewise to so care for their wives, even to be willing to give up power and prestige to secure their welfare. To this care the wife is asked to submit" (ibid.:13). As leaders, Adventist husbands are told not to "stunt their [wives'] potential, or to rob them of individuality," but to "encourage [their] growth, nurture [their] potential, to liberate [them] from all forms of bondage" (ibid.). "As the role of Christ as head is to enable the body to grow and build itself up . . . , so the role of husband as head is to nurture and cherish the wife so she can grow into maturity and strength" (Neall 1992:25).

The apparent ambiguity of this leader/servant model of masculine/feminine marital relationships was reflected by informants in statements such as the following: "I always feel that men should be the leader and the strong one in the household and that I should be there beside him and support him. And I feel that it should be fifty-fifty." While informants generally agreed on ideals for spousal relationships, specific anecdotes and explanations clearly indicated that a great deal of diversity was present in the application of those ideals. While one informant openly deferred to her husband in the interview setting (asking his opinion and approval, for example, before responding to questions), others clearly opined that the marriage relationship ought, ideally, to be one of equality and mutuality. One informant said that in household leadership, she and her husband "take turns": "Maybe he has an opinion and he feels something this time. But also when I have an opinion and I feel like it's right, I feel like he should support me and it's a shared situation. I don't think that it's anymore one should decide than the other. It's basically a shared situation." Another female informant explained, "I feel that women should have their freedom and that if it's [there's] a difference of opinion, you should [both] be able to talk about it and honor what the other person has to say and try to see where they're coming from." If however, no agreement can be reached, "it's the wife's responsibility to submit, because the husband has the final authority" (Kuzma 1992:118).

Gender Ideals and Realities: Resolving Incongruency

The ideal Adventist family, as described by informants, includes a wage-earning father ("provider") and a non-wage-earning mother ("homemaker") who may be employed part-time "after her children leave home." Within this ideal family construct, parents are to assume gender specific responsibilities which allow (purportedly) for the optimal spiritual growth and development of individual family members. Interestingly, though informants concurred overwhelmingly upon ideals for Adventist family life (with two exceptions), Adventists who grew up in homes in which both parents were wage earners did not identify their families of origin as being inconsistent with the ideals that they described. In one instance, an informant explicitly portrayed the ideal Adventist family as a nuclear family in which "the father provide[s] financially for family members" while "the mother care[s] for the house and children and [doesn't] work outside the home" and then insisted that her family of origin, in which both parents were professionals who were employed full-time (and in which the family employed a domestic servant who was "sort of a surrogate mother to me") was consistent with the ideal she had described. Of the fourteen informants who were raised in families in which both parents (throughout the informants' childhood and young adulthood) were full-time employees, only one identified her family as being inconsistent with the ideal of Adventist families because her mother was employed for wages. Most, instead of noting the discrepancy between their own understanding of the ideal SDA family and their experiences, explained that their parents needed to work for financial reasons (the most prominent of which was to send children to

Adventist schools) or were in some way "helping to accomplish God's work" and hastening the advent by working in an institutional or other Adventist capacity. One Adventist man, detailing his mother's reasons for participating in the paid labor force, reasoned that "For the times I was raised in, my parents did the best they could have. I can't fault them. . . . We couldn't have lived on Dad's earnings. Mother worked, so she was home very little. We always attended church schools—that was always very important to my parents, but it was a major sacrifice."

In the same way, while explaining their own or (in the case of male informants) their spouse's wage labor participation, informants accented the practical necessity of wage employment for themselves (or their spouse) in their particular situation. Adventist women explained that they were employed because they "need to work"; that one income was insufficient for their family; that due to the death of a partner or divorce, they were forced to engage in wage labor; or that in order to satisfy intellectual, social, or emotional needs, they were compelled to participate in the paid workforce.[15] Though four non-wage-earning female informants (each with family incomes of above $70,000) did identify female wage labor participation as being antithetical to motherhood, most informants ($N = 43$) upheld the ideal of Adventist womanhood outlined above, but recognized that Adventist women who do not attain that ideal most often work for wages in order to achieve other goals consistent with Adventist ideals (to provide an Adventist education for their children, to assist the local congregation or an Adventist institution) and are therefore not perceived as being outside the realm of the Adventist ideal of the family. One woman, who agreed to be interviewed despite extensive obligations as the mother of two, as a wage earner (with two wage positions), and as the local congregation's music coordinator, said that "life is so complicated nowadays." Explaining that she was employed in order to help meet basic needs (housing, food) of her family, another informant said that "the idea of the man working and paying all of the bills and the woman staying at home to be a mother is just not possible for some Adventists. It's not possible for us [herself and her husband]."

Thus while informants clearly agreed upon an ideal of family life that incorporated gender specific expectations for men and women, informants largely identified exceptions to gender specific components of the ideal as not contradicting, in themselves, that ideal. There were exceptions; in addition to the four women noted above, two Adventist men described employed mothers as being wholly antithetical to ideal SDA family life. Even in these cases, however, one husband commented that his wife wanted to work at home for wages (as a bookkeeper) and explained that wage labor was inconsistent with ideal Adventist motherhood and womanhood only in so far as it preempted her ability to be with her children. In this way, informants identified shared ideals for Adventist family life, recognized discrepancies from this ideal in their own and others' lives, and in most cases, justified those "exceptions" without challenging the ideal.

Changing Gender Norms in the Adventist Family

As the above discussion makes clear, Adventists largely concur that "somebody in the family must bear the ultimate responsibility for the character of the children," and that that person is most often "mother" (Ministerial Association 1988:305). Even some contemporary Adventist writers identified as feminists insist that women were created, like Eve, to be helpers and friends to men, and that women, as such, are intrinsically more capable of caring for and nurturing others; women, more than men, "are genetically endowed with nurturing and caring abilities" (Harris 1992:143). Notwithstanding a history of encouraging women to be submissive to and dependent on men and to "find fulfillment vicariously" through men, Adventists, in the pages of the *Review*, in employment practices and policies, and in everyday life, are beginning to move "away from the guilt-producing stereotype that relegates women to the joys and disappointments of shouldering major responsibility for the home and children while it pushes Dad out the door and into the workplace" (Kuzma 1992:115).

Without explicitly calling gender ideals (developed most forcefully and formally in the 1950s and 1960s) into question (with a few exceptions such as the Association of Adventist Women), Adventist men and women, especially younger Adventists "are choosing to accept whatever responsibilities are necessary in order to meet their families' needs. They are not blindly accepting the role models that were handed down to them from past generations" (Kuzma 1992:115). According to Kuzma, "the secret to happiness in [an Adventist] home today is not following what someone else is doing, or trying to create a Biblical 'ideal.' . . . The secret of fulfillment is in creating your own unique roles based on the two personalities of the couple and the needs of the children" (ibid.:116–17). Even General Conference publications have commenced, in recent years, to explore possibilities for sharing in familial responsibilities: "Just as procreation was not the sole and exclusive right of either Adam or Eve, so neither was parenthood. The latter was also to be a shared responsibility" (Ministerial Association 1988:305). Informants, though most often unfamiliar with specific references to or publications discussing changing gender roles in Adventism, agreed, with only a few exceptions ($N = 4$) that "the role of women in the family has changed. . . . there's more perception now that men and women ought to be *partners*" (emphasis original).

In one recent *Spectrum* article, a prominent Adventist academic critiques traditional Adventist (and non-Adventist) ideals of masculinity and calls upon Adventists to rethink definitions of, and expectations for, men (*"strong, strict, controlling, forceful, disciplined, and authoritarian"* [emphasis original]) (Daily 1990:2). The author relays, and criticizes as limiting, expectations with which he was presented by his father as a boy: "My father taught me to be a man. He taught me that boys were tough, that they didn't cry. We [boys] all learned how to control and suppress our emotions" (ibid.:23). The author insists that Adventism, if it fails to keep pace with contemporary secular reconsideration of masculinity, will be unable to "meet both the male and female needs of its younger generation" (ibid.). Adventism, he concludes, needs to participate in an "overdue attempt to redefine manhood in the wake of the sexual revolution"; to embrace positive "male" (strong, independent and competent) and "female" (nurturing, caring, compassionate) qualities in order to become "more authentically Christ-like for young adult males" (ibid.:29).

Adventists who have publicly challenged SDA (and non-SDA) definitions of masculinity specifically associate their critiques with recent changes in social, familial, economic, and religious roles of Adventist women. James Londis, for example, argues that as women increasingly participate in wage labor, Adventist men need to more actively take part in duties thought to be within the "feminine sphere": "I need the freedom to play [my wife's] traditional role and she needs the freedom to play mine; for if women cannot break into the power of corporate suites, men cannot stay at home and know the power of being caring fathers. If women do not know how to be assertive in the business world, men do not know how to be sensitive in the personal world. If women are denied leadership 'over' men in the church, men never experience the blessings of supporting women in church leadership" (Londis 1987:30).

Informants also identified changing Adventist expectations of masculinity as being "in response to women's changing roles" (especially in the paid workforce) and recognized two primary categories of change. Adventist men in the family, according to informants, were more willing to (1) express and demonstrate emotion and (2) complete everyday housekeeping tasks. One informant explained that, having grown up with an "authoritarian, dictatorial" father, he made a conscious effort, when parenting his own children, "not to be overbearing" because he "wanted [his] kids to be able to respond and interact" and to be "able to express [their] feelings" with him. Another informant felt that this change has resulted because "men realize now that women *can* do things" beyond the mother/homemaker sphere: "Men are less dogmatic now, not as rigid, more open to discussion. It used to be that if a man said something, it was taken as authentic [authoritative?]. Today, men's views are expressed as 'this is my viewpoint.' Men are less authoritarian. Basically similar changes to what has happened in society." Another informant agreed that "men's roles have changed . . . in smaller ways [than women's roles]":

I think . . . men are feeling freer to care for their children more, to spend time with their families, to try more nontraditional careers for men. I think that men are finding it okay now to be compassionate and to express their feelings more. When they're sick to say, "I feel crummy," to express characteristics that have been traditionally thought of as feminine and therefore weak, undesirable. I think it's pretty much a reflection of what's occurring in the larger society. But I think it's a deeper thing though because of the spiritual component—because people are acknowledging that God is more than just male, more than just father, overseer, judge; that he is also tender and compassionate. The nurturing side of God [is being acknowledged].

In addition to being "much more willing to share feelings with and to nurture their children and their spouses," informants concluded that men are "more willing to do household chores." This willingness to share responsibility for housekeeping tasks was directly associated, by interviewees, with women's participation in the paid labor force: "Since I started working full-time . . . I had a talk with him [my husband] once and I said, 'I am supporting this family [financially] as much as you are now and there are other responsibilities at home that are full-time that have always been mine and we need to share them. It's not fair [that] I do this by myself anymore.' Since then he's been really good that way." Men interviewed insisted overwhelmingly ($N = 9$) that they contribute significantly to the completion of housekeeping responsibilities, and female informants generally agreed: "I feel that men have become more helpful in the home, much more. They share the responsibilities because women have to go out and work. There are two-person incomes in the family so men have accepted helping with the home and with the children, because it's [housework and child care] too much for just one person." Rather than explicitly redefine household responsibilities as the equal and shared duty of both marriage partners, however, informants described men's contributions to child care and (especially) housework as "helping," and women were implicitly recognized by both male and female informants as carrying the primary responsibility for housekeeping and child care. In the only exception to this generally accepted division of responsibility, one informant said that "sometimes now the woman might make [earn] more than the man and he might be a, um, a house person and she might be the wage earner." Nonetheless, male informants were quick to explain how they "help around the house," and female informants, too, discussed men's household work and contributions to child care as relieving some of "women's" responsibilities: "If I have to hurry and clean the house well, he'll vacuum or shake the rugs for me. And I'll hurry and clean the bathroom. Sometimes he's cleaned the bathroom."

Adventists interviewed, as indicated in transcription excerpts above, found changing gender definitions in Adventism to be "about the same as the changes occurring in society," although seven female informants perceived gender role changes occurring among Adventists as not being similar to wider social changes but as reflecting a specifically Adventist concern for "greater equality in Christ." One informant found: "A philosophical difference [between non-Adventist and Adventist rethinking of gender norms, ideals and behaviors] in that we [Adventists] have traditionally believed that the role of women in the church, as we assigned it, was limited, and we have had to restudy the Scripture and realize that there's no Jew or Gentile, male or female in Christ." Another informant concurred, "I think in some ways we [Adventists, in redefining male and female ideal roles] are reflecting the change in the wider society. We are part—we live in the world. But I do think that we recognized that we had to restudy our standards." The majority of informants found recent SDA consideration of gender norms and behaviors to be "probably right along with the national average." One Adventist man remembered, "when I was growing up, even in academy, I couldn't imagine a woman delivering a sermon. Now the pastor's wife we have sometimes delivers the sermon. The role of women [in Adventism] has changed along with the changing times we're in." Another noted, "in the past you never saw men helping with the housework. Now I know lots of families where the woman and mother is working and the men do their share and the women do their share. . . . I think it's a reflection of society." One informant called Adventism's contemporary contemplation of gender appropriate spheres "hesitant": "Unfortunately, [I] don't think the Adventist church has taken a leadership role there. It would be nice to think that they led out in this area, but I don't think they did."

Throughout this contemporary struggle to define appropriate gendered realms of behavior, Adventists have grappled with the movement's admonitions to, and precedents for, Seventh-day Adventist men and women. Although this point will be explored in greater detail below, it is important at this juncture to recognize that informants, in discussing modern SDA delimitations (especially changing delimitations) of gender, identified changing gender norms as reflecting developing gender norms in the wider society (the world), but *did not* identify recently questioned gender expectations (man as "breadwinner," woman as mother/homemaker) as arising from the world. Instead, those expectations were termed "traditional" and were characterized, by informants, as being specifically associated with Adventism's distinct (sectarian) identity.

This redefinition differs from that identified by other sociologists of religion in relation to fundamentalist groups considering parameters of gender relations within the family. Although Kaufman, for example (in a prominent recent examination of gender as defined within the context of Fundamentalism), found that evangelical religion allows women "greater claims upon men as husbands and fathers" in completing household and child care obligations by reshaping traditional notions of masculinity (i.e., by placing the husband/wife relationship, as opposed to the husband/father role, in a position of prominence and importance), Adventist redefinition of masculinity exceeds the boundaries of this model (see Kaufman 1991:137). Because SDA men are assuming care-giving and housekeeping duties *in response* to women's increased participation in wage labor and to secular pressure to rethink appropriate gender behaviors, Adventists justify men's altered gender ideal not only by noting the centrality of the husband/wife relationship in families (though that is one important component of new gender demarcations [see Ministerial Association 1988:304]) but by specifically referring to ideals of equality and mutuality put forward by non-Adventist advocates of gender equity. Thus, Adventist men, by the 1980s and 1990s, are, according to Adventist literature, assuming new roles and responsibilities not only because duties associated with being a husband/father are of particular importance but *because equality in itself* is increasingly defined by Adventists as being a desirable (and specifically "Christian") goal: "[Adventists are challenged] to live our strengths and not our weaknesses, beyond imposed roles and definitions, revealing our God-likeness as creatures in God's image. . . . Some of our most destructive [limits appear] as gender-role stereotyping" (Yob 1989:43; see also Londis 1987:39–40).

Notes

1. The "family," for the purposes of this discussion, refers, as the term is used in Adventist literature and worship, to the heterosexual, consanguineal/affinal, nuclear family. While I am acutely aware that "family" incorporates a much broader range of social relationships than that demarcated, to avoid confusion in this context this definition will be assumed.

2. One Adventist woman explained that her family has a daily devotional "at breakfast": "We have a devotional text that we share. It's very short; you can't have it very long because everyone has a time frame. It's just a pause."

3. Consequently, Adventist women, who outnumber SDA men (60 percent to 40 percent), even if they desire to marry, are often unable to find a suitable mate and choose to remain unmarried. (Seventh-day Adventist men may also remain unmarried and in good standing as Adventists, but unmarried Adventist women are most often recognized and portrayed in SDA periodicals and literature.)

4. One informant explained that prior to her marriage her future husband drew a picture of a house, asking her what the household would look like and referring, eventually, to the house they planned as "our house." Before they were married, in her words, "life was all set out."

5. Adventist fertility may also be relatively low due to the uncertainty with which Adventists view the future of the planet (particularly with reference to the conflict which is expected to precede the advent) and the relatively high degree of participation by Adventists in higher education, normally found to correlate with lower birth rates (see Pearson 1990:84).

6. One 1891 *Review* author declared that at marriage, husbands and wives were joined for eternity, and though the introduction of sin into the world had caused death, "God intended for the husband and wife to remain united forever" (Gros 1891:101). In 1894 another *Review* author called divorce the "most dangerous of human vices" (T. 1894b).

7. A. V. Olson, a vice-president of the General Conference, argued at the 1949 spring General Conference meeting that because adultery ended marriage, the notion of continual adultery was inconsistent and Adventists should readmit members disfellowshiped following divorce (Winslow 1975:6).

8. There is evidence that Adventist ministerial attitudes toward divorce have changed dramatically in the last two decades. Robert W. Gardner completed two surveys of pastors serving in the North Pacific Union Conference and concluded that Adventism is moving away from its previously more distinct sectarian understanding of divorce and remarriage. Asking pastors about their preferred response in a hypothetical situation in which an Adventist man "falls in love" with a woman and divorces his wife to marry her, Gardner and Gerald Winslow found an overall increase in tolerance between their first (1973) and second (1984) survey (1986).

9. In cases of divorce resulting from domestic abuse, the authors conclude, neither party has the "scriptural right" to remarry unless the other dies, remarries, or commits adultery or "fornication" (General Conference 1983:10).

10. This informant related Adventism's increasing tendency to accept the divorced into fellowship to the destruction of (sectarian) group boundaries: "Adventism allow[s] it [divorce]. The church has gotten too lenient. God is merciful, but I think our church has got to be stronger in requiring people to do right. We are too lenient. Even clubs have rules and keep people out." Gardner and Winslow, after studying changing Adventist ministerial attitudes toward divorce, agreed: "To the extent that sectarian

boundaries have been maintained in the past through strict standards concerning divorce and remarriage and the exclusion from membership of former members now in second marriages, those sectarian boundaries appear to be eroding" (1986:33).

11. Interestingly, while female informants outlined ideal womanhood with rather vague reference to "service," male informants discussed ideal Adventist womanhood most often with reference to specific services performed. One Adventist man described an ideal Adventist woman as "someone who cooks good meals and makes cookies," while another saw ideal SDA women as "pianists—they're often in charge of the music—or Sabbath school teachers." Another explained that an Adventist woman should "be a homemaker; [she should] know how to be a good hostess and prepare nice meals." Yet another informant explained that though he understood that there were times for "women to wear slacks," he "prefer[s] to see women in dresses." Generally male informants agreed that "the ideal Adventist woman would be the same as the man, Christ-like, except she should recognize her place in society without trying to take over the man's role. . . . Men should be the primary providers."

12. According to an informant, "women have things to offer the church and the world when they don't have children. Women can be doctors and things and can contribute way more than others in those areas if they don't have children. But when women become mothers, that should come first."

13. Careers pursued most often by male informants included teaching, medical work, and the ministry.

14. One informant cautioned that the Adventist ideal of masculinity, if not tempered by "kindness and understanding," would lead Adventist men to become "rigid and dogmatic." "The stereotypical ideal of an Adventist man is someone who is a good provider, is the spiritual head of the home, [who is] not influenced by feelings. . . . [He] doesn't make decisions based on how he feels about things, but on the facts. [He is] rigid and dogmatic. [He is] someone who takes the standards that Ellen White has set and says, 'This is the way things were and if it was good enough for our founding fathers, its good enough for me.' This kind of person comes up if they see someone wearing jewelry, or short skirts, or playing Frisbee or swimming on the Sabbath, comes up and says, 'That's wrong.' That's what I mean by rigid and dogmatic."

15. Three informants adamantly insisted that most employed Adventist women work for wages in order to attain superfluous material goods and therefore do not "need" to work. One stated, for example, "I think mothers should teach their children; but unfortunately mothers have to work, or they *think* they have to work. Whatever, some actually *do* have to work, but most, people want more things" (emphasis original).

7

Drawing the Line:
Gender, Homosexuality, and the Adventist Definition
of Appropriate Sexuality

The Adventist conception of appropriate expression of sexuality has been framed with reference to perceptions and ideals of family, gender roles, relationships within the family, and the position of the family vis-à-vis the world. Although original admonitions within Adventism concerning sexuality were constructed in a specific historical context (Victorian North America) and consequently reflected a Victorian concern with restraining the presumably peculiar and distinct sexual natures of women and men, Adventist definitions of appropriate sexuality have evolved dramatically since the early years of the movement. Nonetheless, despite a redefinition of proper expression of sexuality, Adventists continue to define and delimit notions of sexuality with careful attention to shared notions of family, gender, and the place of the family in the world.

Ellen White, Sexuality, and the Family

Ellen White, raised a Methodist in Victorian New England, adopted assumptions about sexuality prominent in Victorian thinking. White believed that women were sexual temptresses who, through their actions, led men to transgress the "law of God," and consequently she cautioned female Adventists to "refrain both in word and in act from exciting the animal [sexual] passions of [your] husband" (Bull and Lockhart 1989:133). At the same time, according to White's writings, men experienced almost uncontrollable "animal [sexual] urges," and it was the responsibility of women to dwell on spiritual matters and to resist amorous advances, thereby allowing men to control their inherently sinful sexual natures. While White advocated strict control of sexuality rather than abstinence, she left no doubt that it was the responsibility of women to constrain and control men's sexual activity. "Women, she wrote, 'Could soften [a man's] stern nature . . . leading him to strive earnestly to govern his passions. . . . If the wife feels that in order to please her husband she must come down to his standard, when animal passion is the principle basis of his love . . . she displeases God'" (quoted in Lindén 1978:273–74).

The home (family) in Victorian America was to be a haven, a refuge from the hostile world, in which women exerted their virtuous influence for the moral betterment of men. Ellen White and other Adventist writers who specifically addressed sexuality (most notably, John Harvey Kellogg),[1] adopted Victorian assumptions concerning the family and the relationship of the family (harmonious, moral) to the world (antagonistic, immoral), and shaped an understanding of appropriate expression of sexuality compatible with conclusions drawn from that assessment. Kellogg, for example, in addition to concluding that sexual behavior (especially coitus and masturbation) had serious negative physical consequences for participants (including ossification of bones, exhaustion of the body, and retardation and weakening of the intellect), determined that courtship, dating, flirting, and so on were "dangerous" and that a greater share of blame for participation in these behaviors lay with women, who tempted men sexually (Daily 1985:141, 142).

In her later writings on sexuality, White shifted the focus of her criticism from women to men, urging husbands to "act considerately" toward their wives who, in sexual matters (especially in circumstances in which they were being exploited sexually) were justified in acting "promptly and independently" in resolving "the situation" (Pearson 1990:67). As early as 1868, White criticized the "irresponsible sexual behavior of men" when it kept families "in a perpetual state of poverty, damaged the health of the mother, and meant that the children often lacked education, affection and spiritual discipline" (ibid.:59). White encouraged Adventist couples to limit the number of children born to their families in order that the mother's health might be spared and that children might be adequately cared for. She nonetheless placed the major burden for control of sexuality with women and generally agreed with other Victorian writers that men had difficulty stifling their "animal natures."

Ellen White's (and John Harvey Kellogg's) admonitions against participation in sexual activity were informed by the Victorian assumption that each person had a limited reserve of life-giving force ("vital force") located in the brain and that that supply, which could not be replenished and whose absence caused death, was decreased each time an individual experienced orgasm. Women, who were thought to possess less vital force than men, were more threatened, according to White, by the depletion of this crucial substance. White's writings on sex, therefore, generally moralistic and not well informed, made an especial effort to condemn masturbation (termed an "unnatural vice"), particularly by women (Graveson 1983). "During periods of her adult life," according to Numbers, Ellen White "found sexuality a morbidly fascinating topic," especially in discussions of masturbation (1992:221). In her book *An Appeal to Mothers: The Great Cause of the Physical, Mental and Moral Ruin of Many of the Children of Our Time,* White described in graphic detail the horrors and physical deformities resulting from masturbation, most especially in females.[2] In vision "Everywhere I looked I saw imbecility, dwarfed forms, crippled limbs, misshapen heads, and deformity of every description. Sins and crimes, and the violation of nature's laws, were shown to me as the causes of this accumulation of human woe and suffering" (quoted in Lindén 1978:325). In girls who engaged in masturbation, White warned, "the head often decays inwardly. Cancerous humor, which lay dormant in the system [previously] is inflamed, and commences its eating, destructive work. The mind is often utterly ruined, and insanity takes place [sic]" (Numbers 1992:206). Adventist parents were informed by White that masturbation was ten times more harmful than premarital promiscuity, general licentiousness, or "marital excess" (excess of sexual intercourse within marriage) and were cautioned to watch anxiously for signs of "self-abuse." In addition to eliminating "stimulating" foods from the family's diet (including dairy products, meat, spices, and condiments), Adventist parents were warned not to let children sleep in close proximity to playmates, and Kellogg counseled parents to deter children from "unnatural vice" by "bandaging the parts," "tying the hands," or "covering the organs with a cage" (Daily 1985:144).

Family, Gender, and Contemporary Notions of Sexuality

In the same way that Adventist notions of propriety in sexual expression were shaped by Victorian ideals not only of sex but of the family and of appropriate gender behavior of men and women, modern SDA delimitation of appropriate sexual behavior is profoundly influenced by predominant cultural norms and expectations. Adventists continue, however, to discuss sexuality in a manner which seeks to distinguish Adventist expectations of sexual behavior from those of the world. Further, Adventists continue to demarcate appropriate sexuality within the confines of ideals of family and gender roles, and in opposition to the world.

Optimal expression of Adventist sexuality, according to contemporary SDA writers, is (1) relational (masturbation remains widely discouraged), (2) permanent (within a committed, long-term relationship), (3) exclusive (monogamous), and (4) heterosexual. The ideal setting for Adventist expression of sexuality, then, is within a monogamous, heterosexual marital relationship.[3]

Adventists generally embrace this ideal and point to marriage as the means by which societies control the sexual behavior of members: "A world without marriage," wrote Robert Weiland in 1985, "is a world virtually without sexual responsibility or self-control" (9).[4] Within the heterosexual marital relationship, gender specific attributes are perceived as creating attraction between spouses. C. E. Wittschiebe insists, for example, that feminine characteristics (demonstration of emotion) displayed by men, or masculine characteristics (demonstration of physical strength) by women, would lead to a decline of physical attraction within the marital relationship (1970a; 1970b). Though some contemporary Adventist writers explicitly disagree with this sentiment (see, for example, Banks 1992), informants noted often that gender specific behavioral differences between spouses were crucial to the perpetuation of marriage and, within marriage, of sexual attraction and appropriate sexual expression.

Although older Adventists often retain a tendency to associate sex specifically and exclusively with procreation, and though Adventist publications continue, on occasion, to hold women responsible for men's sexual behavior, SDA attitudes toward sex have changed dramatically, especially since the sexual revolution of the late 1960s.[5] As early as 1931, Loma Linda medical evangelists publicly called intercourse and other expressions of sexuality "demonstrations of love within marriage" and argued that the notion of sex purely for procreative purposes was "untenable." At that time also, however, Loma Linda evangelists continued to urge sexual restraint within marriage, as unrestrained sexuality was considered harmful to women's health (see Bull and Lockhart 1989:134). Doctor Harold Shyrock, in *Happiness for Husbands and Wives* (1949), argued that marital sex was an expression of love which served to increase marital happiness, and was therefore desirable within the marital union, thus pointing to new ideals of sexuality within marriage.

The family was originally portrayed by Adventists as a haven from the world within which sexuality was controlled; following the sexual revolution of the 1960s, sexuality became a "gift from God," expression of which was to demonstrate love and to strengthen the marital relationship (Bull and Lockhart 1989:136). Adventist authors exploring appropriate expression of sexuality continued to portray the Adventist family as a haven or "sacred circle," but increasingly concluded that sexual relations between married spouses contributed to (as opposed to detracting from) the morality, sacredness, love, and emotional closeness necessary to protect the home (the family) from the world (see Van Pelt 1979; Kubo 1980).

It should be noted that Adventists did not move quickly or easily from an ideology emphasizing control and restraint of sexuality to one advocating sexual relations as a necessary and desirable component of marital relationships. Indeed, Adventists struggled, particularly during the 1970s, with changing definitions of appropriate sexual behavior and their ability to maintain a distinctly Adventist attitude toward sexual relations without seeming to capitulate to worldly standards. Wittschiebe wrote in 1970 that "in dealing with [sexuality], the people of God are faced almost with a dilemma—how to maintain the purity expected by God without being 'puritanical,' and how to stress the importance and value of sex without seeming to surrender to pagan philosophy permeating the world's thinking" (1970b:4).

In spite of concern expressed over the possibility of appearing to embrace worldly standards of sexual permissiveness, Adventists began, following the sexual revolution of the late 1960s, to criticize previous SDA prohibitions against sexual relations in marriage. "A number of the early church fathers," noted Wittschiebe, "viewed [sexual relations within] marriage as an almost degraded form of existence. Its only justification was [reproduction]. The function was not intended to be a happy one, but a necessity, and only this objective [reproduction] could erase the possible . . . pleasure it provided" (1970b:4). Daily observes further that "our traditional views about sex have often served to heighten tensions over what is sexually appropriate in marriage" and to induce guilt (1990:28). Tom Dybdahl and Mike Hanson agree: "Many people still feel guilty about what is really a normal, happy expression of sex. Many Adventists feel this because of their upbringing. You know, they were taught that sex was dirty and nice people indulge in it only in a dark room, partly clothed, and then with great reluctance and regret and apologies. . . . [Many Adventists] are struggling with neurotic inhibition" (1975:11). In an attempt to redefine sexual intercourse and other sexual activities within marriage as both appropriate and beneficial to the marital relationship, Adventist publications began to attempt to portray marital sex as "no more connected with sin than eating or drinking or thinking" and asserted that sexual intercourse could, in marriage, "be a thing of joy, of laughter, of playfulness" (Wittschiebe, 1970b:4, 5).

Adventist publications (including the *Review*) thus adopted a construct of sexuality which not only failed to discourage sexual expression within the marital relationship but specifically identified a "successful Christian marriage" as one in which partners actively sought sexual relations. Sex was no longer to be strictly avoided, but was one method of creating a strong marital bond and, in so doing, making a good Adventist home. "Each husband and wife have the right and privileges of enjoying to the fullest every expression of sex possible in their marriage (under the broad control of reason and con-science). The Lord intended sex to be enjoyed" (Wittschiebe, 1970b:6). Het-erosexual, marital sex was, following the sexual revolution, a God-given gift to Christians: "The Creator designed both bodies—male and female—so that together they might enjoy the maximum functioning of all the sensory and motor nerves involved in the art of love" (ibid.:6). Dybdahl and Hanson in-sisted that "[God] want[s] to have you [Adventists] enjoy sex all your lives after you are married" (1975:10). Adventists were instructed further that sexual in-tercourse was appropriate only within the bounds of heterosexual marriage and could only be fully enjoyed within this context: "Who else but a Chris-tian husband and wife, grounded in their loyalty to God, secure in their per-manent union, trusting each other implicitly, living for the happiness of each other, can reach the highest level of pleasure possible in sex? [Others'] sexual hedonism does not compare with the pleasure open to sexually mature and healthy Christians" (Wittschiebe 1970b:5).

No longer exclusively, or even primarily, for reproductive purposes, sex be-came, for Adventists in the 1970s and 1980s, a celebration of intimacy within marriage. Celibacy was discouraged and called "a horrible thing to try and impose on people" (Dybdahl and Hanson 1975:10).[6] Adventists were told that sexual intimacy within marriage "should be characterized by warmth, joy and delight" (Ministerial Association 1988:298) and that they were "spiritually in-complete without the opposite sex" (Fowler 1990:155).[7]

Unmarried Adventists

Recent Adventist interpretation of sexuality as being necessary not only for successful intimate (marital) relationships but for full personal spiritual de-velopment, and as occurring acceptably only within the bounds of hetero-sexual, "permanent" marriage has served to further exclude from Adventism's mainstream those SDAs who do not easily fit the definition of "family" inher-ent in the above delimitation. Although the Adventist "family" has long been assumed to consist preeminently of a heterosexual couple, recent emphasis on personal and spiritual growth resulting from intimate sexual relations within marriage fails to include those Adventists who are unmarried or who do not participate in a heterosexual marriage relationship.

Adventism, which from its inception strongly encouraged endogamy, had, by the 1970s, a membership in which women outnumbered men. Consequently some female Adventists choose to marry a nonmember and later attempt to convert their spouse, or to remain unmarried. Those Adventists who choose not to marry are faced, if they remain active participants in Adventism, with constant reminders that the optimal life for Adventists is heterosexual married life. "Single" Adventists, according to various authors, feel "left out" due to the "family orientation" of Seventh-day Adventism. One unmarried Adventist wrote that: "On Friday night and Sabbath, families do things together. Church social events center around family. Activities center around family and children. . . . Singles wake up alone, go to church alone, listen to 'how to be a good parent/spouse' sermons alone . . . and realize that they don't fit in" (Taylor 1989:10).

While Bull and Lockhart observed recent emphasis by General Conference leaders on including single adults in worship services, Adventist publications, sermons, Sabbath school lessons, and so on continue to assume marriage as the norm and to largely ignore Adventists who do not participate in such familial relations (1989). In one 1988 General Conference publication, for example, a thirteen-page chapter on family devotes one paragraph (on the last page of the chapter) to "singles" (Ministerial Association 1988:308). Further, as the number of unmarried Adventists rapidly increases (largely due to increasing numbers of divorces [Nicoll 1990]), Adventism continues to be unable to "integrate [unmarried SDAs] as needed participants" (Vasquez 1990:13). Various authors have proposed possible methods for inclusion of unmarried adults into Adventism, including sharing Sabbath meals with single adults, serving as role models for the children of unmarried parents, and assisting single parents with parenting, and the General Conference has organized services for unmarried adults including Adventist Singles Ministry (a NAD-based organization which provides social and spiritual activities for single Adventist adults) and Adventist Contact (a computer dating service for single SDAs) (see Pearson 1990:36).

Crossing the Line: Lesbian and Gay Adventists

Adventist definitions of appropriate expression of sexuality most explicitly discourage homosexual relationships. Grounded in the assumption that gender difference (and adherence to gender specific roles) is necessary for the success of an intimate relationship involving sexual expression, the Adventist ideal of marriage and family precludes the possibility of same sex relationships. Consequently, formal and informal informants were quick to point out that homosexuality is "unacceptable before God" because such relationships were perceived as "destroying the foundation of the family—the man and the woman [the heterosexual dyad]."

Informants, when asked to clarify Adventism's position on homosexuality, often responded in a manner which demonstrated personal dislike of lesbians and gay men, then incorporated reference to the Adventist understanding of appropriate sexual behavior. One informant, when asked to summarize Adventism's position on homosexuality, said, "I don't like it [homosexuality]. It's not healthy. Visually it makes me cringe. I don't think we were designed that way. God made Adam and Eve opposites." Another agreed: "I find homosexuality repulsive, although I have tried to develop a tolerance. It's something I just don't understand. I don't think that's the way God created us. Besides, promiscuity is not okay." Although these attitudes are not out of keeping with Adventism's official policy toward lesbians and gay men,[8] informants had difficulty clarifying the source of their knowledge.[9] Informants agreed that "homosexuality [is] unbiblical":

> My understanding is that the church is definitely opposed for biblical reasons to [homosexuality]. God never intended it.
>
> That's [homosexuality is] wrong. The Bible says it's wrong.
>
> The church is against it [homosexuality]. It's against the Bible.
>
> It's [homosexuality is] deviant behavior. It's not approved by the Bible.

At the same time, informants were rarely familiar with specific injunctions condemning homosexuality, as responses such as the following demonstrated: "The Bible is really clear on homosexuality. I don't know the direct statement, but it is clear."

Formal and informal informants agreed with Adventist leaders that "heterosexuality is divinely innate" and unanimously attributed homosexual behavior to the introduction of sin into the universe by Satan (see Ministerial Association 1988:303).[10] Informants most often made unspecified reference to "biblical condemnation" of homosexuality in rebuking same sex sexual behavior. In addition to insisting that "the Bible denounces [homosexuals]," informants indicated repeatedly that to condone homosexuality would require basic "liberalization" of Adventist belief, to the extent even that "the fundamental teachings of [Adventism] would be left without foundation" (see Hallock 1989:39). When asked to explain the perceived threat posed to Adventist identity and doctrine by exculpation of homosexuality, interviewees contended consistently that homosexuality entails: (1) "perverse" sexual behaviors—primarily promiscuity and pedophilia; and (2) that same sex sexual relations "destroy the family," primarily by threatening the dichotomy of gender specific behaviors and ideals believed necessary to the marital dyad.

First, informants identified homosexuality as embodying a number of behaviors deemed "perverse," primarily promiscuous activities, including sadomasochism, anonymous sexual encounters, sexual activity involving multiple partners, anal sex, and pedophilia.[11] Homosexual men (lesbians were included in discussion by only one interviewee) were perceived by informants as solely sexual beings (neither long-term, monogamous relationships nor nonsexual activity [employment, intellectual, recreational, esthetic, etc.] was noted). Further, informants identified the "perversity" of homosexuality in contrast to presumed normalcy of heterosexual relationships which were described by informants as absenting "abnormal sexual passions." Whereas heterosexual sexual activity was associated by informants with exclusivity (monogamy) and substantiality, homosexual sexual behavior was identified by informants as involving promiscuity and sexual perversity. In this manner, informants wove understanding of gay men into a pattern, in the words of one interview participant, of "sexual misconduct and perversity that is really the opposite of what God wants for us."

At the same time, informants justified animadversion of homosexuality by insisting not only that homosexuality precludes "God's ideal" for Adventists (monogamous, long-term, heterosexual marriage) but that same sex intimacy involving a sexual relationship threatens distinction by opposition perceived as being necessary within the marital dyad. Informants noted that gender differences create "romance and attraction" and ensure "that the partners need each other."

> The man and the woman need each other in marriage because they are different; they compliment each other. The man's strengths protect the family and keep it safe [while] the woman is able to nurture the family and build it up that way.

> In marriage you have the man and the woman. The man without the woman lacks the softness and beauty of life. In marriage the man gets that and the woman benefits from the man [as well].

> There is a division between man and wom[a]n that is important so that they can compliment and benefit each other. With this in mind [one] can see how marriage is important, because it makes both [men and women] useful to each other.

Identifying men and women as exhibiting fundamentally distinct gender specific behaviors, and maintaining that those differences are necessary to the successful functioning of marital (indeed, any sexual) relationships, informants inherently precluded homosexual relations from the parameters of acceptable intimate or sexual partnerships. Stated simply, informants identified gender (behavioral) differences as being essential to heterosexual relationships, and perceived gay and lesbian relationships, in which gender differences were not clearly defined or were nonexistent, as leading to the destruction of gender specific norms and behaviors and, therefore, the destruction of accepted delimitations of gender appropriate behaviors and spheres. One Adventist man clarified this sentiment: "You see, it's like this—men are men; they do men things, like work [for wages], take care of the family, provide for them and the like. Women, well, they do the cooking, the cleaning, caring for the kids. If you have homosexuals, all of this breaks down. Where do you draw the line?"

Homosexuality, then, is deemed sinful and ultimately unacceptable by a majority of informants because it is assessed as antithetical to the clear division of gender appropriate behaviors and spheres which a large number of Adventists continue to judge necessary for the smooth functioning of the family (and within the family, sexual relations) and of society as a whole. In this way, same sex expressions of sexuality were perceived by informants, and portrayed in SDA literature, as threatening "the basic social unit"—the heterosexual nuclear family. As one leading SDA thinker explains, homosexuality, although it involves consenting adults, is not a "victimless crime" because "the social order itself may be the victim": "What is threatened here is the family structure and thus a basic fabric of society" (Provonsha 1977:47). In this way, Adventists extend notions of family and gender to define appropriate sexual behavior outside of the realm that members generally recognize as constituting the appropriate sphere for expression of sexuality. Thus, homosexuality, though considered a sin in itself, is most detested as it provides an alternative to (and therefore presumably detracts from) the ideal of the family as the mechanism for social control of sexuality and reconstitution of gender norms and ideals. Jack Provonsha, a prominent Adventist ethicist, determined that gay men and lesbians should be restricted because "no structure has yet been discovered that adequately substitutes for a mom and a dad," and because same sex expression of sexuality "separates expression of sexuality from the family" and thereby promotes an alternative to the heterosexual nuclear family which "undermines" the family (ibid.:50).

Informants almost unanimously shared Provonsha's conclusions, citing gay men (especially) and lesbians as a threat to family and, ultimately, social, cohesion. One informant was "very opposed to homosexuality being touted as a desirable lifestyle in front of young people or anybody else" and another objected that "if homosexuals have rights—to be teachers, to have children, to do any job they want or live where they want—it will break apart the family." Adventist authors have expressed similar sentiments: "Today we see the family, the nucleus of society, being invaded, divided and destroyed [by] certain groups who are demanding their 'rights' as individuals" (Campbell 1975:17). In this way, the Adventist construction of sexuality is used not only to determine the realm within which sexual expression is appropriate and thereby to delimit inappropriate expression of sexuality but to draw conclusions which ultimately do not involve sexuality, such as provision of employment and housing opportunities. As one informant concluded, "We can't have the family falling apart. We can't have society going to pot because some homosexual thinks they have a right to make their own determination of the job they'll do. You have to have rules. Society has to decide what is unacceptable and then stamp it out. In the church we're just more clear about pointing to sin, like we point to homosexuals, and say, 'that's wrong' [sic]."

Despite unanimous agreement among informants that homosexual relationships were "wrong" or "sinful" (though one informant clearly specified that some expressions of same sex affection, such as "hugging and kissing" might be acceptable or even healthy, but that coitus between individuals of the same sex was "definitely wrong"), many informants ($N = 31$) were careful to note in some way that "homosexuals can change": "They can be changed and saved by God's grace." Adventist leaders instructed in 1988, after condemning lesbians and gay men, that "Christians will deal redemptively with those who are afflicted by this disorder [homosexuality]. No behavior is beyond the reach of God's healing grace" (Ministerial Association 1988:303). Informants agreed that "some [gays and lesbians] need help and then they can change" and that "the church is trying to help and change homosexuals." Dybdahl and Hanson wrote that although Adventism "has been behind in knowing how to deal with people with these troubles [gay men and lesbians]" and has "made them think that the message [of Adventism] was not for them," that "we must have compassion and sympathy for these people and still hold up Biblical principles": "In other words," they wrote, "we must mix therapy with evangelism and therapy with pastoring" (1975:11). The *Review* also, after labeling "homosexual practice" "a perversion" and calling for "church discipline" of lesbians and gay men, instructed that in local congregations "every effort should be made to restore [lesbians and gay men] to a satisfactory [Adventist] experience" ("SDA Church Moves against Homosexual Support Group" 1988:6).

In an ambitious attempt to implement this policy of "therapy mixed with pastoring," the General Conference in the 1980s funded and in other ways contributed to the founding and operation of the Quest Learning Center, a residential counseling center claiming to successfully change the sexual orientation of homosexuals (almost exclusively gay men). Quest was founded and overseen by Colin Cook,[12] a former Adventist pastor who had been forced from the Adventist ministry in 1974 when his homosexuality was discovered but who had been "restored to heterosexuality" through "God's grace to the homo-sexual"[13] and was married in 1978.[14] Offering a seven-week counseling pro-gram, including weekly peer counseling and Homosexuals Anonymous meet-ings, group counseling sessions, Bible fellowships with host families, and participation in worship services, Quest had, by 1986, served between seven and eight hundred gay men in sixty local chapters, 40 percent of whom were Adventist. Quest, like Adventism, maintained that "homosexual activity is not in harmony with the will of God" and that "the universal creation norm is heterosexuality" (Cook 1980:47). "Nonetheless," concluded Cook, "the great message of righteousness by faith in Christ brings mercy and hope to all people in homosexuality": "Quest holds that the orientation may be healed and that all who desire it may realize . . . heterosexuality, thus opening the way for het-erosexual marriage and family" (ibid.).

Though Cook repeatedly claimed success in "breaking . . . the power of the homosexual orientation," the Quest endeavor failed by Adventist standards of assessment (Cook 1980:47). In a 1986 report to the General Conference, David R. Larson, who studied the Quest experiment in detail, explained that "coun-selees said the Quest program led them to accept and feel good about their homosexuality": "Before they came to [Quest] they had no meaningful gay friendships—their guilt was typically so great that any sexual activity was anonymous. . . . But at Quest they discussed their homosexuality openly, mixed regularly with others like themselves, felt less guilt and shame, formed friendships, were active sexually with these friends, and sometimes for the first time fell in love. These new experiences significantly fostered affirmation and self-acceptance" (Larson 1983:17). Furthermore, extensive independent inter-views with Quest participants found that none had "changed sexual orienta-tion" (Dwyer 1986:9). In 1986, after Cook was forced to resign from Quest (fol-lowing public disclosure of his sexual relationships with clients), the General Conference voted to close Quest but continued to asseverate that it had "no reservations about the basic counseling philosophy of Quest" (ibid.).[15]

The philosophy of sexual reorientation has been questioned, however, by some Adventists who find the leadership's position toward homosexuality to be poorly informed. Insisting that Adventist leaders "have decided the issue without studying it," critics of the official SDA response to homosexuality have noted that Adventist publications which address homosexuality concentrate almost exclusively on explicit discussion of sexual acts (ignoring any consid-eration of monogamous relationships), often misuse terminology, relay bib-lical proof with no reference to cultural or historical context of texts, and focus on gay men to the exclusion of mention of lesbians (see Hallock 1989). More specifically, critics have observed that in addition to addressing homosexuality in a "condemnatory and judgmental" manner, Adventist publications consistently suggest that treatment programs seeking to change sexual orientation are successful, a claim contradicted by extensive research (Graveson 1983:20). Critics within the periphery of the Adventist mainstream (intellectuals and academics) have also attempted to introduce information regarding homosexuality to Adventists, primarily through *Spectrum*. Larson, for example, discussed social science research indicating that gay men and lesbians can be "happy, healthy and successfully adjusted" (1983:17).

Interestingly, the paradigm of family inherent in the Adventist delimitation of appropriate sexuality has not been abandoned by Adventist writers seeking to inform SDAs about lesbians and gay men. Rather, these writers have attempted to portray gay and lesbian relationships not only as failing to threaten the family but as one variant (albeit a less desirable variant) of the family: "Homosexuals involved in unions which function much like wholesome heterosexual marriages tend to be the happiest, healthiest, and most successfully adjusted. Christians therefore have every reason to encourage homosexuals who are honestly convinced that they should neither attempt to function heterosexually nor remain celibate to form Close-Coupled [monogamous, permanent] homosexual unions, even though similar heterosexual relationships should remain Christianity's first hope for all believers" (Larson 1983:16)

Perhaps the most effective critics of the official SDA position toward homosexuality are gay and lesbian Adventists, who have repeatedly expressed feelings of isolation and persecution within Adventism. Gay and lesbian Adventists, as a result of official SDA indictments of homosexuality, most often attempt to hide their sexual orientation: "Whoever was the first homosexual [Adventist] probably kept the fact very quiet for the same reason that most homosexual Adventists still do: his or her church membership would have been in jeopardy if it were known that he or she were gay" (Benton 1980:32). Gay and lesbian Adventists generally identify their only options as hiding their sexual orientation or being disfellowshiped (ibid.). Because a disproportionate number of Adventists are educated in Adventist schools, colleges, and universities for later employment in Adventist institutions, the threat of being disfellowshiped is also often a threat of job loss. Moreover, Adventism's official policy toward homosexuals actively encourages local congregations to disfellowship gay or lesbian members. In one instance, a local church was threatened with expulsion from Seventh-day Adventism if the congregation agreed to accept into fellowship an openly gay man transferring from another congregation (ibid.:37). A leading layman told the congregation to "let them [homosexuals] worship somewhere else. We don't want them here" (ibid.). Another Adventist, suspected of being gay by his local congregation, lost his job (at an SDA institution), was encouraged to participate (and eventually did) in aversion therapy, and was disfellowshiped.

Lesbian and gay Adventists experience a profound sense of isolation. One informal interviewee confided that she was a lesbian and urged me to convey "the loneliness of being gay and being Adventist": "Here I am, twenty-three years-old and even though I've known that I was a lesbian since, well at least since I was fourteen, you're the first person I've ever told. Do you have any idea of the loneliness? Or the abandonment I feel? Or the confusion? With no one to trust, no one to talk to or confide in, I'm forced to present a pretense to everyone. I would like to talk to someone in the church, but I don't think that I could without being condemned." A gay man agreed; having grown up gay "as long as [he could] remember" he "felt several times like going and talking to someone, but I decided there was simply no one I could discuss the matter with in confidence and who would try to help me as an individual and not act like a hellfire-and-brimstone preacher" (Spectrum Editors 1980a:39). A lesbian concurred that "within the church . . . I often feel isolated" and another contended that as a lesbian woman there was no place for her within Adventism: "Some people in the church, I think, know about my being gay; but there's no real place where I fit in the church. I'm forty-one years old so I don't belong with the youth. I'm a single parent in the Adventist church, so what place is there for me? There's a young married people's club, and they graciously allow people up into the forties to be in that. But in what way could I bring my lover, whom I feel married to, to the young married people's club in the Adventist church?" (ibid.:42) One lesbian, at an SDA Kinship Kampmeeting, concluded that the most effective way to end gay and lesbian feelings of isolation was to replace ignorance, fear and hostility with understanding and acceptance: "If people could accept the fact that I was a lesbian, then yes, that's what makes the difference. If people could accept that, too, then I would feel a lot closer to them. If people around me would accept my lesbianism, I would relate to them in a different way. But as it is, I close myself off. So I wish that it would get to the point where a person could be accepted by the membership as a member, as a Christian, without this barrier of being a homosexual and therefore being unapproachable or somebody to be avoided" (ibid.).

Adventist admonitions against homosexuality are not ostensibly constructed as barriers to lesbian and gay members. Instead, the official Adventist understanding and portrayal of homosexuality is intended to reinforce carefully delimited parameters of the appropriate arena for expression of sexuality. More specifically, official Adventist denunciations of lesbians and gay men are rooted within, and intended to perpetuate, notions of appropriate gendered behavior within the heterosexual marital unit. Adventist criticisms of homosexuality inevitably are explicitly undergirded by the "fact of creation": "God created man and woman, *man and woman*, that's how he intended it to be" (emphasis original). Adventists who expressed strong aversion to homosexuality inevitably justified their homophobia by referring to "God's plan." Because "God created Adam and Eve," noted one interviewee, "God intends for there to be men and women. Men and women are different, not just physically, but in other important ways. That difference is needed; it's very important for the attraction to be right."

There is some evidence that as Adventists begin to question strict separation of gendered spheres and behaviors (see chapter 6) widespread aversion to homosexuality will also abate. *Spectrum,* for example, the most prominent (though unofficial) vehicle for promulgation of new ideas among members, has increasingly begun to explore changing gender roles (and associated issues such as the ordination of women to Adventist pastoral positions) and concomitantly to question broad condemnation of homosexuality and, more often, of individual homosexuals. One *Spectrum* author, who personalized AIDS in the periodical by sharing an account of his brother's battle with the disease, asked rhetorically, "Why can't we [Adventists] at least try to love the sinner and not the sin?" (Phillips 1986:3). An informant stated that while "the Bible clearly says that [homosexuality] is wrong" she felt unqualified to condemn individual gay men and lesbians:

> Who are we to turn anyone away from God, because God is just the reaper of souls? I would certainly not turn [gays and lesbians] away from my door. And I have no right to tell them they cannot come in and worship in my church, because it's God's church and his house. . . . I don't *agree* with that lifestyle. I cannot understand the attraction, but I'm not going to condemn anybody. Therefore, I'd just have to leave it alone. They're human beings. God created them just as much as he created us. They don't have to agree with my lifestyle anymore than I have to agree with theirs. (emphasis original)

This informant's comments, while rare in their demonstration of tolerance among interviewees, were indicative of what another informant called "the changing tide in Adventism." "As we struggle with things like righteousness by faith [justification vs. sanctification] and ordination of women and all of these modern controversies," she said, "we Adventists are going to have to do some soul-searching to determine if we are just doing things because they've always been [done] that way, or if we're doing it to be different than the world, or if it is truly a Christian thing to do. You take homosexuality which you [Vance] just asked about. Now that is wrong. But would Christ turn those people away? Turn them out of the church? Maybe we need to think more about that."

Conclusions

In the same way that Adventist definition of appropriate sexuality has been historically constructed with reference to ideals and expectations of family, gender, and the place of the family vis-à-vis the world, so too changing contemporary notions of sexuality (as necessary for creating an intimate, loving marital relationship, and as such as being an important component of strong family relationships) rely on shared SDA conceptions of family, gender, and the relationship of the family to the world. Most importantly, Adventists have defined appropriate expression of sexuality as being concomitant with family, especially ideals of masculinity and femininity that were (and to a lesser extent, are) to be adhered to by Adventists within the family. In this way Adventists historically (most especially Ellen White) concurred with Victorian prescriptions of sexuality which identified men as inherently needing to be restrained sexually and women as essentially moral and responsible for controlling men's sexuality. So too, modern Adventists, though they have redefined marital sex as "joyful" and "pleasurable" (something in which married couples *ought* to engage in order to create intimacy), continue to equate appropriate expression of sexuality with gender specific ideals of behavior. Men and women, informants concurred, are socially and behaviorally different, and are therefore sexually attractive and necessary to one another. This extraction of expected behavior from stated ideals extends beyond definition of appropriate sexuality to justification of condemnation of expressions of sexuality (and attraction or emotion associated with those sexual relationships) which are deemed inappropriate. By defining appropriate expression of sexuality with reference to gender ideals and, more broadly, the family, Adventists have not only delimited sexuality but confined expressions of sexuality which they deem inappropriate (most notably homosexuality) to a realm outside of SDA notions of family, marriage, and so on. Thus while lesbian and gay Adventists may view long-term, committed relationships as being familial in nature, Adventists, by defining family and gender in terms of specific expressions of sexuality, and sexuality in terms of family and gender, have simultaneously identified other types of relationships as being nonfamilial, and in fact antithetical to family.

Notes

1. John Harvey Kellogg, a prominent health reformer, was one of the first Adventists to be trained as a physician (at Ellen White's urging) and oversaw the Battle Creek Sanitarium, Adventism's first medical facility. Kellogg eventually left Seventh-day Adventism in the midst of conflict surrounding his religious views (which SDA leaders contended were pantheistic). Kellogg is perhaps best known as the inventor of (Kellogg's) prepared cereal products.

2. As with many of her works, White's *Appeal to Mothers* was not published until after her death in 1915.

3. One informant noted simply that "marriage is the ideal and it's for a lifetime. People should not be sexual with each other if they're not married."

4. In one survey, Leonore Johnson (1987) found that students at Adventist colleges and universities disapproved of premarital intercourse far more often (70 percent) than did students attending secular institutions of higher education (15 percent).

5. Kistler, for example, wrote in 1987: "If a wife withholds sexual intercourse from her husband . . . and in such a situation the husband succumbs to the needs of the flesh through intimacy with another woman, which of the marriage mates is 'innocent' and which is 'guilty'?" (134).

6. Dybdahl and Hanson observed that an Adventist man "recently talked to a group of conference workers and advocated generally abstaining from sex. . . . That is a heresy of major proportions" (1975:10).

7. Roy G. Graveson has contended that contemporary Adventist publications which reinterpret Ellen White's writings criticizing "animal passions" as applying only to "copulation unconnected with a pleasuring, endearing love relationship" (as many do) fail "to accurately reflect [Ellen White's] intended meaning" (1983:20). Indeed, though Ellen White's writings can be construed as supporting modern interpretations of appropriate sexual relations (primarily by redefining "animal passions"), it is clear that Adventist ideals of sexual relations have evolved to include a far more permissive attitude toward acceptance of sexual intercourse within marriage than that endorsed by early Adventist leaders, particularly Ellen White.

8. Adventist leadership has chosen to target gay men and lesbians for criticism at least in part because such a position "is not perceived as challenging the unity of [SDA] membership" (Pearson 1990:34). The *Review,* for example, in 1988, stated specifically that "Official SDA church standards classify homosexual and lesbian [*sic*] practices . . . as 'obvious perversions of God's original plan.'"

9. "The *Seventh-day Adventist Church Manual* lists homosexuality *and other perversions* as grievous sins for which members shall be subject to discipline" ("SDA Church Moves against Homosexual Support Group" 1988:6; emphasis added).

10. It seemed to make little difference if informants perceived homosexuality to be a "choice" or to be (presumably, like heterosexuality) innate. In both cases informants concluded that homosexuality was "sinful." One woman explained that if homosexuality was genetic, as she believed it to be, then she must simply conclude that "Satan has gotten to the level of the gene."

11. For a discussion of homosexuality see Marcus 1993.

12. According to Bonnie Dwyer, "during the 1980s the [Adventist] church's actions toward homosexuals were bound up with the dramatic chronicle of Quest, Homosexuals Anonymous and Colin Cook's personal struggles" (1986:5).

13. "God's Grace to the Homosexual" was the title of a 1976 three-part series Cook authored in *Insight* magazine.

14. Cook presented a five-page proposal for funding of Quest to the General Conference via Duncan Eva in March of 1981, after which the General Conference appropriated $47,500 per year for the center.

15. In part due to the overwhelming advocation by Adventist leadership of Cook's philosophy (Benton, for example, wrote that Adventist "officials at every level are speaking out in support of Colin Cook's . . . thesis . . . that God loves homosexual people and calls them to find their heterosexual identity in Christ through the training of their faith" [1980:37]), Adventist leadership opposed efforts to create groups offering support for gay men and lesbians. Specifically, SDA leadership opposed SDA Kinship, a group formed in the mid-1970s by gay and lesbian Adventists. SDA Kinship, with a current membership of over twelve hundred, regards stable gay and lesbian relationships as "compatible with Adventism" and holds annual "Kampmeetings" to celebrate spirituality in the context of gay and lesbian relationships. In addition to openly attacking lesbians and gay men in prominent periodicals (most notable the *Review* and *Ministry*), Adventist leaders sued SDA Kinship in 1986 in an attempt to prevent the group from openly associating itself with Seventh-day Adventism. Though SDA Kinship agreed to drop "SDA" from its title if Adventist leaders would agree to include discussion of homosexuality in parochial sex education courses and publish balanced articles dealing with homosexuality in *Review* and *Ministry,* Adventist leaders refused SDA Kinship's offer, and Adventist leaders lost their suit. Further, as a result of continued scandal surrounding Cook (including numerous allegations of sexual abuse of counselees), the General Conference recently indicated in the *Review and Herald* that it no longer supports his ministry.

8

Becoming like the World:
Adventist Women and Wage Labor

Contemporary Adventist definitions of family and gender that preclude specific activities based upon gender have not been advocated consistently throughout the history of the movement (see chapter 5). As secular definitions of gender and gender norms of behavior have evolved, so too have Adventists altered gender expectations specifically advocated for men and women. Nonetheless, modern NAD Adventists are largely unaware of the positions and roles that Adventist women assumed in the early movement, particularly prior to 1915, and often define recent changes in gender norms as arising in response to secular pressure and as challenging earlier norms (those perpetuated in the *Review* during the 1920s, 1930s, mid- to late 1940s, and especially 1950s and 1960s) which are widely believed to have been exclusively advocated in early (1850s–1915) Adventism. This chapter will explore roles and positions of women in early SDA history, discuss the evolution of women's "place" in SDA education and employment, and examine informants' understanding of the relationship between the historical and contemporary roles of SDA women.

Women's Declining Contribution to Adventism

"Many women held high positions and made outstanding contributions in early Seventh-day Adventist history" (Running 1972:54); particularly prior to the 1940s and 1950s, Adventist "women enjoyed greater freedom to serve in all parts of the work of the church" (Pearson 1990:145). According to data gathered pertaining to the number of women serving in various positions in Adventism throughout the movement's history, "something happened to women in the Seventh-day Adventist church, beginning in 1915 and sharply accelerating in the mid-1940s, that led, [by 1950,] to the almost total exclusion of women from leadership positions in the church." Bertha Dasher, who collected data from Adventist *Yearbooks* concerning numbers of women filling leadership positions in the NAD between 1905 and 1980, found that: "Many women were church leaders during the early years of the century; we had the highest number in 1915. However, as the church became larger and more prestigious, men began taking over leadership positions. By 1950 there were no women in administrative or departmental leadership in any conference in the North American Division" (Dasher 1983:35). In addition to Ellen White, who "taught publicly, preached, counseled, and rebuked men as well as women," Adventist women held conference leadership positions, served as conference secretaries and treasurers, departmental leaders, departmental directors, and held positions of leadership in SDA institutions (see figures 2–7 [information in figures dating prior to 1982 compiled using data from Dasher [1983]; remaining data compiled from *SDA Yearbooks*]).

Despite the relative abundance of opportunity available to SDA women, especially prior to the 1930s, the number of Adventist women in leadership began a dramatic and uninterrupted decline in 1915. (As figures 2–7 demonstrate, this decline was most marked in the 1940s, and by 1950 was complete.) Dasher has observed that the decline of women serving in positions of leadership in Adventism was contrary (particularly during the 1920s) to secular trends: "During the same decades when American women were gaining legal, educational, financial, and professional recognition, women within the Seventh-day Adventist church steadily lost leadership positions" (Dasher 1992:75).

Explanations for this decline are not lacking. First, it is apparent that "during the years 1920–1950, women who worked with selfless devotion [within Adventism] seem to have been convinced (how easily is hard to judge) that the best interests of the church would be served by their being replaced by male ordained ministers" (Dasher 1992:76). In addition, the education (especially postsecondary education) of women "seems to have been adversely affected during the years 1920–1970" (ibid.:78).[1] At Loma Linda medical school, for example, 20 percent of graduates were women in the years immediately following Ellen White's death in 1915. That figure fell to 10 percent during the 1920s and declined further in the following decades, rising again to 20 percent only in the 1970s (Clark 1982). Rather than directly causing the decline in women's participation in leadership positions within Adventism, however, stagnating enrollments at Adventist colleges and universities appear to have been a simultaneous symptom of a broader cause.

Other explanations for the decline have been offered by Patrick Allen and Kit Watts. Allen attributes the dramatic decrease in the number of women working in Adventist leadership to the Great Depression and Adventism's consequently difficult financial situation during the late 1920s and early 1930s. According to Allen, during the depression, the General Conference limited

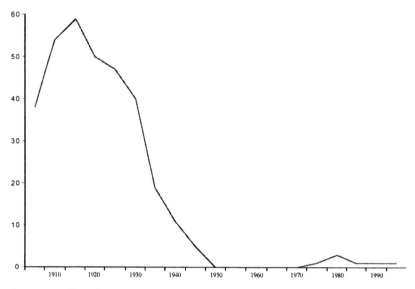

Figure 2. Number of Women Serving as SDA Departmental Secretaries, 1905–90

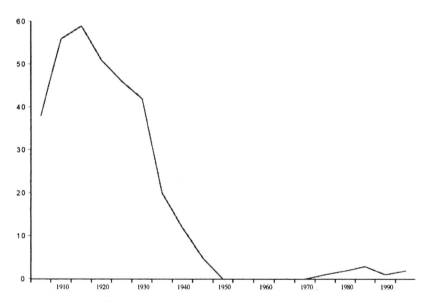

Figure 3. Number of Women Serving as SDA Sabbath School Department Leaders, 1905–90

Figure 4. Number of Women Serving as SDA Education Department Leaders, 1910–90

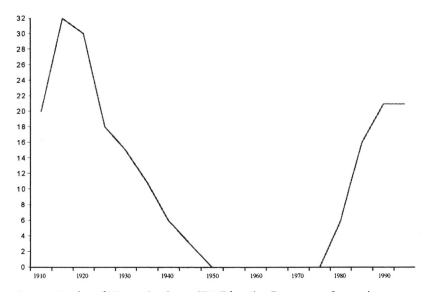

Figure 5. Number of Women Serving as SDA Education Department Secretaries, 1910–90

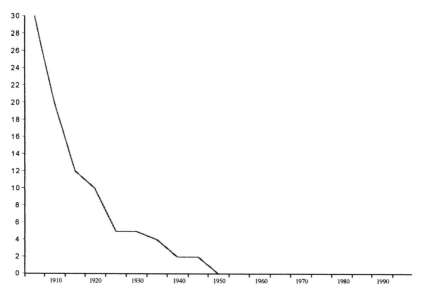

Figure 6. Number of Women Serving as SDA Conference Secretaries, 1905–90

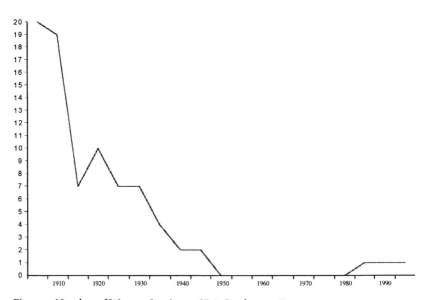

Figure 7. Number of Women Serving as SDA Conference Treasurers, 1905–90

176

tenure of departmental positions, and when women left positions of employment, they were replaced by men. Further, in the early to mid-1930s, SDA conferences merged, and women consequently lost paid positions. (In all cases of
merger of conferences except one, female employees were replaced by men.)
Last, because women were not ordained, they were first to lose their positions
when pastoral staffs were trimmed. Between 1931 and 1933 the number of
Adventist women employed as pastors dropped from six to none (see Allen
1984).

Allen's explanation of reasons for the decline of female SDA employees,
while certainly illuminating the differential effects of the Great Depression for
Adventist women and men, fails in its ability to consider not *that* women were
replaced by men but why *women* were forced to relinquish their positions.[2]
Allen notes that the decline of women serving in positions of leadership commenced prior to the depression but fails to explain why or how, if the depression was cause for this decline, the decline preceded the depression. Perhaps
more seriously, Allen fails to explain why, if financial hardship was cause for
the dismissal of female employees, the total number of credentialed and licensed female SDA employees slipped from 500 to 350 between 1930 and 1935,
while the total number of credentialed and licensed male Adventist employees *increased* from 2,000 to 2,250 during the same period. Additionally, though
Adventist women began, in the 1920s, to lose positions of leadership and authority, the number of women serving as colporteurs—a relatively low wage,
low prestige position—increased during the same period. Thus, while Allen
cites "societal attitudes" as contributing, in part, to changes in the Adventist
workforce, he fails to consider their impact adequately.

In contrast to Allen, Watts relates the decline of Adventist women in leadership to Ellen White's death. The death of Ellen White left Adventist women
without a visible role model or advocate: "Since Ellen White died [in 1915]
women's voices—their needs their dreams, their hopes—have seldom been
heard in the council chambers of church leaders" (Watts 1990c:5).[3] While Ellen
White undoubtedly did provide a voice for the concerns of Adventist women
in decision-making bodies of the Adventist hierarchy, as Dasher pointed out
in 1992 (and as is clear from the review of changing Adventist gender expectations in chapter 5), Adventist women were encouraged to leave positions of
paid employment between 1920 and the 1960s as a result of the change in
emphasis on appropriate gender specific expectations for men and women in
Adventism and, simultaneously, Adventism's increasing accommodation to the
world (as evidenced most obviously in rapid institutionalization, decreasing
emphasis on sectarian separation, and increased concern for and attention to

evangelism). As Bull and Lockhart noted in 1989, the decreasing numbers of SDA women serving Adventism in leadership capacities occurred in conjunction with White's death, with the increasing restriction of appropriate gender role activities for Adventist women, and with Adventism's newfound willingness (after the turn of the century) to participate in (even encourage) expanding bureaucracy.

Returning to Leadership, 1970–90s: Continued Struggle

Adventist reification of gender appropriate spheres was not questioned in the context of concomitant secular emphasis on the propriety of separate and distinct gender spheres (men, "breadwinners"; women, mothers and housewives) following World War II. In the 1960s, however, following "the beginning of change in cultural attitudes toward women, and the expanded [secular] areas open to them," some Adventist women began to prepare themselves to participate in Adventist employment by enrolling in university undergraduate and graduate programs (Dasher 1992:76). In the 1970s, the number of women employed by the General Conference in positions of leadership began to increase, though this increase became more pronounced in the 1980s and 1990s. In 1970, for example, seventeen women served in General Conference, North American Division, Union and Conference leadership positions. By 1991, that number had risen to 131 (Perez-Greek 1992).[4] Between 1970 and 1981, women served Adventism as directors of communication, education, health and temperance, public relations, and Sabbath school (ibid.). While "no woman has ever been elected as president of a conference, union, or division," since the early 1980s women have served as vice president of the NAD, associate treasurer of the General Conference, associate secretary of the NAD, field secretary for the NAD, regional treasurer, conference treasurer, and conference secretary-treasurer (see ibid.:92).

Despite the appearance, since the 1980s, of Adventist women serving in leadership capacities within the movement, Adventists within the NAD are by no means unanimous in their support of recently increased (though still limited) opportunities for women. Indeed, controversy surrounding appropriate gender specific behavior—especially dispute concerning the propriety of ordaining women to the ministry—is commonly discussed in SDA books, periodicals, conversations, and even sermons. Adventists do not generally acknowledge, nor are they generally aware of, the relatively prominent role that SDA women played in the early decades of the movement (with the exception, obviously, of recognizing Ellen White's work and contributions). Though some researchers have noted the disparity between positions available to Adventist women prior to the 1920s, and even prior to the 1950s, and positions available since that time (see Dasher 1983, 1985, 1992), there has been little recognition of the irony of the claim made by many Adventists (and by a majority of interviewees [$N = 46$]) that the recent assumption of leadership positions by women within Adventism reflects capitulation (be it bad or good) to secular norms. One interviewee, for example, explained that "times are changing where there are a lot more Adventist women in church leadership than ever before. Mostly that's a result of the church responding to [the] Women's Lib[eration movement]." Another said that "feminism has opened the way for women in the church to go into areas that maybe were strictly always [for] men." The majority of informants expressed similar sentiments. Predominant secular attitudes assumed by Adventists in the 1920s–60s which served to limit the public sphere of authority available to Adventist women were identified by interviewees as being, if not uniquely Adventist, at least true to Adventism's original message. However, as William G. Johnsson demonstrated in 1988, the position toward which Adventism is currently moving (in attempting, though hesitantly, to more fully include women in positions of leadership) is more consistent with the movement's original practice: "Our spiritual forebears did not see the reiteration of marriage and home as incompatible with giving women a public role in worship and gospel work. In taking this position, they were at odds with much of society of their day" (4). As Iris Yob further observed, "the church has lost touch with its women pioneers and has lost much in so doing" (1988:51).

Although some early Adventists were offended by the prominent, public positions assumed by Adventist women and quoted Pauline scriptural prohibitions in an attempt to limit their activities, Adventist leaders, including James White, J. N. Andrews, and Uriah Smith "frequently defended Adventist practice on the basis of scripture. As early as the August 18, 1868 issue of the *Review*, M. H. Howard reflected on 'that conservatism which so readily takes flight at the prominence accorded a woman.'" In contemporary Adventism, leadership is not often so quick to defend women who assume positions of authority (see below). Instead, modern SDA conservatism is challenged by academics and intellectuals who are most often labeled feminist (and most often the label is applied pejoratively). Within Adventism: "Some men are reluctant to advance women; some women are uncomfortable seeing other women in leadership. And some men and women continue to argue that placing women in public leadership roles denies their Biblical place. These members need to take a hard look at the Adventist church of the last century" (Yob 1988:51). Indeed, as Johnsson claimed in 1988, within Adventism "something has happened": "Those days [when SDA women filled leadership positions within the movement] have gone. Few women occupy leadership positions in today's church; some [Adventist women] so misconstrue Paul's words that they even refuse to read the scripture or teach a Sabbath school lesson if a man is present. . . . I do not know why we have departed so far from the pattern of the pioneers. But I am sure that we are the poorer for it" (4).

Ellen White on Employed Women

Certainly it would be misleading to conclude that early Adventist women were not encouraged and expected to fulfill gender specific responsibilities (primarily associated with motherhood and wifehood) in the domestic sphere (see chapter 5). However, it would be equally misleading to fail to note that these expectations did not preclude the possibility, and even the expectation, that women, like men, would engage in work considered essential to furthering the message of Adventism and thus hastening the advent. While Ellen White's writings (especially prior to the 1870s) obviously contributed to delimitation of women's activities within the domestic sphere, her later writings (1870s–1915) more frequently encouraged Adventist women to engage in "public gospel work," and Adventist employers to treat female employees well and pay them equitably. Though Graybill (1983) and others (especially Daily [1985]) have insisted that Ellen White's "theology lacked feminist relevance" (Graybill 1983:37), it is important to consider that: (1) Ellen White's feminist contemporaries (with rare exceptions, such as Victoria Woodhull) placed emphasis on achieving goals constructed and communicated so as to not be perceived as threatening widely accepted social norms (specifically the woman's role as wife and mother); (2) Ellen White enthusiastically encouraged women's participation in Adventism (see below); (3) while Ellen White advocated Victorian notions of gender and sexuality, she concomitantly encouraged more active public roles for women and strongly encouraged men to be "housebands," active and contributing parents; and (4) she called for equal wages for women employed in Adventist labors. Leona G. Running did not find Ellen White's writings to lack feminist relevance; indeed, she found them eminently applicable but often ignored (or used selectively) in contemporary disputes surrounding gender: "In trying here to make the men of the church aware of the thinking of women of the church—and of the nation and of the world—I thus draw attention to the fact that the principles about which people are concerned today [gender equality] are principles clearly set forth many years ago by this respected church leader [Ellen White]" (1972:60).

Ellen White, most notably, was a proponent of equitable wages for women "employed in the work." She wrote: "Those who work earnestly and unselfishly, be they men or women, bring sheaves to the Master; and [those] converted by their labor will bring their tithes to the treasury. When self-denial is required because of a dearth of means, do not let a few hard-working women do all the sacrificing. Let all share in making the sacrifice. God declares, I hate robbery for burnt offering" (White 1946:482). More specifically:

> Women who work in the cause of God should be given wages proportionate to the time they give to the work. God is a God of justice, and if ministers receive a salary for their work, their wives, who devote themselves just as interestedly to the work as laborers together with God, should be paid in addition to the wage their husbands receive, notwithstanding that they may not ask this. As the devoted minister and his wife engage in the work, they should be paid wages proportionate to two distinct workers, that they may have means to use as both see fit in the cause of God. The Lord has put His spirit upon them both. If the husband should die and leave his wife, she is fitted to continue her work in the cause of God, and receive wages for the labor she performs. (ibid.:59)

Ellen White urged that female physicians be paid equitable wages and be treated professionally (Daily 1985:229, 232). Further, she threatened to withhold her personal tithes in order to create a fund from which to pay female workers whom she felt were being economically exploited by male church leaders (see Pearson 1990:142).[5]

Ellen White also encouraged women to actively participate in forwarding the work:

> A great work is to be done in our world, and every talent is to be used in accordance with righteous principles. If a woman is appointed by the Lord to do a certain work, her work is to be estimated according to its value. Every laborer is to receive his or her just due. (White 1946:491)

> The Lord will use intelligent women in the work of teaching. And let none feel that these women, who understand the word, and who have the ability to teach, should not receive remuneration for their labors. They should be paid as verily as their husbands. There is a great work for women to do in the cause of present truth. (ibid.)

> Seventh-day Adventists are not in any way to belittle women's work. [If a woman] puts her housework in the hands of a faithful, prudent helper, and leaves her children in good care, while she engages in the work, the conference should have wisdom to understand the justice of her receiving wages. (1915:452–53)

Gender Discrimination in Adventist Wage Labor

According to Running, Ellen White "made some enlightened statements" regarding the "place" and potential roles of Adventist women within Seventh-day Adventism that "have been well ignored": "Men pay lip service to the inspired guidance of Ellen White, but conveniently they ignore the clear statements that deal with the principles that are basic to bringing about a change in the status of women in the church" (1972:60). Indeed, there is ample evidence that those in the employ of Seventh-day Adventism are treated differently on the basis of sex, and that women face discrimination as SDA employees. This discrimination, manifested most blatantly in wage disparity, has been legally challenged and Adventist leaders are currently attempting to rectify some of the most obvious examples of gender employment inequity.

Adventist women, like women generally in North America, work most often due to economic necessity (Kuzma 1992:119). Adventist parents face financial strain due to the shared assumption that children should be educated in Adventist parochial schools, and Adventist women are often employed for wages in order, in part, to provide funds necessary for children's tuition (and often in the case of secondary students, room and board) (see Crider and Kistler 1979:198). Seventh-day Adventist women also work for wages in order to help staff SDA institutions, to better achieve personal intellectual and emotional fulfillment, or in order to support themselves as unmarried women, or following the death of a spouse, or divorce or separation (see Kuzma 1992:119).

Regardless of why they choose to participate in wage labor, Adventist women face barriers to full and equal status in Adventist employ at every level of participation. In hiring, "some women employed by the church feel that only menial jobs are available to them; they do not have equal opportunity based on ability" (Hegstad 1970c:12). Many Adventist women, including a number of interviewees ($N = 27$), observed that "the church . . . is a man's world" in which men have been given preference in hiring and in salary. Female SDA employees were systematically denied equitable wages between the 1940s and the 1970s by Adventism's Head of Household wage category, under which whomever was defined as the head of household received wages and benefits in excess of other employees. This differential most profited married men, then unmarried men, then single women, and most disadvantaged married women (Watts 1990a). Furthermore, positions within Adventism filled almost universally by women—stenographers and secretaries—continue to receive hourly wages which allow employers to avoid being legally required to provide benefits. In addition to these wage disparities, Adventist women are beginning to articulate concern with restrictions they face in attempting to advance their careers.[6] Ottilie Stafford described this "glass ceiling" that SDA women confront: Adventist women "in denominational employ . . . feel their heads bumping against a ceiling and . . . know that at a certain level of accomplishment their male colleagues, however able or lacking in ability, will rise around them while they would remain where they were" (Stafford 1983:32).

One 1989 survey of 1,872 female Adventist employees substantiated anecdotal evidence of the differential opportunities available to women in Adventist employ.[7] Although respondents were generally satisfied with their positions of employment, and though 67 percent of respondents felt that their colleagues "accepted [them] as equal professionals," between 25 and 33 percent identified the following as major areas of dissatisfaction: (1) advancement opportunities, (2) salary/benefits, (3) availability of support services/equipment, and (4) growth/educational opportunities (Flowers 1989:15). Fifty percent of survey respondents felt that women had access to fewer opportunities "in denominational employ" than men; 59 percent had experienced gender discrimination "in at least some areas of denominational employment"; 63 percent of respondents expressed concern with equality of wages and benefits; 47 percent were concerned about increasing opportunities for personal development; and 35 percent expressed explicit concern about gender discrimination (ibid.).[8] Karen Flowers observed that survey respondents "want to believe the best about men in leadership with whom they work. . . . And . . . care deeply about the well being of the church" (ibid.:16). So much so, in fact, that respondents indicated a willingness to "make personal sacrifices" in order to participate in SDA employ. One respondent wrote that: "Most women who work for the church are not expecting high wages. Those do not come with the territory. What they are expecting is exactly the same wages and benefits that a man in the same position would receive. This is not about money, it's about equality" (ibid.:17). Survey participants indicated that: "More than anything they want to feel that their church respects and appreciates their intelligence, competence, and trustworthiness. They need assurance that the church gives its full support to women employees" (ibid.). Nonetheless, female SDA employees, according to survey results, "continue to pick up on the subtle and not-so-subtle messages that make them feel like second class citizens in the kingdom" (ibid.).

Despite apparent concern on the part of female employees with the lack of gender equality in Adventist employment, "some see the church's only responsibility [to employed women] as that of saying more loudly that mothers should stay home with their children" (Shell 1992:160). Instead of attempting to rectify wage and hiring discrepancies: "They would like to turn back the clock They are uncomfortable with the fact that society has changed, that the problem exists" (ibid.). Again, though Adventist critics of employment reform "would like to turn back the clock," they express sentiments more in keeping with Adventism's delimitation of gendered spheres as expressed in the 1950s than with those promulgated by SDA leaders and publications in the early decades of the movement. Edna Maye Loveless, for example, in response to Running's article (cited above) demanded that men and women should not have equal employment opportunities because they are "different" and because women should "choose the greatest of all professions, motherhood" (1972:65). Original SDA understanding of women's obligations as mothers, as advocated early in Adventism's history, not only failed to preclude women's (and mothers') active participation in work deemed necessary to hasten the advent but encouraged such participation. Contemporary response to women "attempting to break into leadership" has, nonetheless, "been condescending at best" (Vasquez 1990:13). Although the exclusion of women from the paid labor force, the institution of unequal wage, benefit, and hiring practices, and the collateral attempt to relegate women exclusively to the domestic sphere are inconsistent with early SDA ideals for women, such practices persist.[9] "For the most part," Adventism's female employees "have served with little recognition": "Their salaries have ordinarily been much less than those of men. They have rarely petitioned for higher responsibility or titles. They have done virtually everything [and] asked virtually nothing" (Allen 1984:48). Although women began, in the 1970s, to enter the Adventist workforce in unprecedented numbers, most fields of employment, including the pastorate, are still dominated by men (see Carroll et al. 1983:50–56).

The disparity between the expectations of Adventist women who prepare for careers within Adventism and gender inequality in SDA employment is cause for disillusionment in many cases: "We educate women right alongside men in our schools. When you educate a person, you empower that person. You give him or her a dream of service for the church. Then we tell women that the ladder they are climbing is much shorter than the one their [male] classmates are climbing" (Flowers 1989:17).[10] Women are often discouraged by the lack of opportunity available to them as Adventist employees and consequently, "the brightest [SDA] young women these days are looking toward the secular world for opportunities in areas like law, business and medicine" (Stafford 1983:32): "Adventist women are giving up on their church. While deeply committed Adventist women feel constrained to use their professional expertise elsewhere, others, despite inequalities, continue in church employ.

Both groups express frustration at not being able to serve their church more fully" (Daffern 1980:43).

Though not unaware of frustration arising from discriminatory employment practices, Adventist leadership chose not to alter wage or hiring practices between the late 1970s and the mid-1980s. Running warned Adventist leadership in 1972 that Adventism should institute a policy of pay equity for female employees before government action became necessary because such policy change would be "good, right and fair" (60). "In recognition of the fact that society is changing," Running insisted (adopting implicitly the presupposition of opponents of gender equality within Adventism; that adherence to changing norms equaled capitulation to secular standards and therefore constituted a fundamental change in Adventism), women in Adventist employ should be allowed equality of opportunity, pay, benefits, and representation in Adventist leadership structures (ibid.:61). Watts, in a 1990 *Review* article, assumed a different premise—that gender discrimination prevalent in Adventism was a result of surrender to dominant social norms. "Many of the actions [taken by Adventist leadership in the late 1980s in an attempt to institute more gender equity in employment] closely parallel social concerns or laws in the United States or Canada. Our *environment* rather than our moral *convictions* seems to have moved us forward. In addition we took some steps only in the wake of unfortunate lawsuits, public demands, or painful confrontations among ourselves" (Watts 1990a:5; emphasis original).

"Secular Feminism" as Opposition: The Silver Case

One such lawsuit, Adventism's most notorious confrontation involving gender inequality in employment, was initiated by a Pacific Press employee, Merikay Silver, who as a married woman did not qualify for head of household status (and therefore received wages equaling about two-thirds of those of her male colleagues completing comparable work).[11] Though Silver originally filed an individual suit, following repeated personal confrontations with press management and no consequent employment policy changes, she agreed to allow the Equal Employment Opportunities Commission (EEOC) to pursue a class action suit on behalf of all female press employees.[12] The suit, which Silver and co-litigant Lorna Tobler eventually won, claimed that the press violated Title VII legislation because: (1) press employee pay was based not on performance but on sex; (2) female press employees were not paid according to the actual job category of the work they completed; (3) women were denied benefits due to the head of household policy; and (4) the press had retaliated against those filing charges of discrimination in an attempt to force them to forfeit attempt at legal remedy (see Dybdahl 1975). In addition, Silver and Tobler challenged the press's practice of placing employees in specific jobs based on sex. While the press had six categories of workers, for example, ranging from hourly workers to managerial and supervisory staff, only two women were employed in the highest three categories, though in the three lowest wage categories almost all employees were women.

Adventist leaders, who considered Adventism, while within the bounds of the law, to be an entity outside of the purview of state control, viewed Silver's suit as a challenge to Adventism's religious liberty.[13] The General Conference argued that all SDA church (institutional) workers are "ministers," that therefore Silver was a "minister," and hence that the dispute between Silver and the press (Adventism) was a matter of "church government and administration . . . beyond the purview of civil authorities" (Dybdahl 1975:49). The press attempted to argue "that this case was not primarily a case of discrimination against women, but rather a case of whether the government had the right to become involved in the internal affairs [of Seventh-day Adventism]" (ibid.). "The entire problem was termed a church controversy which ought to be resolved within the church and according to the doctrine of the church" (ibid.). In order to combat Silver's suit, General Conference leaders insisted that Adventism was hierarchical and thus that Silver's complaint would be more appropriately dealt with within the context of that hierarchy to which she, by her participation in Adventism as a "minister," was subject.[14] The General Conference claimed further that "individual believers, so long as they are parcel of the remnant church . . . must yield in matters of faith, doctrine, practice and discipline to the authority of the whole church speaking through the General Conference" (Welebir 1977b:7). "The church," on the other hand, General Conference president Neal Wilson insisted, "is free to ignore, even to flout, measures which bind all others. . . . The church claims exemption from all civil laws in all its religious institutions; although it seeks accommodation, it draws a line of its own when dealing with Caesar" (ibid.).

The court disagreed, awarding monetary reimbursement not only to Silver and Tobler but eventually to numerous female press employees. Nonetheless, Silver's suit was closely aligned, by opponents, with secular feminism and, consequently, the world. General Conference leaders opposed Silver's suit not only to protect a wage practice which financially benefited Adventism as an employer in relation to its female employees but to prevent the world (in the form of the secular judicial system) from making decisions for the movement. The Silver lawsuit "was one of the first signs that feminism had things to say to the Adventist church about the equality of women that had to be taken seriously," but due to the hostile nature in which the suit was resolved, and the fact that it was adjudicated by a secular institution, the suit did not generally alter attitudes within Adventism with regard to employment equity but instead widely solidified resolve against secular feminism.[15]

Conclusions

Surveys as early as 1981 clearly indicate that Adventists agree overwhelmingly that Adventist "women should have opportunities for job equality" (women, 96 percent yes; men, 88.4 percent yes). In 1985, when the debate concerning the ordination of Adventist women to pastoral work reached the General Conference, "the almost total absence of any women in [General Conference] leadership posts," and therefore the almost total absence of women in decision-making positions, was brought to the attention of the General Conference. Consequently, the conference adopted an affirmative action statement "to urge that 'affirmative action' for the involvement of women in the church be a priority plan with church leadership and to request leaders to use their executive influence to open to women all aspects of the ministry in the church that do not require ordination" (Johnsson 1988:4).[16] In the context of the struggle to share their concerns and, more importantly, to insure equity of opportunity at all levels of participation within Adventism, "several groups of Adventist women have concluded the same thing: women's concerns will not be heard until women themselves have voice and vote where decisions are made" (Watts 1990c:5). Despite this shared sentiment, and despite the General Conference's 1985 call for implementation of affirmative action policies, the number of women elected to leadership positions at the General Conference world headquarters—"post[s] in which they [would serve as] members of the General Conference committee and [have] the right to speak and vote— has not increased" (ibid.).[17]

In 1988 the General Conference expanded its commitment to gender equity, adopting a sexual harassment policy which outlined procedures for reporting incidents and halting offenses. Later, in 1989, Adventist leadership moved further, embracing an equal opportunity for service policy which "commits the NAD to seek qualified women, minorities, and the handicapped as church employees" (Watts 1990c:5). The policy recommends that "promotion, salary and other benefits . . . be given without regard for race, color, gender, national origin, ancestry, physical handicap, age, height, weight, marital status, or prior military service" (ibid.). Efforts to promote equality appear to have had, since their implementation, only limited success.[18] According to one interviewee with substantial experience working in SDA institutions: "Most of the key positions in our church, in our whole church structure, are still carried by men. Associates and assistants are women. [As a result,] often women carry the work without getting paid for it. So in this sense women's salaries may not reflect their contribution[s]. Legally the church must pay men and women equal wages; but the church did not do this until they were made to do it. And disparities persist." She explained further that "Women's wages are unequal in two ways. One is when a woman is doing the work that the man is being paid for—she is an assistant or associate—and making the decisions. The other is when a woman is well qualified to hold a key position and when she is held back because it would be 'inconvenient' [to have a woman in that position]."[19] Although Adventist leadership made an effort in the late 1980s to encourage equity in Adventist employment, policies adopted by the General Conference dealing with gender discrimination in employment apply only within the North American Division, and even there, policies may or may not be enforced depending on local and institutional leadership (Watts 1990c). As Johnsson observed with regard to the position of women in Adventism following the late 1980s policy amendments, "little has changed so far" (1988:4).[20]

Notes

1. Specific statistics regarding the relative numbers of men and women participating in postsecondary education at Adventist colleges and universities between 1920 and 1950 are not available. In order to assess the accuracy of Dasher's observation, I sent letters requesting information concerning the number of male and female enrollees in and graduates from SDA colleges and universities in the NAD between the turn of the century and 1990. Although statistics were not available from the majority of respondents, Southwestern Adventist College and Pacific Union College sent records substantiating Dasher's assertion. Between the turn of the century and 1930, for example, both colleges graduated slightly more female than male students. This proportion decreased after 1930, until in 1950, male graduates far outnumbered female graduates (46:4 at Southwestern). The number of female graduates began to climb during the 1960s and (especially) 1970s, until by 1980, female graduates again slightly outnumbered male graduates (108:105).

2. In a related example, the General Conference voted in 1931 to withdraw furlough privileges from female overseas workers who married indigenous people but not to revoke those of men in similar circumstances.

3. Graybill wrote in 1983 that because Ellen White's position of authority was dependent upon her unique access to visions, Adventist women are "unable to use her career as a model": "Her womanhood as such had nothing to do with her leadership"

(1983:173). Recognizing the validity of Graybill's observation (Adventists regularly note that Ellen White was "chosen" only after two other potential messengers, both men, had refused to serve in the capacity—God, in other words, settled for a woman), I disagree based on fieldwork observation. Female Adventists with whom I spoke did often ($N = 33$) specifically identify Ellen White as either a personal role model or as a role model for Adventist women generally. Stafford, for example, wrote, "certainly Ellen White provides Adventists with a powerful example of a woman who not only did all these things herself [managed to care for her children, ran her households and succeeded in her career], but urged other women to do the same" (1983:33).

4. Debra J. Clark wrote in 1990, "The new decade is bringing unprecedented opportunities for women within [Adventism]" (17).

5. "I . . . feel it my duty to create a fund from my tithe money, to pay these women who are accomplishing just as essential work as the ministers are doing" (White in Haloviak 1988:29; see chapter 9).

6. Stafford noted, for example, "there was a time when my salary was about two-thirds of even the young, beginning male teachers in the department I chaired" (1983:32).

7. Flowers's 1989 "Seventh-day Adventist Women Employees Survey" had a response rate of 47 percent. Forty percent of respondents were members of the North American Division. Respondents ranged in age from thirty-six to fifty years old; 32 percent were unmarried; 50 percent had no dependents; and 50 percent had worked in Adventist employ for at least twenty years (Flowers 1989:15).

8. Seventy-seven percent of respondents indicated that they were employed in order to meet financial needs, though 86 percent of employees surveyed indicated that even if they did not need to work in order to meet financial obligations, they would still choose to pursue a career as an Adventist employee. Fifty-eight percent of employees felt that their careers benefited their family life, while only 14 percent found their wage employment to be a detriment to family life (Flowers 1989:15).

9. In addition, the ideal of domesticity presented to SDA women assumes marriage and the ability of the male partner to provide financially and independently for family members. The number of women adhering to Adventism's official (though changing) ideal for women is so small, according to Stafford, "that to anchor a policy on them is ridiculous" (1983:33).

10. There is some evidence that this disparity may soon become more apparent. Yob's 1988 study of SDA school materials (readers and workbooks) for grades K–8 found that gender stereotypes were frequently embraced by text authors and Yob called for revision of Adventist school materials to more positively and realistically portray women and girls. In a separate examination of similar 1993 materials, I found that gender stereotypes had been largely eliminated from Adventist K–8 readers and textbooks. Indeed, text authors demonstrated conscious effort to question stereotypes and to portray females and males as being equally capable of strength and compassion. In particular, Adventist school readers employed nonsexist language ("firefighters,"

"people build buildings"), portrayed women in nontraditional occupations (such as dentistry and construction), portrayed men doing housework, and featured girls who insisted that "girls can be anything they want; that's the way it is now." While this development is positive, it introduces the possibility that unless SDA employment practices are also altered, there will likely be an increase in frustration among Adventist women in response to employment discrimination.

	Yob 1988	Vance 1993
In texts:		
Girls helpless	88%	50%
Girls victimized or humiliated	70	50
Girls needing help	92	60
Girls creative or inventive	34	41.6
Girls problem-solvers	29	51.4
In illustrations:		
Girls passive	63	51.6
Girls playing sports	5	52

11. In another important case, Loma Linda University agreed in the late 1970s to pay all employees "in accordance with the provisions" of the Fair Labor Standards Act (Welebir 1977a).

12. The Pacific Press and the General Conference Executive Committee took a number of actions to discourage Silver and co-litigant Tobler in their suit. Press managerial staff publicly ridiculed Silver and Tobler, causing other employees to fear expressing public agreement with the suit lest "they would be called names and have fellow workers turn their backs on them, and be embarrassed in public, as happened with Lorna [Tobler] and Merikay [Silver]" (Dybdahl 1975:48).

13. Adventists mistrust government for a number of reasons, including the assumption that the final controversy preceding the advent will involve government coalition with religious bodies that oppose Seventh-day Adventism, as well as historical conflict with the United States government surrounding enforcement of Sunday laws during the late nineteenth and early twentieth centuries.

14. One General Conference response to Silver's suit included amending the *Church Manual* to include the following: "Instigating or continuing legal action against the church or any of its organizations or institutions [is] contrary to Biblical and Ellen G. White counsels." Though the amendment had been considered prior to the press case, it was implemented in response to Silver's suit. Further, as Elvin Benton noted: "The significance of any amendment to the Church Manual cannot be overemphasized. The Church Manual is more than an advisory handbook. It is a rule book that claims the highest earthly credential, setting forth the fundamentals and regulations of the church with the authority of the body's claim to heaven-sent mandate—approval by the General Conference in session" (1975:3; see chapter 3).

15. The General Conference Executive Committee, for example, voted on February 14, 1975, to dismiss Silver and Tobler because in initiating suit the two women had "gone

against scriptural admonition to settle grievances without involving the law." Though both were reinstated following a court order, Silver and Tobler were constantly attacked throughout the suit.

16. As a result of the 1985 affirmative action resolution, Betty Holbrook (who was at the time of the passage of the resolution employed by the General Conference Church Ministries Department) was appointed chair of the Women's Ministries Advisory Committee. (She was succeeded by Karen Flowers in 1988.) Also, Elizabeth Sterndale was invited by the General Conference to attend division officers' meetings and to share women's concerns and problems at those meetings.

17. Between 1980 and 1990, eight women held these decision-making positions; in 1990, four women were elected to such posts, though only one was eligible to sit on the General Conference executive committee (Watts 1990c).

18. In one exception, in 1996, Rose Otis was elected vice president of the North American Division of the General Conference. This is the highest office yet held by an Adventist woman.

19. Other examples of continuing, not explicitly employment related, gender discrimination include: (1) the lack of availability of institutionally provided child care for two-income SDA families (though this problem is slowly beginning to be addressed [Shell 1992:159–60]); and (2) continued, though decreasing, sexism in Adventist advertising. Bull and Lockhart observed in 1989 that women are used frequently, and in some cases sexually, in SDA advertising and that "this display of women is at odds with the advice in Adventist literature which encourages women to be modest and discreet" (187). In one egregious example of the (mis)use of women in SDA advertising, a woman's feet and legs extend upside-down from a large garbage can. The copy reads: "I used to get his attention. Not anymore. I've been dumped. But not for another girl. Would you believe, a book? . . . It's almost more than a girl can compete with. Almost" (*Insight* 1 [10]).

20. Some obvious changes *have* been made with regard to gender related policies. Three women were appointed to the Church Hymnal Committee, which met between 1982 and 1985 and raised concerns about sexist language in the SDA hymnal. Ottilie Stafford, working with the committee to revise the hymnal, made neutral much, though not all, of the previously exclusive language. Though this policy of use of gender inclusive language has not always been implemented, "Concerned feminists in the church are grateful for the commitment to inclusive language that [Adventist publications, especially the *Review,* have] made, at least in policy, if not always in practice" (Yob 1988:35). At its 1990 annual session the General Conference Church Manual Committee also voted to use inclusive (gender neutral) language in all gender references where appropriate.

9

The Struggle for Ordination: Women and the Adventist Ministry

Controversy surrounding the question of whether Adventist women should have the opportunity to be ordained has been the most persistent and pervasive dispute among Adventists (with the possible exception of the dispute concerning the relative degree to which justification and sanctification are necessary for salvation; see chapter 4) in the last decade.[1] Because ordination entails, according to Adventist teaching, public acknowledgment of gifts that have already been divinely bestowed on the ordinee as well as of divine calling for ministerial service, Adventist ordination is not as much a bestowal of gifts or power as a public recognition of gifts. Nonetheless, ordination is the door through which an individual must pass in order to be fully authorized to "act for the church" (Gordon 1985:6; Davidson and MacCarty 1987:31; Haloviak 1988:35).

Ordination: SDA Attitudes

Adventist opinion is generally in opposition to the ordination of women. One 1977 study indicated that 56 percent of NAD Adventists opposed ordination, while 29 percent favored ordination and 15 percent expressed no opinion (in Pearson 1990:167). A 1981 survey, on the other hand, found 74.6 percent of SDA women and 67.7 percent of SDA men in support of the ordination of women (in Daily 1985:256), though a 1985 study indicated 56 percent of Adventists opposed ordination of women while only 29 percent favored ordination and 11 percent were neutral (in Pearson 1990:167).[2]

In part as a result of this widespread disagreement, Adventists on both sides of this controversy have turned to the writings of Ellen White to substantiate differing opinions concerning the propriety of the ordination of women.[3] As proponents of the ordination of women have noted, Ellen White left her children on many occasions for extended periods to carry out her ministry (Graybill 1983:60; Pearson 1990:138–39). Opponents of women's ordination, on the other hand, argue that because Ellen White was never ordained, she must have opposed the idea of the ordination of women generally. Evidence indicates that while White received her ministerial credentials (in 1883 and 1885 with the word "ordained" omitted, and in 1887 with the word "ordained" included) and a ministerial stipend, she was never ordained, though her name appeared in the 1895 General Conference Bulletin with those of eighty other licensed ministers (see Gordon 1985).[4] Nonetheless, despite her powerful public position in early Adventism, when Pauline admonitions that "women keep silent in the churches" were raised (most often by non-Adventists), Ellen White let her male associates respond to critics. Further, Ellen White never advocated full ordination for women in the pastorate (though Daily has asserted that she failed to do so primarily because such a step would have been seen as self-serving and would have served to divide Adventists [Daily 1985:233]). White seems to have refused the laying on of hands because she considered herself to have been ordained by God; ordination by men was therefore unnecessary. Ellen White did argue by 1900 that women "shouldn't be denied professional status," and between 1900 and 1915 White's commitment to broadening opportunities for Adventist women increased in both expression and degree.

Ellen White on Women in the Ministry

Between 1850 and 1860, in adventism's first decade (though prior to legal organization), Ellen White said "virtually nothing about the role of female ministry" within adventism (Daily 1985:228). Regardless, "between 1865, when James White defined the ministry and 1871, [there was] an apparent widening of the SDA ministerial doors to women. They received training and were licensed as ministers" (Haloviak 1988:4). During this time (1860s–70s), Adventist men and women most often evangelized in husband/wife ministerial teams. Ministers didn't pastor a specific congregation (or group of congregations) but traveled constantly, evangelizing in various locals (ibid.:3).

At the 1870 and 1871 General Conference sessions, Ellen White advocated ministerial reform; she urged Adventists to adopt a more beneficent, pastoral type of ministry. At the same time, Adventist leaders, in their attempt to allow only qualified ministers to represent Adventism, instituted a course of study for ministers, which women were encouraged to attend, and instituted a system of wages for ministers, which women received (Haloviak 1988:3–4). At the same time, Ellen White increasingly "began to encourage Adventist women to become gospel workers outside the home" (Daily 1985:222). By the close of the 1870s, Ellen White increased her calls for female participation in Adventism's public work to an unprecedented level. In 1878 she argued that women were better qualified than men to perform a host of tasks which ranged from clerical work to home visitation and personal ministry. She maintained that women could reach a class that male ministers were unable to access effectively and urged women to participate in the "many branches of missionary work" that were being neglected by men (White 1878:190). In 1879, Ellen White wrote that "women can be instruments of righteousness, rendering holy service": "It was Mary who first preached a risen Jesus. . . . If there were twenty women where there now is one, who would make this holy mission their cherished work, we should see many more converted to the truth" (White 1879:2). Indeed, by the late 1870s, Ellen White regularly wrote articles exhorting Adventist women to "extend their missionary work beyond neighborhood welfare work to a more public form of ministry" (in Pearson 1990:140). White castigated Adventist women who used domestic activities as an excuse for ignoring evangelical responsibilities and lamented that Christian sisters were failing to complete the work that she had identified as their duty. Advocating a public role for women in Adventist ministry, White encouraged women to work as Bible instructors (now associate pastors) and as colporteurs (a position used by early Adventists to prepare participants for pastoral work) (Haloviak 1988:15).

The seeming contradiction of White's admonitions, life, and advice are not easily reconciled. White referred to the ministry as a male domain; "on the other hand, [she] called for a greater leadership role for women in the church, and advised individual women who raised questions about public ministry to 'address the crowds whenever you can [and] to teach, counsel, and function as man's equal and co-worker'" (Daily 1985:226). In 1886, White again noted the "superior ability" of women to complete specific work, especially Sabbath school work, and insisted that in Adventist endeavors "Not a hand should be bound, not a soul discouraged, not a voice should be hushed; let every individual labor, privately or publicly, to help forward this grand work. Place the burdens upon men and women of the church, that they may grow by reason of the exercise, and thus become more effective agents in the hand of the Lord for the enlightenment of those who sit in darkness" (White 1895:434).

According to Bert Haloviak, White's understanding of the divine pattern of Adventist evangelism changed before the turn of the century to take a form which more clearly involved and benefited Adventist women (1985:16). While in Australia in 1891, the economic crisis Adventism faced led White to alter her notion of ministry from solely evangelism to evangelism in combination with offers of practical assistance. Termed "Christian help work," this new evangelical approach employed many SDAs not specifically trained as pastors (such as medical practitioners—"medical evangelists") in evangelism, and allowed the ordination of women on an equal basis with men to the work (ibid.:30). Benevolent ministry, or the ministry of caring, articulated by Ellen White in part in an attempt to create a more effective urban evangelizing force, necessitated greater involvement of women in the ministry: "It was the 'ministry of compassion' that naturally brought women to a prominent role in . . . ministerial team efforts. This new style of evangelism, in which Adventist ministers were to visit and care for 'the flock,' rather than just 'sermonize,'" led to increased involvement of women in Adventist ministry and to a more general recognition of women's contributions to pastoral work (Haloviak 1988:23–24).

Ellen White demonstrated her clear approval of women's participation in beneficent pastoring by stating (in 1895) that women involved in this work should be set apart by the laying on of hands and, perhaps more significantly, by insisting repeatedly that the women involved in beneficent pastoring, like their male colleagues, should receive wages from SDA tithe funds, even though Adventist tithes had declined sharply during that period. Adventist women who served as Bible teachers, who instructed other women in missionary/evangelical work, who were medical missionaries, or who were married to ministers and assisted their husbands in ministerial work were all to receive wages from tithing funds, according to White. "Again and again," Ellen White told Adventists, "the Lord has shown me that women teachers are just as greatly needed to do the work *to which he has appointed them* as are men" (in Haloviak 1988:33; emphasis original). White reiterated this sentiment in 1898: "When a great and decisive work is to be done, God chooses men and women to do this work, and it will feel the loss if talents of both are not combined" (White in Pearson 1990:141). By the close of the nineteenth century, "Ellen White clearly considered women as full-fledged ministers in the nineteenth century concept of ministry" (Haloviak 1988:1).

In their attempt to avoid appearing to be similar in any way to Babylon, nineteenth-century Adventists employed traveling (not settled) pastors who constantly moved between gatherings of believers. As this emphasis changed to focus on settled pastoral work (in part in response to James White's concern that Adventism was losing as many believers as it was gaining due to the lack of a consistent source of support for believers), Ellen White encouraged participation by men and women in ministry. She continued to discourage "laws and rules specified by men" and to insist that "There must be no fixed rules; our work is a progressive work, and there must be room left for methods to be improved upon" (White in Haloviak 1985:31). At the same time she held that "this question [of women's participation in the ministry] is not for men to settle. The Lord has settled it" (White 1946:493). Women were, White maintained, called of God in the same way that men were called of God. White was less concerned whether women should be ordained than that women could and *should* minister:

> God calls for earnest women workers, workers who are prudent, warmhearted, tender and true to principle. He calls for persevering women who will take their minds from self and their personal convenience, and will center them on Christ, speaking words of truth, praying with the persons to whom they can gain access, laboring for the conversion of souls. (White in Watts 1992:46)

> The Lord instructed me that our sisters who have received a training that has fitted them for positions of responsibility are to serve with faithfulness and discernment in their calling, using their influence wisely and, with their brethren in the faith, obtaining an experience that will fit them for still greater usefulness. (White 1952:158)

> There are women who should labor in the gospel ministry. In many respects they would do more good than the ministers who neglect to visit the flock of God. (White in Pearson 1990:141)

White was far from being alone in her support of women's ministerial work. Her colleagues regularly published articles like the following (by Robbins in the December 8, 1859, *Review and Herald*): "We are informed on the authority of divine revelation [that] male and female are one in Jesus Christ; that in relation to which they both stand to him, the distinction is completely broken down as between Jew and Gentile, bond and free. . . .The mind of the female is certainly susceptible to all those sensibilities, affections and improvements which constitute the Christian character" (1859:22).

Women, licensed as ministers, were active in Adventist ministry in the movement's early years, serving as Bible workers, as administrative officials, and in husband/wife evangelistic partnerships.[5] The ministerial license, which Adventist leaders granted women beginning in 1868, "was taken very seriously by the denomination since it was seen as the route to the full ordination and reception of ministerial credentials" (Haloviak 1984:52). During the 1870s, strict guidelines were established to ensure that only the most qualified applicants received ministerial licenses and served as representatives of Seventh-day Adventism. The focus of Adventism's official ministry, throughout the 1870s and 1880s, was evangelism, and in order to best accomplish that task "the Adventist church encouraged women to enter the ministry, and made it relatively easy for them to do so" (Haloviak 1987:34).

Although early Adventist women did not baptize or officiate at weddings (only ordained pastors did), women were fully engaged in the primary task of Adventist ministerial efforts—evangelism—and received payment from SDA tithe funds which "Ellen White considered reserved for the official ministry" (Haloviak 1987:34). White often expressed her disappointment that women engaged in ministerial work were not paid fair and equitable salaries and noted that:

> I feel it my duty to create a fund from my tithe money, to pay these women who are accomplishing just as essential work as the ministers are doing, and this tithe I will reserve for work in the same line as that of ministers. . . . I know that the faithful women should be paid wages as is considered proportionate to the pay received by ministers. They carry the burden of souls and should not be treated unjustly. These sisters are giving their time to educating those newly come to the faith and hire their own work done, and pay those who work for them. All these things must be adjusted and set in order, and justice be done to all. (White in Haloviak 1984:58)

Between 1870 and 1900, at least twenty Adventist women received ministerial licenses from their local conferences. Though they were not ordained, "they followed the same path [toward ordination] as that followed by men" and early Adventist leaders struggled with the question of whether to ordain women (Haloviak 1988:7). In 1878, James White asked Stephen Haskell, an SDA authority on Scripture, to assess the biblical role of women in order that Adventist leadership might better be able to determine the appropriate positions Adventist women should fill. Haskell's analysis led him to conclude that the women of the Bible played a major role in early Christianity, baptizing converts and completing other ministerial functions. As women continued to become more involved in Adventist ministry (especially during the 1880s), pressure mounted within the movement to allow the ordination of women. At its 1881 annual session, the General Conference considered the following resolution: "Resolved, that females possessing the necessary qualifications to fill the position, may, with perfect propriety, be set apart by ordination to the work of the Christian ministry." The resolution was considered, tabled, and never raised again, though reasons for its failure are not specifically known. Although Ellen White was, according to Haloviak, "ready during the 1890s for the full ordination of women in the ministry of the church," she failed to support the General Conference's ordination resolution, or even to attend the 1881 General Conference session due to the recent death of her husband, James. Though Ellen White's role in discussions concerning the question of women's ordination in the early movement was "extremely influential," her hesitancy to clearly support or oppose the ordination of women, in conjunction with her repeated admonitions that women's most important work was as mothers, and her frequent, outspoken support for Adventist women serving in public capacities, has fueled the ambiguity and controversy which continue to surround the issue.

The Contemporary Struggle for Ordination

Instead of disappearing, this controversy has, in recent decades, burgeoned into a divisive and, for many, defining issue for Adventism. Although SDA women had disappeared from leadership positions by the 1950s, during the 1970s, as women in North American society generally began to question roles, positions, and options available to them, Adventists demonstrated "renewed concern for the role of women in the church" (Roberts 1982:2). In its first contemporary official attempt to determine whether women should be ordained, Adventism's Biblical Research Institute (BRI) met with Adventist scholars at Camp Mohaven (Ohio) to discuss the role of women in Adventism. The group recommended that Adventist leadership fully support women in ordination, evangelical efforts, Adventist leadership, and the home. Although these recommendations were approved by two General Conference annual counsels, "they were accepted in principle" only, and "significant limitations were imposed to restrict" the ordination of women (Yob 1988:31). The BRI subsequently made available a series of papers by various SDA authors and academics insisting that no biblical injunction against the ordination of women existed and that women should be fully ordained to pastoral positions.

In 1973, following the Camp Mohaven meeting, the General Conference established an ad hoc committee on the role of women in the church and the General Conference annual council voted that "continued study be given to the theological soundness of the election of women to local church offices which require ordination," and that "in areas receptive to such action there be continued recognition of the appropriateness of appointing [but not ordaining] women to pastoral-evangelical work." The following year the annual council requested that the "President's Executive Advisory . . . arrange for a continuing study of the theological and practical implications of ordination of women to the gospel ministry." The 1975 spring council urged caution "on the matter of the ordination of women to the gospel ministry" and asserted that "the world church [non-NAD Adventists] is not yet ready to move forward [and ordain women]" (Daffern 1980:40, 41).

While the General Conference continued to study and discuss whether women should be ordained, congregations supporting the ordination of women began to take steps to place women in positions of pastoral leadership.

In 1972, Josephine Benton was ordained an elder in the Brotherhood SDA Church (Washington, D.C.), with Columbia Union Conference and Potomac Conference presidents officiating. Following her ordination, Benton served in a pastoral capacity with six other staff pastors in the Tacoma Park Church (Maryland).[6] Other Adventist women also began to train for and serve in pastoral positions following continued conclusion by General Conference study committees that there was "no basis in the Bible or in the writings of Ellen White for withholding ordination from women" (Daffern 1980:40). In 1977, Adventist leaders created a category, associate in pastoral care, through which those who participated on pastoral staffs but could not be ordained (women) could be recognized. An internship for associates in pastoral care was established in 1979 and implemented beginning in 1980, and women used the opportunity provided them by the internship to prepare to serve as pastors. One 1981 survey found that at that time, nine women were serving as associates in pastoral care, five were serving as pastors or associate pastors (not in the associates in pastoral care program), and three were serving as pastors or associate pastors holding missionary licenses or credentials (Roberts et al. 1982). (No women held ministerial licenses at that time.) The same survey found that while thirty-three women had been trained in pastoral work and graduated from Andrews University seminary program between 1976 and 1981, only eight had been placed in pastoral-type positions (ibid.).

Despite continued findings by General Conference committees that prohibition of women's ordination had no scriptural basis, the General Conference persisted in denying the full participation of women in Adventism.[7] Again, local conferences supporting ordination of women took steps to grant women the authority to perform ordinances for which ordination was normally a prerequisite. In 1984, three Adventist women in the Potomac conference baptized converts. Although the Church Manual makes provision for nonordained persons to baptize individuals in the absence of an ordained minister, and although unordained Adventist men had been permitted to baptize and perform marriage services for members since the late 1970s, General Conference officers attending the congregations in which the baptisms were held protested strongly against women performing baptism (Nembhard 1983a).[8] After three ensuing baptisms by women, the General Conference intervened and the Potomac Conference agreed to desist further such actions on the condition that the General Conference would reconsider its position on the ordination of women (see Branson with Gainer 1983; Nembhard 1983a; Potomac Conference 1983; Kuehnert 1987:54; Perez-Greek 1992). Following the Potomac Conference's compromise with the General Conference, General Conference officers advised the divisions that they were "free to make provision . . . for the election and ordination of women as local church elders," but reiterated their opposition to the full ordination of women in pastoral capacities and appointed another committee to study the issue of ordination of women (Johnsson 1985:5).

The NAD committee appointed to study the role of female pastors recommended at the 1985 General Conference session that associates in pastoral care be allowed to baptize individuals and solemnize marriages (Coffin 1985). Noting the discrepancy between the practice of allowing unordained men, but not women, to perform baptisms and marriages, committee members stated that they found no scriptural injunction against allowing women to officiate at such ceremonies. North American Division conference presidents, especially of the Columbia Union, Potomac, and Southeastern conferences, strongly supported the committee's findings. In 1986, Loma Linda University pastoral leaders declared that: "[Adventism's] policy of not allowing women to officiate at baptisms and weddings while allowing unordained men to do so has no theological or pragmatic basis, and is therefore discriminatory against women. This discrimination is morally unacceptable" (Davis 1985:26). The Southeastern California Conference also noted pay differentials existing between men and women serving in pastoral capacities, called such discrepancy reprehensible, and voted to institute equitable wage and equal employment opportunity policies.[9] Later, NAD officials agreed, requesting that the General Conference rectify "discrepancies between the responsibilities of and remuneration of licensed ministers [men] and commissioned ministers [women]" (Kuehnert 1987:51).

In recognition of increasing discrepancy between General Conference policies and growing participation of women in pastoral service, the October Annual Council of the General Conference voted in 1989 to accept the following General Conference special commission on ordination proposal: "(a) We do not recommend authorization for women to be ordained to the gospel ministry. (b) Those who have, without regard to gender, been recognized as commissioned ministers or licensed ministers may perform essentially the same functions as an ordained minister to the gospel in the churches to which they are assigned, subject to division authorization of this provision" (Adams 1990a:4). Apparently attempting to allow women to participate in the pastoral role (at least at the local level) while at the same time continuing to restrict ordination by gender, the General Conference's solution "was an accommodation—a compromise" but fully satisfied neither opponents or proponents of women's ordination (ibid.).

In a continuing effort to achieve ordination of women, the Ohio Conference Executive Committee voted 20 to 1 in early 1989 to request permission of its Union to ordain a woman serving as a pastor in the conference. The Columbia Union approved the request in 1990, and in the same year, the Pacific Union Executive Committee (the largest union in the NAD) concurred with the Columbia Union's decision and urged the General Conference to remove remaining barriers to women's ordination: "We strongly encourage the General Conference to eliminate gender as a consideration for ordination to gospel ministry. We endorse the ordination of qualified women to the gospel ministry in divisions, unions and conferences where deemed helpful and appropriate" (Cassano 1987:11). In June of 1990, North American Division presidents ($N = 9$) voted unanimously to endorse the Columbia Union's statement of support for the ordination of women (ibid.:12).

General Conference leaders, concerned at the increasing divisiveness surrounding the ordination issue, used the 1990 General Conference session to urge NAD leaders to delay action on ordination resolutions and to vote to continue to restrict ordination based on gender. While NAD leaders expressed strong support for ordination of women, the world church, especially representatives from developing countries, vehemently opposed such a move (Stirling 1990). Numerous General Conference delegates voiced fears of a division within Seventh-day Adventism if the General Conference voted to allow women to be ordained. Others, primarily NAD delegates, expressed fear of continuing and perhaps increased apostasy if Adventism failed to allow women to participate fully as ordained pastors in SDA congregations, divisions, and unions.[10]

Disturbed by the General Conference's continuing reluctance to fully incorporate women into the Adventist ministry, NAD leaders conveyed their disappointment at the General Conference's failure to act in what they deemed an ethical manner and expressed regret at not being able to act in accordance with their consciences in their congregations, divisions, and unions.[11] The Adventist Women's Institute, in an attempt to demonstrate clear, tangible, and notable opposition to the 1990 General Conference's decision not to ordain women, created an escrow fund to which similarly disconcerted members could contribute tithes.[12] As Fay Blix of the Adventist Women's Institute explained, "we've threatened this for a long time, and we are finally realizing that the bottom line is green" (quoted in "Adventist Women" 1990:1160).

Despite actions of the Adventist Women's Institute and others, the General Conference remains resistant to ordination of women. In 1995, at the fifty-sixth

General Conference session, North American and northern European delegates in support of ordination of women were outvoted overwhelmingly by world delegates (673 to 1,482) who opposed ordination of women (see Scriven 1995).

Far from settling the issue, however, the vote served to inspire disappointed NAD delegates to action at the local level. An enthusiastic Sabbath school class discussion at the Sligo Church in California shortly following the 1995 vote led members to propose the ordination of women to the local church board where it passed by a vote of 138 to 21. Although the Potomac Conference Executive Committee voted against granting women ordained ministers' licenses when Sligo brought the issue before them, the congregation resolved to go forward with the action. On September 23, 1995, three Adventist women, Penny Shell, Norma Osborn, and Kendra Haloviak, participated in an ordination service at Sligo (see Zervos 1995). In December of 1995, La Sierra University Church voted, in the face of opposition from the Southeastern California Conference, to ordain Halcyon Wilson and Madelynn Jones-Haldeman, and the Walla Walla College Church adopted a resolution to approve Leslie Bumgardner for ordination (see Bartlett 1995). Another woman, Margot Pitrone, was ordained on July 6, 1996, in Orange County, California (see Dietrich 1996). Despite widespread and enthusiastic support for these ordinations at the congregational level, regional conferences opposed the actions and it is unclear what their ultimate effect will be.

Opposition to/Support for Ordination of Women to the Adventist Ministry

Opponents of the ordination of women in SDA pastoral work (most often also opponents of women's *participation* in SDA pastoral work) base their opposition to the ordination of women on notions of gender, sexuality, and family not inconsistent with Adventist ideals (discussed in chapters 5 and 6). Opponents clearly distinguish appropriate spheres of gender behavior and responsibility and conclude that ordination, though compatible with the ideal masculine sphere of activity, is inconsistent with ideals and behaviors appropriate for women. Most specifically, those who oppose the ordination of women insist that to incorporate women in Adventist pastoral work would remove women from the home and thereby "threaten the home," which is "primary" to the Adventist "way of life": "A neglect on the part of woman to follow God's plan in her creation, an effort to reach for the important positions which He has not qualified her to fill, leaves vacant the position that she could fill to acceptance" (Lee nd.:15, 16). The ideal of woman as mother, homemaker, and wife precludes, according to this position, ordination, which would disturb "the delicate balance of male/female roles as demonstrated and taught in the scriptures," which, in turn, would disrupt "the well-being of the family, the church, society and the ultimate happiness of God's children" (Rivers 1985:7–8). Any blurring of distinction between well-defined ideals of masculinity and femininity (such as the ordination of women) would, according to opponents, lead to the breakdown of the family and of society: "The breakdown of the family structure as God ordained it has produced a sick society, ridden with emotional problems, weakened wills and characters and sexual perversions" (ibid.:7).

As E. Wilbur Bock and Jackson W. Carroll have observed, "the ministry 'has not only been defined as masculine, but as sacredly masculine'" (in Carroll et al. 1983:9). Because Adventist opponents of the ordination of women so precisely distinguish between gender appropriate norms, and because they so closely identify pastoral work with masculinity, some are unable to differentiate between masculinity and pastoral work, and therefore conclude that women who pursue ordination, "with very few exceptions, . . . desire . . . not to be priests but men—though naturally they [are] unaware of this fact" (Ball 1985:49). Indeed, opponents maintain that if women would simply accept their true natures, they would lose any desire to participate in public ministry; women will "lose their zeal and indeed their interest in this cause when they come to know themselves better" (ibid.).[13]

In addition to questioning the gender identification of women who seek ordination, opponents have consistently and specifically identified an explicit connection between attempts to secure equal access to ordination and secular feminism. Bryan Ball, for example, "fears that the ordination of women is in part, and without recognition, a capitulation to the secular feminist movement": "The move to the ordination of women is unquestionably coming to the church at this time in its history as a result of the pressure of contemporary society" (Ball 1985:50). Those opposing women's ordination claim that their interpretation of Scripture reaffirms divine meaning while Christian feminists reinterpret (and wrongly interpret) Scripture (Bacchiocchi 1987). Christian feminists, they insist, have adopted a liberal theology which is out of keeping with traditional Adventism, and SDAs should therefore be suspect of those seeking the ordination of women (Ball 1985). To those who oppose the ordination of women, "to ordain women as ministers would mean yielding to modern secular pressure" and capitulation to worldly standards (Durand 1990:5).[14] In the same way that feminists are identified by many Adventists as attempting to move women inappropriately beyond their proper realm, opponents of women's ordination accuse those seeking ordination of women of attempting to advance personal interests that are incompatible with those of Adventism as a whole: "I have observed over a number of years . . . that an unhealthy high percentage of the ladies who advocate women's ordination to the ministry appear to give the unfortunate impression of being too eager to demonstrate their capabilities and their equality, and to claim their 'rights'" (Ball 1985:47). "The urge to advance oneself on the basis of one's rights or one's ability is clearly contrary to the concept of ministry as it is set forth in scripture" (ibid.).[15] "The real question," according to opponents, is not whether women are equally qualified, talented, or able to serve as pastors, "but whether God has 'called' women to ministry" (ibid.:48).[16] Because primary contemporary SDA ideals of womanhood discourage participation in wage labor, they also, according to opponents, preclude pastoral work. If women were to be ordained, opponents conclude, the line clearly demarcating gender would be blurred. Other Adventist beliefs and practices would concomitantly be threatened; the "ordinance of humility, the distinction between clean and unclean foods, tithing, even the Sabbath [might] all be argued against" (ibid.:51). In this way, opponents not only equate the ordination of women with secular pressure but perceive the ordination of women as diminishing those beliefs and practices which allow Adventism to maintain a distinct identity, and therefore conclude that the ordination of women, or even the full and equal participation of women in Adventism's public ministry, would irrevocably alter Seventh-day Adventism: "If we have female ordination then . . . we contemplate a major shift in the nature of Adventism . . . the change will not stop with the ordination of women. It cannot, if the fundamental nature of the church and the basis of its theological statements are changed" (ibid.:52).

Writing in support of the ordination of women to pastoral work, on the other hand, proponents note that the ordination of women to pastoral work is important as it conveys that the congregation, the division, the conference, and the union trust the ordinee. In addition, "ordination is access to decision-making power in the church"; conference, union, and General Conference presidents must be ordained so "withholding ordination from women ministers guarantees that they will be excluded from 'line' administration in the church" (Daffern 1980:42). Authors have noted that the claim "that liberal theologians, critical Bible scholars and/or secular feminists have influenced those who favor women's ordination," is "of course, clearly unfair": "No issue can be decided on the basis of who else takes the same position" (Brunt 1985:56).[17] Other writers have questioned the assumption that advocates of the ordination of women are submitting to secular pressures, wondering instead (especially in light of Adventism's history of more active participation by women in public ministry) if cultural conditioning has "instead been in the minds of theologians who for millennia have interpreted scripture with a negative bias toward women" (Neall 1986:54).

Instead of focusing on strict interpretation of gender ideals, those who advocate the ordination of women (such as Haloviak) often attempt to uncover the history of women's contributions to Adventism, especially prior to the 1950s, and to demonstrate that "ordination of women to full gospel ministry is called for by both the historical heritage of the Seventh-day Adventist Church and by the guidance of God through the ministry of Ellen G. White" (Haloviak 1984:52). Proponents also find support in biblical writings, arguing against a literal interpretation of Pauline injunctions and calling for sociohistorical contextual interpretation of Scripture (as did James White and other early Adventist leaders): "We must see how the basic principles and issues intersect with the circumstances of our time. This means asking if we are in line with the direction that the Bible leads, not just with its specific practices. A literal hermeneutic will not do" (Brunt 1985:56). Advocates insist that opponents of the ordination of women use the Bible to incorrectly support a God-Christ/man-woman model of hierarchy, and that they do so by using scripture selectively and inconsistently (see ibid.:57). They have observed, for example, that a consistent interpretation of the argument that because Christ chose only male apostles, only men may be ordained, would lead one to the conclusion that because Christ chose only Jewish apostles, only Jews may be ordained (ibid.). Further, advocates have noted that consistent interpretation of the idea that women cannot be ordained because the world church is not ready would lead one to conclude also that practices in which non-NAD Adventists engage, such as polygyny, should be adopted by NAD Adventists (Branson 1984:4).

In opposition to those who conclude that the ordination of women would threaten Adventism's very nature, advocates of women's ordination argue that to deny women the opportunity to be ordained weakens Adventism. Proponents generally agree that "freeing women to serve society and the church [through ordination] as equals to men will liberate us all" (Londis 1987:38) and indicate to Adventism's female membership that "they not only have equal standing to men, but that their God-given gifts, possible contributions, and particular viewpoints are recognized, valued, and utilized by the church" (Yob 1988:49). According to a number of proponents, Adventism has been and continues to be affected negatively by the refusal to allow women to participate fully in administrative, institutional, and pastoral work: "A church that accepts the gospel commission as a serious challenge and has a vision of a worldwide labor can no longer afford to limit its recognition of particular gifts to only half its membership" (Gordon 1985:12). As long as women are ineligible for ordination they are barred from certain leadership positions: "Because women are excluded from ordination they are also excluded from other roles for which they are well suited, such as editors, administrators, and members of certain decision-making groups" (Yob 1988:30).[18] In a less tangible manner, advocates argue, failure to ordain women weakens Adventism—"even the perception of inequality is devastating to Adventism if it hopes to promote a model of liberation for all people" (Londis 1987:38).[19]

Informants' Perceptions of Women's Role in Public Ministry

Contemporary Adventists demonstrate little familiarity with either historical roles of women within the movement or the context of changes in those roles. When asked about the evolution of women's activities in the movement since "early Adventism" (1850s–1915), informants agreed almost unanimously ($N =$ 47) that Adventist women "have become much more active in the church, mostly in public ministry just in the last two decades" (1970s and 1980s). Though interviewees emphasized different aspects of women's perceived burgeoning involvement in public ministry (some emphasized specific positions to which women may now be appointed, while others noted a general increase in public religious activity by women), they agreed, with only three exceptions, that "women are much more in leadership now" and that "that was never the case in the early days of the church."

Informants, overwhelmingly unaware of the active role played by Adventist women prior to the 1950s and, more especially, prior to the 1920s and 1930s, insisted repeatedly in interviews that "since the 1970s women have taken [on] much more leadership," and that although "Ellen White was a lay minister [and] . . . very active—a leader," "other women stayed at home." Women, informants agreed, were occupied solely with "caring for their children, cooking, cleaning house" and "making candles," and "weren't at all involved in the activities of ministry or missionary work." "Women didn't do the work of the church, that was left up to the men."

Furthermore, informants identified what they perceived to be increasingly prominent positions of SDA women (since the 1970s) with specific changes in secular society (particularly the feminist ["Women's Liberation"] movement), though no association was made by informants between the previous gender prescriptions and corresponding secular norms and expectations (i.e., proscription of wage labor and public activities by women during the 1950s and 1960s). Instead, interviewees agreed that "the role of Adventist women in the church has changed along with the role of women in society"; "[Contemporary] women are more educated, they make a larger contribution to the church and to society." Both interviewees who supported and those who opposed the perceived "increasing visibility" of "women in leadership and ministry" (with the exceptions noted above) agreed that women have only recently gained access to positions of authority and leadership within Adventism (since the 1970s) and that change resulted because "the world forced the church to change its attitude toward women." "Women have taken much more leadership" and "women are more career-oriented" in recent decades, informants agreed, because "social change has imposed itself on Adventism in terms of women's place in the church": "Social changes have really conspired to bring this about because Ellen White always wanted women to be in the home. Women should be in the home." Informants, regardless of differing opinions concerning the appropriate roles of women in the family, religion, and society generally, overwhelmingly concurred that SDA women have become involved, since the 1970s, and especially the 1980s, in evangelical and ministerial work "in a way that they never were before": "This involvement is new. It is a dramatic shift from the original days of the church when women were basically—with the exception of Mrs. White, of course—not involved." "Women have become involved in a major way now that they never were in the past. Women used to be just in the home, never [involved] in the church's work."

Informants, again overwhelmingly ($N = 45$), directly associated this perceived increasing (and heretofore absent) participation as resulting concurrently with, and largely as a consequence of, secular pressures, most specifically pressures resulting from the secular feminist movement or "Women's Lib[eration]": "When women in the world, women's libbers, for example, started making noise about 'rights' and all that, that is when some Adventist women (a minority of them, I think) started clamoring for ordination and things." One male interviewee linked "the fight for women's ordination" and perceived increased involvement of Adventist women in leadership, ministry, and evangelism generally with a broader agenda for social change. Specifically, he said that Adventist women attempting to secure positions of leadership "are connected with all of them in the world pushing for 'rights'—the blacks, the women, Indians—all of them are trying to get special rights so that it's gotten so the white male is the minority." Informants generally perceived Adventist women as having used secular pressures to secure, or at least inspire, movement toward more active participation by women in Adventist ministerial, employment, evangelical, and leadership efforts.

Though perceived changes in expectations of, and opportunities available to, Adventist women were attributed to secular forces, interviewees agreed (though less consistently [N = 39]) that SDA men have also been introduced to changed gender expectations, especially in the last two decades, but insisted that those changes have arisen in response to "changes in women's roles." Whereas women were often thought to be "too competitive with men," contemporary SDA men were portrayed by informants as relinquishing leadership and authority in order to respond to demands made by women. (One informant said: "I feel that sometimes [SDA women] are getting so liberated that they are trying to push the men out. I know that the men have been the ones that have been leading the church and doing these things for years and years.") "Men," informants generally agreed (N = 46) "have always been the leaders," though men are, informants felt, "becoming more accepting of women doing things." In short, informants held that "men's positions" have changed "in connection with the changes in woman's [sic] role. Men are more understanding and tolerant [now] of women in higher positions." Seventh-day Adventist men, according to informants, "are sharing responsibility more. And decision-making . . ." Men are "letting women do more things" and consequently, some informants felt (N = 11), "the effectiveness of the men has gone down as the women take leadership."

Just as there was little recognition by informants of women's prior involvement in SDA ministerial, medical, publishing, evangelical, or educational work or leadership, informants were, with few (N = 2) exceptions, unaware of Ellen White's and early *Review and Herald* admonitions that men be "housebands" and participate actively in housework and care of children. Instead, informants identified men's contribution to housework as a modern expectation, for which Adventism had no precedent, arising in response to women's changing roles and responsibilities in Adventism, and especially in the paid labor force. Thus informants identified not only the controversy surrounding the ordination of women but also the related changes in gender specific expectations as having no root in Adventism but as resulting from secular change. This being the case, those informants opposed to the ordination of women, or to any changes in ideals prescribed for Adventist women, most often substantiated their opinions by citing historical reference to Adventism's forebears. Proponents, on the other hand, were left (with three exceptions) to justify their support of ordination and changing gender ideals by citing abstract ethical and secular philosophical, rational, and intellectual arguments. In this way, informants, unaware of specific components of SDA history, accepted a vision of the past more consistent with Adventist gender ideals promulgated in the 1950s than in the 1850s (or 1860s, 1870s, 1880s, etc.) and attempted to understand modern events from the perspective of that understanding.

Women and Ministry: Survey Results

Without question, the most immediate effect of Adventist understanding of the propriety or impropriety of women's service in public leadership positions is found in the impact that such understanding has on women who attempt to secure and serve in these positions. Most prominently, such understanding influences the experiences of women who serve in pastoral capacities. In an attempt to gauge perceptions and experiences of Adventist women serving in pastoral positions, and to contrast those perceptions and experiences with similar responses of men serving in comparable positions, I have completed a survey of pastors serving in the NAD.

The data on which this analysis is based come from a 1994 survey of all women serving as pastors or associate pastors in the North American Division ($N = 30$) and a simple random sample of men serving in comparable positions ($N = 60$). The North American Division of the Office of Women in Ministry assisted in attaining names and addresses of female respondents, while the SRS sample of male respondents was drawn from the 1994 SDA directory. A larger sample of male respondents was attained in order to draw valid comparisons with the relatively small number of women serving in pastoral capacities. Follow-up procedures yielded a usable survey response rate of 80 percent ($N = 24$) from female subjects and 75 percent ($N = 45$) from male subjects. In addition to specific gender differences in education and employment discussed below, the majority of male respondents held positions as pastors (93 percent), while the majority of female respondents were associate pastors (58 percent). Both male and female respondents ranged in age from 29 to 47 years, but male respondents had a mean age of 44.75 years and female respondents a mean age of 38.6 years. Female respondents were more likely to serve in large metropolitan churches as part of a pastoral staff (81 percent), while male respondents more often served as senior pastors of churches in smaller cities (60 percent).

Survey results demonstrate that women who pursue the pastorate via the traditional Adventist route (i.e.: [1] an undergraduate theology/religion major at an Adventist college or university; [2] sponsorship by an Adventist conference; [3] seminary training at Andrews University; and [4] employ in an Adventist congregation) face gender specific barriers. Although women reported aspiring to the pastorate for reasons identical to those cited by male respondents (primarily, they felt "called" to the ministry), female respondents reported less support from parents, pastors, and peers for their commitment to pastor (see figure 8). Several female respondents noted specifically that they did not *choose* to pastor: wrote one, "It was not something I 'chose' . . . it is how the Lord has led." Despite feeling called to the ministry, 25 percent (N = 6) of Adventist women noted that following the initial decision to pastor, a parent or peer attempted to dissuade the respondent from pursuing such a course. One respondent noted that she "received a direct call from God during my freshman year in college as an answer to my prayers for God's direction. God woke me up in the middle of the night for several weeks in succession, and gave me the same inner conviction—I needed to take a theology major. When I expressed this to my roommate, she took me to a counselor on campus who urged me to change my major." In contrast, no male respondents reported attempts by parents, peers, pastors, or others to discourage participation in the SDA pastorate.

More significantly, as female respondents persisted in preparation for the Adventist pastorate, most often (58 percent [N = 14]) by entering Andrews University seminary, they were confronted by an absence of female peers and faculty role models. Indeed, Andrews University seminary is so skewed by gender as to be classified, according to Rosabeth Kanter, as a uniform group— a group composed of only one significant social type (men). The Andrews University seminary faculty is overwhelmingly male (ranging from a male: female ratio of 30:1 in the 1970s to 40:4 in the 1990s) and respondents reported attending seminary in classes with a male:female ratio of between 450:1 and 450:7. Kanter insists that such skewed underrepresentation encourages

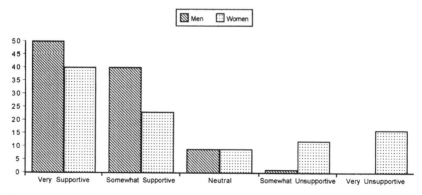

Figure 8. Relative Distribution of Responses to Men and Women Entering the Pastorate

marginalization of and ambivalence toward women (1977:207). Forty-six percent of respondents who attended Andrews University agreed. Female respondents expressed a sense of being excluded from social activities (83 percent [N
= 20]), fear that upon graduation they had little hope of finding employment
in the pastorate (75 percent [N = 18]), "fear of speaking up in class" (25 percent [N = 6]), a sense of having to work particularly diligently in order to
"prove" their ability (17 percent [N = 4]), and the assumption, on the part of
male seminarians, that they were "husband hunting" (8 percent [N = 2]). Sev-
enty-three percent of male respondents, on the other hand, reported that there
was "no difference" between the experiences of male and female seminarians.
Of those male respondents who noted gender differences, 42 percent cited "no
clear future in ministry" for female seminarians (N = 5), 33 percent noted lack
of peer companionship for female seminarians (N = 4), and 33 percent observed the scarcity of female role models in the Andrews University seminary
faculty (N = 4).

The most tangible evidence of gender disparity noted by respondents was
in pastoral employment. While all male respondents were employed prior to
leaving seminary, female respondents, despite equivalent overall academic
records, cited protracted, difficult, and often unsuccessful attempts to procure
employment. Male respondents noted the ease with which they attained spon-
sors and subsequent employment. The following descriptions are typical of
those offered by male respondents:

> I have been very blessed in that I have always been called to the various posts I've
> served. I've never had to send out letters asking for employment.

> Upon graduation from [an] Adventist college with a major in Theology, I was spon-
> sored by a conference ([in] my home area) to attend seminary and then serve that
> conference.

> I was interviewed in seminary by three conferences. I accepted and was sponsored.
> I still work for [this conference]. I had no difficulties securing employment.

> [I] was extended a call before completing college.

> I went to seminary and got called from there.

> I made no attempts [to secure employment]. I received a call.

> Jesus open[ed] the doors. Very little effort on my part was needed.

While four female respondents also noted the ease with which they secured
(associate) pastoral positions, 83 percent of female respondents (N = 20) cited
resistance, particularly on the part of local conferences, boards, elders, and
congregations to hiring a woman as pastor, and all female respondents indi-

cated that Adventist women generally face more difficulty than SDA men in procuring pastoral positions. The following experiences are representative of female respondents' attempts to secure pastoral positions:

> In seminary [a] conference talked of hiring me . . . but [a General Conference leader] was afraid I might baptize someone if God blessed my ministry (God forbid). So they called and asked [a local conference leader] to sign a contract saying I'd preach no time in his church. I raised concern to [the General Conference president] (they already had one lawsuit in the works) and a call was arranged to another conference.

> Placement in the last eight years has been extremely difficult in that [my] conference is allowing local churches to "choose" pastors and no one wants to choose a woman.

> Nine months of rejection letters. Only intervention by a personal friend on my behalf at the conference level . . . brought a job offer.

> I was an undergraduate religion major. The guys in my class were told when the conference personnel would be on campus for interviews. Since they were not used to calling the females, I was not informed. This was corrected and there was an apology. During the interviews I was asked if I wanted to be a Bible worker. No, I didn't. Some also had suggestions of men I could marry so I could be a pastor's wife. I wanted to be a pastor. So I was not offered a call in the regular route.

> The largest church in our conference—I was asked by [the] senior [pastor] to come. Board and elders were opposed—not desirous of having a "female."

> Many doors were closed to me based on my lack of ordination. Churches won't even consider me because I'm female even though my gifts match their needs.

In addition to encountering difficulty in securing pastoral positions, female respondents noted that they experience wage inequality as (associate) pastors. While all male respondents indicated that they received standard full-time wages in their pastoral capacities, 42 percent ($N = 10$) of female respondents reported that they have been paid half salary for a significant period of time (at least one year), and 17 percent ($N = 4$) reported receiving less than half salary for a year or more in their pastoral capacities. Twenty-five percent ($N = 6$) of female respondents observed that accepting lower than standard pastoral wages was, for them, a prerequisite of employment.

> I wanted to be a pastor [but] was not offered a call. . . . I was hired as a task force worker to work as a campus chaplain at a boarding school. They provided room and board and $15/week. . . . At the end of my first year I was hired on a [half] salary to do full-time work (my choice). . . . Money was scarce so after two years I asked to work as an assistant Chaplain in campus ministries and manage the office. . . . The

person who negotiated my salary said the goal was to have me do full-time Chaplain's work. . . . They couldn't pay me the full time rate—but hoped to move there. Two years later things hadn't changed and there was no likelihood that they would. I then accepted a two and one-half year assignment at the General Conference to be director of a project for the North American Division schools. Upon completion of that assignment I was offered a job at the church I currently serve. Ten years after I started—I finally had the job I wanted. Now I wait for my own church.

(1) I was brought on as a Bible worker with no pay (one year); (2) I was later hired as a Bible worker for $600 a month (one year); (3) I was brought on as a Bible worker for full-time pay (six years); I was ordained a local elder and brought on as associate pastor for full-time pay (six years).

The fact that I lived with [one-quarter] salary for several years, even when I had no children, indicates to me that many doors are still closed [to women].

Very easy to receive initial call out of college. Unfortunately, no pay for six months.

Initially it was very easy [for me to secure a pastoral position]. . . . But after seminary, when I chose to marry a fellow pastor, I encountered difficulties because my conference was convinced that we must pastor 'together' at the same church. I agreed to be put on half salary so my husband could be picked up (dumb move). We were associates in a large church for two years, then transferred and my salary was cut to [one-quarter] pay. I have tried sending resumes when there were various openings especially designated for women, but have never had opportunity to actually move and secure full-time work again. . . . I desire very much to work full-time as a pastor—for equal pay!

It is not surprising, given the pervasive absence of female seminarians and faculty at Andrews University seminary, the lower level of support offered women pursuing pastoral training, the difficulty faced by women in procuring pastoral positions, and the concomitant dearth of women in pastoral positions, as well as the divisiveness of the debate surrounding the ordination of women, that women who serve in pastoral capacities might experience at least initial resistance on the part of congregates. In fact, although 98 percent of male associates and pastors indicated that the congregation in which they serve "was pleased to have a man serving in my position and supported me fully," female respondents found congregations less initially receptive (see figure 9). One respondent noted, for example, "People would get up and walk out every other week when I stood to preach. Several others had their doubts." Another respondent wrote that her current position "is a distinct blessing compared to the previous. . . . It took me quite some time to recover. I'd never been treated so unkindly and abusively in my life." A respondent serving as an interim pastor noted that her congregation "is confident they will soon get a 'real' pastor (i.e., male)."

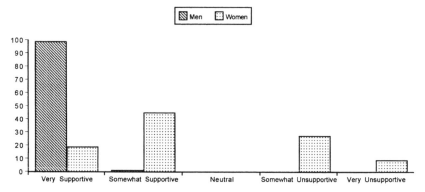

Figure 9. Relative Distribution of Congregations' Initial Responses to Male and Female Pastors/Associate Pastors

Despite initial resistance to women serving in pastoral capacities, female respondents noted a pattern of increased acceptance by congregates over tenure in their positions similar to that previously discussed by social scientists (see Bull and Lockhart 1989). Eighty-nine percent ($N = 40$) of male respondents observed that "the congregation's response to me has not changed" while 83 percent ($N = 20$) of female respondents observed that "the congregation has become far more supportive of me" over time, 8 percent of female respondents noted that "the congregation has become slightly more supportive of me" over time. (Eight percent [$N = 2$] of female respondents reported "no change.") One respondent explained that "over the five years [my husband and I have been here], the climate has warmed. Two of the most critical families transferred out, and several leaders did an in-depth study into the role of women. One man who would go elsewhere on Sabbaths when I preached now takes taped copies of my sermons to distribute to his friends and relatives because he likes my message so much."

While many mainline denominations have worked to eradicate exclusive language, implement affirmative action programs, and promote professionalism of female clergy, Adventist women, denied access to ordination, continue to be grossly underrepresented at every level of pastoral leadership (and are concomitantly barred from participation in a plethora of leadership posts which require ordination) and to receive wages not commensurate with their positions or responsibilities. Certainly research indicates that gender inequity persists in denominations in which women have access to ordination and affirmative action programs. Adventist women, however, confronted by a world church that vehemently opposes their ordination or participation in leadership, and with a North American Division which is sharply divided on the issue, have had little success in attaining even a semblance of parity.

Conclusions

Adventist women continue to confront opposition in attempting to attain positions which would allow them to demonstrate their abilities and to overcome gender stereotypes. Although Adventist women were pivotal in launching the Seventh-day Adventist movement—in coalescing disillusioned Millerites, in organizing the original sabbatarian movement, in undertaking early evangelical efforts, in instigating and contributing to institution building—contemporary Adventists are largely unaware of this history of women in the movement and thus attribute attempts to increase women's involvement in Adventism to secular forces (the world) while at the same time identifying more narrowly defined ideals of womanhood (especially those promulgated between the 1920s and the 1960s) as being both (1) divinely inspired and (2) historically consistent. This being the case, Adventist men and women who recognize that SDA women will never have full and equal access to employment and other opportunities without access to ordination struggle to combat an image of ideal womanhood (and ideal manhood) that Adventism adopted from secular culture after the turn of the century, and most especially during the 1950s, while at the same time trying to promote a level of participation by men and women within Adventism most consistent with the movement as it existed prior to 1915.

Notes

1. A 1985 *Review* series dealing with ordination of women ("for" and "against") prompted 279 written responses from readers, more than any other article in recent years. *Spectrum,* after publishing one issue devoted to discussion of ordination of women, received more letters in response than to any other in the journal's history. Last, in 1986, when Dr. Samuele Bacchiocchi published an article opposing the ordination of women in an Adventist college newspaper, he initiated a debate among students and faculty, carried on in the paper's editorial section, which lasted three months, ceasing only when a majority of college residents left campus for summer vacation.

2. Unpublished studies on the role of women in Adventism have found that Adventists generally oppose inequality based on sex (see Pearson 1990:161–66).

3. "It is a common observation that [Ellen White's] writings are now used to support a wide variety of points of view, many of which are mutually exclusive" (Shull 1974:78).

4. Ellen White accepted papers of ministerial ordination at the 1887 General Conference (Daily 1985:225).

5. In 1869, nine Adventist women met and initiated the Vigilant Missionary Society, which later developed into the Adventist Book Centers (ABCs), Adventism's publishing branch, and Adventism's personal ministries program (Watts 1992:47).

6. A 1975 poll of Dr. Benton's congregation indicted that 62 percent of members felt she had done as good or better job in her position than her male predecessors (Bull and Lockhart 1989:190).

7. At the 1983 General Conference annual council, a General Conference ad hoc committee presented several recommendations, including one that the NAD ordain women. All recommendations of the committee were approved, except that calling for the ordination of women.

8. The general reaction of congregates to the baptisms, however, was positive (Nembhard 1983a).

9. Subsequently, on December 20, 1986, Margaret Hempe, an associate in pastoral care at Loma Linda University Church, baptized two converts.

10. Opposition within the General Conference to the ordination of women comes primarily from delegates from the developing world, but that opposition is supported by some delegates of the NAD.

11. "Many North American delegates do not relish returning to another session begging for permission to act in their division with simple fairness and respect toward their fellow members, including women" (Branson 1988:7).

12. Interest collected on tithes contributed to the institute is used to fund scholarship and other programs for Adventist women.

13. Some opponents of women's ordination go so far as to suggest that women who seek equality in Adventism in the form of ordination are mentally unbalanced: "There is evidence . . . that the whole question of the female psyche is of profound significance in [the ordination] debate. . . . [I]t is evident that there is a very real and urgent need for a thoroughly professional and objective study of the psychology of female sexuality in relation to this whole question of women's ordination before any final decision is taken" (Ball 1985:49).

14. "Today the Seventh-day Adventist church faces the question 'Shall we ordain women because of the demands of our society?'" (Rivers 1985:1).

15. The accusation that women seeking ordination are self-promoting is so prevalent that Johnsson, in a 1988 editorial, found it necessary to write that Adventist women in pastoral ministry "aren't rebels or crusaders" (4).

16. As this quote makes apparent, opponents of the ordination of women also oppose women serving unordained in pastoral capacities, as this work, too, denies the strict separation of gender appropriate activities.

17. Brunt observed further that by employing the hermeneutic arguments posed by anti-ordinationists, one could justify slavery (1985:56).

18. Running postulated that women are barred from ordination, in part, because by so doing SDA institutions and their employers are able to hire women to serve in capacities as trained pastors or in other positions of responsibility without being required to pay those employees the wages of an ordained worker (1972:60).

19. The full ordination of women has become, for many Adventists, the symbol of women's attempt within the movement to achieve equity. Though certainly debate surrounding the controversy invokes larger questions of gender, social roles, and family, it is clear that ordination in itself does not represent the full gamut of inequalities Adventist women face. As Manuel Vasquez wrote, "the issue is not simply that of ordination of women, but rather of the entire role[s] of women in the church. The issue concerns the equal treatment of women, and their place, alongside men, in helping to finish the work" (1990:13). The danger for Adventist women in achieving ordination lies, according to Yob, in cessation of further struggle for gender parity beyond ordination (1988:32–33).

Conclusion:
Routinization and the Place of Women
in Sectarian Movements

A system of religious ideas can be understood as a dialectic between the
ordering of the world it creates and the everyday social interactions of the people
who inhabit that world, ideas and social interactions each influencing the other.
—Ammerman 1987:40

This work has explored various facets of Seventh-day Adventism with attention to evidence of tension within the movement between the tendencies toward sectarian distinction and denominationalism, and the ways in which this
tension has influenced gender ideals and expectations as outlined by Adventist
leadership. This tension is best understood in the context of examination of
Adventist history, institutionalization, evolution of theology, and development
of movement organization. As Adventism originally adopted components of
organization and belief necessary for the movement to continue in the face
of the delayed advent—legal organization, distinct beliefs, a name, standards
for admitting new believers, an educational system, health care facilities, and
so on—its response to the world concomitantly underwent a subtle shift.
Adventism's emerging belief system (incorporating understanding of the seventh-day Sabbath, the cleansing of the sanctuary, the investigative judgment,
the spirit of prophecy, the advent) allowed Adventists to create and maintain
a distinct identity in the face of "continuing time," and Adventist institutionalization created physical structures that served to reinforce that identity while
meeting temporal needs. Within this context of "continuing" until the advent,
Adventists gradually began to adopt a more accommodating response to the
world.

Although increasing acceptance of movement-wide organization, rapid institutionalization, and a shift in membership due to extensive evangelical success indicate movement toward accommodation, the relationship between
gender and sectarian change within Adventism has been neither completely
linear nor totally predictable. Crises of faith in Adventism, for example, most
especially those instigated by increased SDA participation in secular graduate education during the 1960s, led Adventists, during the 1970s and 1980s, to

a level of discourse unprecedented in the movement. When long accepted hallmarks of Adventist belief and distinction—Ellen White's role as prophetess, the sanctuary doctrine, the investigative judgment, the relative importance of justification and sanctification—were critically analyzed, Adventism's leaders defended belief and attempted to reassert sectarian identity. These conflicts briefly challenged movement toward accommodation, which was accelerated in the 1950s (especially with the publication of *Questions on Doctrine*), and instigated a backlash by Adventist leaders eager to reassert "traditional" Adventism, in the form of "standards" (and sanctification), which they perceived as being threatened.

Within this context of questioning of belief and changing response to the world, Adventists have defined gender in a manner influenced by evolving identity. Examination of the *Adventist Review* illustrates the way in which SDA leadership shifted from advocating ideals inconsistent with those promulgated in the wider society in a time of strong sectarian response to the world (especially with regard to women), only to later embrace (and claim as their own) secular expectations of gender when Adventism adopted a more accommodating response to the world. When SDA leadership perceived threats to distinct Adventist beliefs during the 1970s and 1980s, leaders resisted accommodation—they reaffirmed White's role as divine messenger, discharged Desmond Ford, advocated adherence to SDA standards, and discouraged variance from gender ideals outlined for Adventist women most vociferously during the 1950s and 1960s. Thus, in returning to "traditional," "fundamental" Adventist belief, Adventist women and men were presented with gender ideals advocated most explicitly within the movement during a period of relative accommodation, and deviation from those ideals was associated with secular society (most especially the modern feminist movement).

Modern gender ideals delimited within the Adventist family, too, are consistent with those embraced in Adventism during periods of greater accommodation following the turn of the century. Women within the family, Adventists were told (especially during the 1950s and 1960s), were to be mothers and homemakers to the exclusion of participation in wage labor. Further, women were taught to assume gender specific responsibilities (child care, homemaking) in a manner that framed those responsibilities with reference to eternal consequences, and thus identified secular ideals specifically with Adventist definitions of behavior within the family. Although women's lives were often inconsistent with those ideals, deviations from expected norms were framed, by informants, in the context of the ideal, and women identified themselves, regardless of responsibilities they assumed beyond the parameters of the ideal (wage labor participation, for example), as being primarily responsible for housekeeping and child care. Men, on the other hand, were identified by informants as being the "provider" for the family and as offering spiritual leadership within the family. Although Adventists have renegotiated the marital relationship as women have continued to participate in wage labor—so that men are currently expected to contribute more to the functioning (housekeeping, child care) of the family—such change is attributed to modification of gender roles in secular society and is not associated with notions of participatory fathering present in Adventism historically.

Framed most explicitly in the context of the family, gender ideals also serve to delimit appropriate expression of sexuality. Though marital sex is no longer deemed expedient solely for procreative purposes, gender distinction is considered a central and defining component of sexual/marital partnerships. As such, nonmarital relationships, most especially gay and lesbian relationships, are denounced. Called "unbiblical," these relationships are most rebuked as a threat to distinction of gender roles within the family and as, in turn, jeopardizing social cohesion.

Regardless of this contemporary emphasis on gender distinction and assumption of "appropriate" gender roles and responsibilities, early in the movement's history (a time of strong sectarian response to the world), in the arenas of family, wage labor, and the ministry, Adventist leadership encouraged participation of men and women in a manner inconsistent with wider social mores (asking men to be active, participating fathers, and promoting women's participation in public religious work and wage labor). Prior to 1915, women played an active role in Adventist leadership, and were defended, in so doing, by prominent Adventists. Despite this history, informants overwhelmingly depicted early Adventist women (1850–1915) in a manner consistent with ideals advocated for women during the 1920s and 1930s, and especially following the close of World War II, during the late 1940s, the 1950s, and the 1960s. Even personal knowledge of family members (mothers, grandmothers, and great-grandmothers) whose lives were inconsistent with these ideals did not alter the perception of ideal as reality. As a result of this shared perception, the contemporary move in Adventism for equal opportunity without regard to gender has been identified by opponents and, often, supporters as being inspired and influenced by the secular feminist movement.

The sociological theory of sectarian development, although it has not heretofore considered questions of gender, can provide insight in attempting to understand and explain the relationship, within Adventism, between the movement's advocation of specific gender ideals and its evolving response to the world. Weber asserted that sectarian movements originally "allot equal-ity" to women and other disprivileged groups because, in identifying them-selves through hostility to the world (secular society), sectarians maintain identity by contrast. This being the case, sectarians may institute norms of behavior and ideals not only dissimilar from those of secular society but dis-tinctly in contrast to those of the world. The sociological theory of sectarian development also notes, however, that as sectarian movements become bureau-cratized and seek accommodation to secular society, positions of leadership and authority available to women diminish.

The evolution of Adventist women's "place" (and more broadly of gender norms and ideals generally) may be understood within this theoretical con-struct of sectarian development. Seventh-day Adventism originally arose as a small, scattered band of believers came together in an attempt to institute minimal legal organization to ensure that they could collectively own prop-erty. As former Millerites, early adventists knew that Christ would soon come to the earth, making extensive worldly involvement, in either proselytizing or property ownership, unnecessary. The group was characteristic of a sect—adventists despised secular involvement and found a collective identity in re-pudiating the world. Even after formal organization (1860) and eventual (lim-ited) participation in evangelical activity and institution building, Adventists believed themselves the sole possessors of truth and defined "'true Protestant-ism' in terms that could only include Seventh-day Adventists" (Land 1986c: 169).

In this context of a carefully delimited sectarian identity—the most impor-tant aspect of which was the urgency surrounding Christ's imminent return—all Adventists were counted necessary to the work; men and women, old and young, black and white, all were encouraged and expected to further efforts deemed necessary to hasten Christ's coming. Soon, institution building was identified as being not only important but essential to furthering goals identified by Adventist leadership. Institutionalization became synonymous with evangelism and "as various departments [within Adventism] grew, and more responsibilities were heaped upon the individuals in charge of these departments, women generally disappeared from all leadership spots" (Daily 1985:240). Adventist growth toward institutionalization and denomination-alization began in earnest following World War II and burgeoned through the 1950s and 1960s, with greatly increased evangelical efforts, expansion of Ad-ventism in mass media, and an overall deemphasis of the unique sectarian characteristics of Seventh-day Adventism. For women, these developments signaled more limited opportunities: "The growing professionalism of the whole structure . . . served effectively to exclude women from positions of responsibility" (Pearson 1990:153). During the 1970s, in the face of internal challenges to some of Adventism's most basic unique beliefs, growing numbers of Adventists, particularly prominent SDA writers, thinkers, and leaders, began to associate Adventism's move away from its distinct sectarian heritage with an unwanted capitulation to worldliness, and to call for a return to sectarian distinction. Traditionalists of the 1970s, 1980s, and 1990s, however, while seeking to re-institute what they perceived to be Adventism's original (and therefore correct) theology, also advocated a return to socioreligious norms most prevalent in Adventism during the 1950s and 1960s (norms which during those decades actually reflected popular secular trends) because those norms were seen as being the antithesis of norms advocated by more recent secular movements (i.e., feminism). Adventist women, who had begun to lose positions of responsibility and leadership early in the century (and who were forced from those positions completely by 1950), had proportionately fewer positions of leadership by 1973 than SDA women had had during the 1930s and 1940s (and certainly fewer positions than they had had prior to those decades) and were, furthermore, confronted with ideals of womanhood that severely restricted their options, in addition to being informed that those ideals were not secular but divine. Adventism experienced, then, "a direct correlation between the growth of hierarchical church structure and the decline of female participation and lay involvement in the decision making processes of the church" (Daily 1985:234).

Perhaps most important, Adventists were told (and largely convinced, according to interview data) that movement toward gender equity was inconsistent with Adventism's historical tradition; that to attempt to secure equal pay or equal opportunity (especially ordination) was to align oneself with the world. This was aptly demonstrated at the 1990 General Conference session at which delegates debated whether to allow women access to ordination, and argued that the central issue involved in the possible ordination of women was "whether the Seventh-day Adventist church will allow itself to be governed by rules and influenced by sociological factors or whether we will just simply go by 'thus saith the Lord'" (Spectrum Editors 1988:31). Some delegates claimed that the idea of ordaining women originated in "secularism and its influence on other churches, especially Protestant churches" and that "the influence of liberal theology, in its many forms, is clearly evident in the writings of many who advocate women's ordination. It is the pervasive influence of liberalism that should deter Seventh-day Adventists from moving precipitately in the direction of female ordination" (Ball 1985:42).[1]

These claims, coupled with a historically accurate understanding of the relatively prominent positions held by Adventist women before the 1920s (and even until the 1940s), lead one to conclude with Stafford that: "We perceive the past in strange ways, and then we shape the future by those distortions we have placed upon past events. In looking at what has happened to women in [Adventism], we assume that things are better today than they were yesterday, that our age is enlightened and the past was dark. Yet in many ways [Adventism's] treatment of its women today is less generous than was its treatment of our mothers and grandmothers" (Stafford 1983:31).

A few Adventist scholars, particularly those who have given specific attention to positions assumed by women in Adventism historically, have observed that "too often [contemporary Adventist] theological formulations reflect the contemporary culture rather than play a part in reshaping the status quo" (Spangenberg 1974:73). These authors have observed, as did Shell in 1992, that "it is a strange thing to hear some today object to using women's talents in administration and ministry because this is 'following after the world'" and have suggested instead that Adventism's status quo was been influenced by secular norms: "For years the SDA church has been following after the world in repressing women's contributions and constricting their roles" (165); "In holding this attitude of a subordinate position for women the Seventh-day Adventist church . . . reflected the prevailing attitudes of American culture" (Allen 1984:54).

Regardless of contemporary interpretations of the direction, extent, or influence of secular forces, modern Adventism underwent, most especially following World War II, a dramatic redefinition and subsequent limitation of gender specific expectations for men and women. This shift coincided with, and was precipitated by, Adventist movement away from sectarian isolation and toward denominationalization and accommodation. The attenuative importance and predominance of women's leadership and active participation in positions of authority in Adventism "coincided with the breakdown of distinctive cultural and behavioral patterns that helped to sustain [a] separate subculture [sect] in which patterns such as the ministry of women were preserved against a hostile culture [the world]. Successive generations, embarrassed by such 'strange' and 'unnatural' practices, . . . accommodated to the dominant culture becoming in some ways the sort of [religious organization] against which their forefathers and foremothers had protested" (Sider and Dayton 1975:20).

Stated simply, as Adventism consolidated a unique identity in opposition to secular society, space was created for freedoms not allowed in the world, particularly for members of groups disadvantaged in the larger society (i.e., women, people of color). As Adventism became institutionalized, however, and began increasingly to attempt to accommodate to the world, secular norms and expectations were adopted.[2]

Carroll et al. outline this process of development, implicitly adopting the sociological model of sectarian change outlined above, and attempt to identify specific, predictable, corollary developments of religious movements and women's evolving place within them. Adumbrating first an initial sectarian response to the world, they outline the "charismatic stage"—a stage in which a new vision is introduced by a prophet and members of the movement see themselves as being "in direct contact with the divine" and therefore informed of unique and essential truths (1983:21). These new truths unite believers against nonbelievers (the world) and allow them freedom to define expression of spiritual gifts in a manner sometimes unacceptable to the world. In this stage of development, women are encouraged to participate fully in the movement: "When a religious movement is at its charismatic phase, 'women's place' is not an issue" (ibid.).

The authors' second phase of development is "one of consolidation and organization" which, according to Carroll et al., is initiated by the maturation of the sect's second generation: "If adherents of the movement become active participants in the status system of the wider society, organization and respectability become important goals; and the *role definitions of society at large become the natural order to which the group would grant religious legitimacy*" (1983:22; emphasis added). As sectarians become more aware of, and more concerned with, societal norms and expectations (as a result, for example, of interaction with the world necessitated by proselytizing, participation in secular higher education programs, operation of mass media services, etc.), they become concerned with the impropriety with which the world views women's participation in leadership, and "respectability demands that women be put in their place" (ibid.:23). Women are thus removed from positions of leadership as authority is increasingly identified as being synonymous with masculinity. Whereas gender appropriate behaviors may have been largely undifferentiated, or differentiated in a way that had few practical or deleterious implications for women prior to this stage, as the movement seeks to accommodate secular society, gender specific activities and behaviors are carefully delimited in a manner consistent with secular norms, and deviations from those norms are discouraged.

According to Carroll et al., "the third phase of the development of a religious movement" "[i]s that of maturity, of institutionalization, when [the movement] no longer must seek respectability, when its boundaries blur into the general social structure. No longer under the critical eye of some other 'establishment,' the church can now relax some of its standards and allow variations within its broader limits; it may now tolerate mildly prophetic expressions of social conscience, and attempt to lead rather than adapt to the larger society" (1983:23). Thus, mature religious movements may, like their forebears, attempt to instigate social change rather than maintain hostility with the world (phase one) or adapt to prevailing social customs (phase two). In summary:

> Women have typically been permitted freedom of expression and exercise of leadership in the first early phase of the movement. . . . However, as the movement becomes older and larger, it enters into its "consolidation and organization phase" in which women are absorbed into a system dominated by men and not allowed much autonomy of expression, organization or decision-making. Further development of the religious movement into a well-established denomination typically creates conditions favorable for the reemergence of women as visible leaders, as the denomination and its churches become more complex and less differentiated in structure, membership, and values from the general society. (ibid.:47)

This model, like the traditional sociological model of sectarian development which it assumes, tends to oversimplify and overgeneralize observable patterns of change in relation to women's place in sectarian movements over time. Like any model which tries to account for disparate and often diverse examples, Carroll et al.'s explanatory scheme is unable to account for individual nuances and the diversity of specific sectarian groups. It is unable to explain, for example, variations in the rate or degree of the changes noted, or reversals of the expected pattern.[3] Furthermore, the authors' model seems unable to explain two characteristics of Adventism's changing understanding of women's "place": (1) the tendency of Adventists to identify recent definitions of ideal gender roles, behaviors, and realms as being consistent with Adventism's original ideals for men and women (and, relatedly, to ignore Adventism's history of more equitable participation based on gender); and (2) the tendency of Adventists to cling to recent, more limiting definitions of ideal gender roles/behaviors/realms, to specifically associate these with Adventism's unique identity as a sectarian movement, and to explicitly claim that any threat to these is both (a) posed by secular society and (b) a threat to Adventism's unique history and sectarian nature. Despite these limitations, it is clear that Carroll et al.'s model accomplishes much in delimiting the dimensions and general correlations of sectarian/denominational change and the accompanying change of status of women in religious movements.[4] Their model is restricted by some of the limitations of the denominationalization thesis the authors assume;

most obviously, by the assumption that sectarian development is linear and predictable, when in fact it is not. In the case of Seventh-day Adventism, for example, conflicts (such as those explored in chapter 7) created a sense of urgency among some NAD Adventists to return to "traditional Adventism" in an attempt to preserve standards that they perceived as being endangered most especially during the 1970s and early 1980s. These Adventists also identified the increasing involvement of women in SDA leadership (during the 1970s and 1980s) as a threat to Adventism's unique (sectarian) identity and attempted to "preserve" notions of ideal gender behaviors and realms made popular in the movement between the 1920s and 1960s (primarily between the end of World War II and the late 1960s). In this way they associated insistence upon sectarian distinction and concomitant *limitation* of women's involvement in positions of authority in the movement. The relationship, then, between sectarian development and women's roles within sects is too complex to be fully explained by Carroll et al.'s three-phase model. The model, nonetheless, provides a more than adequate point of departure for attempting to unravel such relationships.

It is clear that just as sectarian development is neither completely linear nor totally predictable, women's place in such movements is constantly evolving. In the case of Adventism, routinization, expressed in part in institutionalization and development of formalized belief, served to supplement a changing ideology of gender and to reinforce new notions of propriety which limited women's participation in leadership and public activity generally. As Adventists have become participants, to varying degrees, in secular society—as they have established institutions, participated in mass evangelism, evolved uniform statements of belief—they have accommodated themselves, in different forms and to different extents, to the world.[5] As they have done so, they have adopted secular notions of women's place and then claimed those notions, and accompanying limitations, as their own. One Adventist scholar wrote that: "In our early days as a movement we indeed appeared to affirm an eschatological otherworldliness that informed an altruistic this-worldliness. . . . In our more recent days we appear to articulate an eschatological otherworldliness and to use the same as a rationale for not challenging those social structures which reward us with greater life chances" (Teel 1980:44). Adventists, through their participation in the world, have become invested in what *is;* though Christ is still at the door, the imminence of his coming is mitigated by demands of the present. Within this context, propriety, between the 1920s and 1960s, assumed importance and women were removed from leadership. When Adventism's basic beliefs seemed to be challenged during the 1970s, SDA conservatives retrenched; stressing standards and fundamental beliefs, they sought a return to basic Adventism but succeeded in reintroducing rules of behavior, not the original fervor or enthusiasm of the sect, and women, according to the rules they emphasized, were not to play a public role in the movement. In their attempt to reinforce the standards of early Adventism, the reformers succeeded in instigating a backlash, leaving power and public authority in the movement almost exclusively in the hands of men.

It is unclear whether Adventism will soon embark upon Carroll et al.'s third phase of development and dare to create greater equality of opportunity for disprivileged groups within the movement. Certainly ongoing controversy surrounding the ordination of women serves to call attention to the disparity of opinion within Adventism regarding the propriety of women's full and equal participation in the leadership of the movement: There remain serious rifts among NAD Adventists, with accommodationists advocating acceptance of increased participation by women in movement leadership and traditionalists (sectarians) struggling to retain gender specific notions adopted by the movement during the twentieth century. Further, this work considers only NAD Adventists; the world church (particularly in developing countries) presents far more formidable resistance to changing notions of gender than do NAD anti-ordinationists. Yet even the highly emotional debate regarding ordination of women fails to address crucial questions of changing definitions of gender which extend beyond the boundaries of incorporating women into current hierarchy, challenging instead basic notions of propriety, responsibility, family, and gender. As one informal informant said, "Ordination of women in Adventism would not be so radical. Women in the [secular] world participate in leadership; lots of Protestant denominations ordain women. If we truly want to *lead* the world we must consider more than just the ordination of women."

Adventists, particularly those in university and college settings, have begun to explore the possibility of using religious conviction and belief to lead secular society in critical examination of gender (and racial/ethnic) constructs which limit possibility for some. Although Iris Yob is perhaps the best known of these, others, including Steve Daily, have called into question restrictive gender delimitations and accompanying ideals as unacceptable. In attempting to redefine basic notions of gender, family, work, marriage, and sexuality, these Adventists move beyond the realm of accepted ideology within Adventism. Only such debate can advance Adventism beyond the confines created by decades of adherence to secular notions of limitation based upon gender, and toward an ethic that is more genuinely consistent with Adventism's heritage.

Notes

1. Ball argued further that "it should be recognized that there is a direct line of connection between the women's liberation movement, the Christian feminist's movement in the church at large, and the movement for women's ordination within the Seventh-day Adventist church" (Ball 1985:49).

2. In this way, argue Lucille Sider and Donald Dayton, "during the last couple of centuries evangelicals led the way in granting a major role to women in the churches. . . . [The practice of encouraging/allowing women to assume positions of authority], however, has declined in recent years, especially since W.W.II" (1975:20).

3. As recently as October of 1993, for example, the Church of Jesus Christ of Latter-day Saints excommunicated a number of adherents for promulgating "feminism." Carroll et al.'s model seems unable to explain why this particular religious movement, having progressed far on the road of denominationalism, would cling so adamantly to a strict delimitation of women's "role" which serves to isolate and distinguish Latter-day Saints from contemporary secular society and even from mainline Protestantism.

4. "[S]imilar processes have repeated again and again as new sectarian groups have formed. In the earliest Baptist churches in the south, women were ordained as deaconesses, and some preached without ordination. In the eighteenth century, Separate Baptists allowed what has been described as 'remarkable freedom of participation by women.' After 1800, however, that freedom diminished as that body merged with the Regular Baptists" (Carroll et al. 1983:22).

5. One SDA sociologist told Adventist leaders that "By the mid-twentieth century . . . it appears that no small accommodation [to the world] has occurred" (Teel 1980:43–44). According to Ronald Lawson, Adventist accommodation is further evidenced by extensive institutionalization; accreditation of SDA educational institutions; Adventist participation in noncombatant military positions; a general warming of relations between Adventism and the United States government; decreasing adherence to SDA dietary guidelines, particularly vegetarianism; and modification of Adventism's apocalyptic outlook (Lawson 1997).

Bibliography

AAF Board. 1983. "The AAF Board Responds: A Reaffirmation of Purpose." *Spectrum* 15 (4):28–30.

Adams, Roy. 1981. *The Sanctuary Doctrine: Three Approaches in the Seventh-day Adventist Church.* Berrien Springs, Mich.: Andrews University Press.

———. 1990a. "The Annual Counsel's Vote on Women—I." *Adventist Review* 167 (5):4.

———. 1990b. "The Annual Counsel's Vote on Women—II." *Adventist Review* 167 (8):4.

———. 1993. *The Sanctuary.* Hagerston, Md.: Review and Herald Publishing Association.

"Adventist Women." 1990. *Christian Century* 107 (36):1160.

Allen, Patrick. 1984. "The Depression and the Role of Women in the Seventh-day Adventist Church." *Adventist Heritage* 11 (2):48–54.

Ammerman, Nancy Tatom. 1987. *Bible Believers: Fundamentalists in the Modern World.* New Brunswick, N. J.: Rutgers University Press.

Anderson, Eric. 1977. "Ellen White and the Reformation Historians." *Spectrum* 9 (3):23–26.

———. 1981. "Johnsson on the Future of the Adventist Review." *Spectrum* 13 (4):43–48.

———. 1987. "The Millerite Use of Prophecy." In *The Disappointed: Millerism and Millenarianism in the Nineteenth Century,* ed. Ronald Numbers and Jonathan M. Butler, 78–91. Bloomington: Indiana University Press.

Anderson, Godfrey T. 1974. "Make Us a Name." *Adventist Heritage* 1 (2):28–35.

———. 1986. "Sectarianism and Organization: 1846–1864." In *Adventism in America: A History,* ed. Gary Land, 36–65. Grand Rapids, Mich.: William B. Eerdmans Publishing Co.

Anderson, J. Brush. 1920. "Wanted—Men and Women." *Advent Review and Sabbath Herald* 97 (38):73.

Andreassen, Karen. 1989. "I Am Appalled." *Ponderings,* no. 2:5–6.

Andrews, J. N. 1879. "May Women Speak in Meeting?" *Advent Review and Sabbath Herald* 45 (3):54.

Andross, E. E. 1940. "And She Is a Minister's Wife?" *Adventist Review and Sabbath Herald* 117 (46):12–14.

Armory. 1890. "Only My Mother." *Advent Review and Sabbath Herald* 67 (33):517.

Arthur, David T. 1974. "After the Great Disappointment." *Adventist Heritage* 1 (1):5–10, 58.

———. 1987. "Joshua V. Himes and the Cause of Adventism." In *The Disappointed: Millerism and Millenarianism in the Nineteenth Century,* ed. Ronald Numbers and Jonathan M. Butler, 36–58. Bloomington: Indiana University Press.

Ashaway. 1925. "Proud of Him." *Advent Review and Sabbath Herald* 102 (15):13.

Ashbaugh, Kraid I. 1980. "The Truth." *Adventist Review* 157 (12):14.

B., F. L. 1935. "One Thing at a Time." *Advent Review and Sabbath Herald* 112 (37):17.

Bacchiocchi, Samuele. 1987. *Women in the Church: A Biblical Study on the Role of Women in the Church.* Berrien Springs, Mich.: Biblical Perspectives.

Baer, Hans. 1993. "The Limited Empowerment of Women in Black Spiritual Churches: An Alternative Vehicle to Religious Leadership." *Sociology of Religion* 54 (1):65–82.

Bakker, Jean. 1980. "Queen for a Day." *Adventist Review* 157 (27):14.

Ball, Bryan. 1985. "The Ordination of Women: A Plea for Caution." *Spectrum* 17 (2):39–54.

Ballis, Peter H. 1985. *In and Out of the World: Seventh-day Adventists in New Zealand.* Palmerston North, N.Z.: Dunmore Press Limited.

Banks, Olive. 1981. *Faces of Feminism: A Study of Feminism as a Social Movement.* New York: St. Martin's Press.

Banks, Rosa Taylor. 1992. *A Woman's Place: Seventh-day Adventist Women in Church and Society.* Hagerston, Md.: Review and Herald Publishing Association.

Barclay, James S., et al. 1972. "Organization: A Discussion of the Seventh-day Adventist Church." *Spectrum* 4 (2):42–62.

Barfoot, Charles H., and Gerald T. Sheppard. 1980. "Prophetic vs. Priestly Religion: The Changing Role of Women Clergy in Classical Pentecostal Churches." *Review of Religious Research* 22 (1):2–17.

Bartlett, Skye. 1995. "From Sligo to La Sierra." *Spectrum* 25 (2):51–59.

Battisone, Joseph. 1981. "The Great Controversy Theme in E. G. White's Writings." *Spectrum* 13 (4):56–57.

Beach, B. B. 1965. "The Church and the World." *Advent Review and Sabbath Herald* 142 (7):2–4.

Beach, Walter Raymond. 1970. "Academic Freedom in Action." *Review* 147 (54):5–7.

Beckford, James A. 1975. *A Trumpet of Prophecy: A Sociological Study of Jehovah's Witnesses.* New York: Wiley.

Bee, Bessie M. 1899. "Young Women and Foreign Missions." *Advent Review and Sabbath Herald* 76 (13):198–99.

Bennett, Douglas. 1980. "Are You Ready for Marriage?" *Adventist Review* 157 (52):8–10.

Benton, Elvin. 1975. "Lawsuits and the Church: Notes on the Vienna Decision." *Spectrum* 7 (3):2–8.

———. 1980. "Adventists Face Homosexuality." *Spectrum* 12 (3):32–38.

Benton, Josephine. 1984. "God Called a Woman." *Spectrum* 16 (5):44–50.

Berger, Peter L. 1954. "The Sociological Study of Sectarianism." *Social Research* 21 (Winter):467–85.

———. 1958. "Sectarianism and Religious Sociation." *American Journal of Sociology* 64 (1):41–44.

Berger, Peter, and Thomas Luckman. 1967. *The Social Construction of Reality.* Garden City, N.Y.: Anchor Books.

Bietz, A. L. 1955. "Why Homes Crumble." *Advent Review and Sabbath Herald* 132 (8):12–13.

Bietz, Gordon. 1985. "Dream or Die!" *Adventist Review* 162 (36):5–7.

Bietz, R. R. 1975. "Preserving the SDA Home." *Adventist Review* 152 (February 6):12–13.

Bird, Herbert S. 1961. *Theology of Seventh-day Adventism.* Grand Rapids, Mich.: William B. Eerdmans Publishing Co.

Bland, Flora C. 1895. "How Are We Training Our Children?" *Advent Review and Sabbath Herald* 72 (29):454.

Bland, W. T. 1895. "Some Examples of Home Training." *Advent Review and Sabbath Herald* 72 (35):551.

Blodgett, Ralph. 1984. *How Will It End?* Boise, Idaho: Pacific Press Publishing Association.

Bowers, N. J. 1881. "May Women Publicly Labor in the Cause of Christ?" *The Advent Review and Sabbath Herald* 57 (24):372–73.

Bradford, C. E. 1980. "Formula for Change." *Adventist Review* 157(April 20):11–15.

Bradley, Mae Carberry. 1945. "The Head of the Household." *Advent Review and Sabbath Herald* 122 (24):14–15.

———. 1955. "The Seventh-day Adventist Home." *Advent Review and Sabbath Herald* 132 (32):12–13.

Bradley, Paul W. 1971. "Ellen G. White and Her Writings." *Spectrum* 3 (2):43–64.

Brannaka, Marjorie. 1980. "Love Can Be Learned." *Adventist Review* 157 (53):10–11.

Branson, Roy E. 1972. "Coming of Age." *Spectrum* 4 (1):5–8.

———. 1976. "Adventists between the Times: The Shift in the Church's Eschatology." *Spectrum* 8 (1):15–26.

———. 1981. "A Time for Healing." *Spectrum* 13 (2):2–3.

———. 1984. "You Are My Witness." *Spectrum* 16 (1):2–4.

———. 1988. "From the Editor's Notebook." *Spectrum* 20 (5):2–7.

Branson, Roy, with Diane Gainer. 1983. "Potomac Conference Yields: Baptisms by Women Halted." *Spectrum* 15 (3):2–4.

Branson, Roy E., and Harold D. Weiss. 1970. "Ellen G. White: A Subject for Adventist Scholarship." *Spectrum* 2 (4):30–33.

Branson, W. H. 1940. "A Bible Woman's Witness in War." *Advent Review and Sabbath Herald* 117 (17):12.

Braude, Ann. 1989. *Radical Spirits: Spiritualism and Women's Rights in Nineteenth Century America.* Boston: Beacon Press.

Brimsmead, Robert D. 1980. *Judged by the Gospel: A Review of Adventism*. Fallbrook, Calif.: Verdict Publications.

Brodie, Fawn M. 1976. "Ellen White's Emotional Life: A Psychological Portrait of Ellen White." *Spectrum* 8 (2):13–15.

Brown, Elsie N. 1895. "Mothers, Don't Underestimate Your Privileges." *Advent Review and Sabbath Herald* 72 (25):390.

Brunt, John C. 1981. "What Does the New Testament Say about Divorce?" *Spectrum* 13 (4):15–21.

———. 1985. "Adventists against Ordination: A Critical Review." *Spectrum* 17 (2):55–62.

Brunt, Larry. 1989. "Challenging Adventism. In Campus Thought: Walla Walla's *Collegian*, 1988–1989." *Spectrum* 20 (1):9–10.

Bull, Malcolm. 1988. "Eschatology and Manners in Seventh-day Adventism." *Archives de Sciences Sociales des Religions* 165 (1):145–59.

Bull, Malcolm, and Keith Lockhart. 1986. "The Intellectual World of Adventist Theologians." *Spectrum* 18 (1):32–37.

———. 1989. *Seeking a Sanctuary: Seventh-day Adventism and the American Dream*. San Francisco: Harper and Row Publishers.

Butka, Brenda J. 1971. "Women's Liberation." *Spectrum* 3 (4):22–28.

Butler, Jonathan. 1976. "When Prophecy Fails: The Validity of Apocalypticism." *Spectrum* 8 (1):7–14.

———. 1978. "The World of Ellen G. White and the End of the World." *Spectrum* 10 (2):2–13.

———. 1987. "The Making of a New Order: Millerism and the Origins of Seventh-day Adventism." In *The Disappointed: Millerism and Millenarianism in the Nineteenth Century*, ed. Ronald Numbers and Jonathan M. Butler, 189–208. Bloomington: Indiana University Press.

———. 1989. "Seeking a Sanctuary: Review." *Spectrum* 21 (1):44–45.

———. 1991. "Prophecy, Gender and Culture: Ellen Gould Harmon [White] and the Roots of Seventh-day Adventism." *Religion and American Culture* 1 (1):3–29.

———. 1992. "Introduction: The Historian as Heretic." In *Prophetess of Health: Ellen G. White and the Origins of Seventh-day Adventist Health Reform*, ed. Ronald Numbers, xxv–lxvii. Knoxville: University of Tennessee Press.

Butler, Jonathan M., and Ronald L. Numbers. 1987. "Seventh-day Adventism." In *The Encyclopedia of Religion*, ed. Mircea Eliade. New York: Macmillan Publishing Co.

C., J. N. 1985. "Women of the Cloth?" *Adventist Review* 162 (9):15–16.

C., R. F. 1960. "Mental Illness." *Advent Review and Sabbath Herald* 137 (42):3.

Callahan, Valma. 1993. "A Journey from Fear to Faith." *Adventist Review* 170 (36):11.

Campbell, Alma L. 1975. "Sodom and Tomorrow." *Review and Herald* 152 (Mar. 6):17–18.

Caro, Edgar. 1895a. "The Mother." *Advent Review and Sabbath Herald* 73 (1):7.

———. 1895b. "The Father." *Advent Review and Sabbath Herald* 73 (52):822.

Carr, Inez Storie. 1965. "Every Marriage Needs This 'Third Party.'" *Advent Review and Sabbath Herald* 142 (7): 10–11.

Carroll, Jackson W., et al. 1983. *Women of the Cloth: A New Opportunity for the Churches.* San Francisco: Harper and Row Publishers.

Carscallen, Lois Koth. 1977. "Standards of Family Life among Seventh-day Adventists in Northwestern United States." Ph.D. dissertation, Walden University.

Casebolt, Donald. 1980. "Is Ellen White's Interpretation of Biblical Prophecy Final?" *Spectrum* 12 (4):2–9.

Casey, Bonnie L. 1982. "Graybill's Exit: Turning Point at the White Estate?" *Spectrum* 14 (4):2–8.

Cassano, Christopher. 1987. "Women Pastors Expand Role in World Church." *Spectrum* 19 (5):11–13.

Chartier, Gary. 1990. "Southeastern Will Ordain Women—Someday." *Spectrum* 22 (4):56–57.

Clark, Debra J. 1990. "Church Elects Women to Important Posts." *Adventist Review* 167 (41):17–18.

Clark, Walter. 1982. "Women Graduates from Loma Linda University School of Medicine." Unpublished manuscript, Loma Linda, Calif.

Clark, Walter B. 1950. "Home's Greatest Charm." *Advent Review and Herald of the Sabbath* 127 (17):14–15.

Clarke, Jos. 1871. "City Working Women." *Advent Review and Herald of the Sabbath* 37 (7):83.

———. 1874. "Divorces." *Advent Review and Herald of the Sabbath* 44 (5):35.

Clinton, Catherine. 1984. *The Other Civil War: American Women in the Nineteenth Century.* New York: Hill and Wang.

Coffin, James. 1985. "Council to Women Pastors: Baptisms No, Tax Break Yes." *Adventist Review.* 162 (50):5–7.

Cook, Colin D. 1980. "Church Funds Program for Homosexuals." *Spectrum* 12 (3):46–48.

Cottrell, R. F. 1860. "Making Us a Name." *Advent Review and Sabbath Herald* 15 (18):140.

———. 1862. "Organized." *Advent Review and Sabbath Herald* 19 (6):46.

Cottrell, Raymond F. 1973. "The Eschaton: The Seventh-day Adventist Perspective on the Second Coming." *Spectrum* 5 (1):7–31.

———. 1980. "The Sanctuary Review Committee and Its New Consensus." *Spectrum* 11 (2):2–26.

———. 1982. "The Varieties of Church Structure." *Spectrum* 14 (4):40–53.

Couperus, Molleurus. 1978. "Tensions between Religion and Science." *Spectrum* 10 (4):74–88.

Covert, William. 1894. "The Homestead." *Advent Review and Sabbath Herald* 71 (33):514.

Craley, Noreen Suriner. 1990. "Surviving Ministry from a Woman's Perspective: Celebrating the Joys and the Pitfalls." In *Surviving in Ministry,* ed. Robert L. Lutz and Bruce T. Taylor. Mahwah, N.J.: Paulist Press.

Crider, Charles, and Robert C. Kistler. 1979. *The Seventh-day Adventist Family: An Empirical Study.* Berrien Springs, Mich.: Andrews University Press.

Crosby, Timothy. 1976. "Do the Authorities Conflict on Perfectionism?" *Spectrum* 8 (2):62–64.

Cross, Whitney R. 1986 [1950]. *The Burned-over District.* New York: Harper and Row.

D., E. F. 1985. "$10,000 Witness." *Adventist Review* 162 (18):13–14.

Daffern, Janice Eiseman. 1980. "How Long Must Women Wait? Prospects for Adventist Church Leadership." *Spectrum* 12 (4):39–43.

Daily, Steve. 1985. "The Irony of Adventism: The Role of Ellen G. White and Other Adventist Women in Nineteenth Century America." Ph.D. dissertation, School of Theology at Claremont.

———. 1990. "Where's Papa? What's Masculinity?" *Spectrum* 22 (2):22–29.

Dakar, Sidney. 1975. "Outward Splendor without Internal Purity." *Adventist Review* (Feb. 27):6–7.

Damsteegt, P. Gerard. 1977. *Foundations of the Seventh-day Adventist Message and Mission.* Grand Rapids, Mich.: William B. Eerdmans Publishing Co.

———. 1989. "The Adventist Message." In *Doctrine of the Sanctuary: A Historical Survey,* ed. Frank B. Holbrook. Silver Springs, Md.: Biblical Research Institute.

Dasher, Bertha. 1983. "Leadership Positions: A Declining Opportunity?" *Spectrum* 15 (4):35–37.

———. 1985. "Adventist Women of Yesterday." *Adventist Review* 162 (44):10–11.

———. 1992. "Women's Leadership, 1915–1970: The Waning Years." In *A Woman's Place: Seventh-day Adventist Women in Church and Society,* ed. Rosa Taylor Banks, 75–84. Hagerstown, Md.: Review and Herald Publishing Association.

Davidman, Lynn. 1991. *Tradition in a Rootless World: Women Turn to Orthodox Judaism.* Berkeley and Los Angeles: University of California Press.

Davidson, Richard, and Skip MacCarty. 1987. "Biblical Questions on Women and Ministry." *Spectrum* 19 (5):29–32.

Davis, Clark. 1985. "Women Pastors and Baptism: Loma Linda University Church Takes the Plunge." *Spectrum* 17 (3):25–28.

Degler, Carl. 1980. *At Odds: Women and the Family in America from the Revolution to the Present.* New York: New York University Press.

Dick, Everett N. 1986. "The Millerite Movement: 1830–1845." In *Adventism in America: A History,* ed. Gary Land. 1–35. Grand Rapids, Mich.: William B. Eerdmans Publishing Co.

Dickson, Louis K. 1955. "What Is the Essential Qualification?" *Advent Review and Sabbath Herald* 134 (4):3.

Dietrich, Pam. 1996. "Southeastern California Churches Ordain, Advance Women." *Spectrum* 25 (5):55–56.

Doan, Ruth Alden. 1987a. "Millerism and Evangelical Culture." In *The Disappointed: Millerism and Millenarianism in the Nineteenth Century,* ed. Ronald Numbers and Jonathan M. Butler, 118–38. Bloomington: Indiana University Press.

———. 1987b. *The Miller Heresy, Millennialism, and American Culture.* Philadelphia: Temple University Press.

Doherty, Ivy R. 1975. "Heart Cry: A Surrogate Mother Reacts to the Heart-Cry of Children Left in Her Care by Working Mothers." *Review and Herald* 152 (Sept. 4):14–15.

Douglass, Herbert E. 1977. "Paxton's Misunderstanding of Adventism." *Spectrum* 9 (3):31–36.

———. 1979. *The End: Unique Voice of Adventists about the Return of Jesus.* Mountain View, Calif.: Pacific Press Publishing Association.

"Dress of Civilized Women, The." 1873. *Advent Review and Herald of the Sabbath* 42 (24):191.

Dudley, Roger L. 1985. "The Church and Human Relations." *Adventist Review* 162 (55):5–7.

———. 1986. *The World—Love It or Leave It?* Boise, Idaho: Pacific Press.

Dudley, Roger L., et al. 1983. "A Study of Women in the Seventh-Day Adventist Church." Unpublished paper, the Institute of Church Ministry, Andrews University.

———. 1990. "Public Issues: Where Do US Adventists Stand?" *Adventist Review* 167 (13):14–18.

Dudley, Roger L., and C. Robert Laurent. 1988. "Alienation from Religion in Church-Related Adolescents." *Sociological Analysis* 49 (4):408–20.

Durand, Eugene. 1990. "The Other Side." *Adventist Review* 167 (14):5.

Durkheim, Emile. 1965. *The Elementary Forms of Religious Life.* New York: Free Press.

Dwyer, Bonnie. 1986. "Lawsuits and Scandals—Adventist Homosexuals Not So Anonymous Anymore." *Spectrum* 18 (4):4–12.

Dybdahl, Tom. 1975. "Merikay and the Pacific Press: Money, Courts and Church Authority." *Spectrum* 7 (2):44–53.

———. 1976a. "How to Wait for the Second Coming." *Spectrum* 8 (1):33–35.

———. 1976b. "Merikay and the Pacific Press: An Update." *Spectrum* 8 (1):44–45.

———. 1976c. "We SHOULD Be Involved in Politics." *Spectrum* 8 (3):33–37.

———. 1979. "Court Verdict on Pacific Press Case." *Spectrum* 11 (1):14–17.

———. 1980. "Bad Business: The Davenport Fiasco." *Spectrum* 12 (1):50–61.

Dybdahl, Tom, and Mike Hanson. 1975. "Sex and Adventism: An Interview with Charles Wittschiebe." *Spectrum* 7 (3):9–12.

Editors, *Advent Review and Sabbath Herald.* 1887. "Suppression and the Shut Door." *Advent Review and Sabbath Herald* 64 (29):456–57.

Emmerson, Richard. 1980. "The Continuing Crisis." *Spectrum* 12 (1):40–44.

Emmerson, W. L. 1965. "Unity or Truth." *Review and Herald* 142 (18):2–3, 8.

———. 1983. *The Reformation and the Advent Movement.* Washington, D.C.: Review and Herald Publishing Association.

Engelkemier, Joe. 1967. "Training for Marriage." *Advent Review and Sabbath Herald* 144 (33):12–13.

Evans, Newton Gordon, et al., eds. 1931. *The Home Physician and Guide to Healthcare.* Mountain View, Calif.: Pacific Press Publishing Association.

Faris, Ellsworth. 1955. "The Sect and the Sectarian." *American Journal of Sociology* 60 (6):75–89.

Farnsworth, Vesta J. 1920a. "Honor Thy Father." *Advent Review and Sabbath Herald* 97 (13):19–20.

———. 1920b. "What Have They Seen in Thine House?" *Advent Review and Sabbath Herald* 97 (34):20–21.

"Father in the Home, The." 1925. *Advent Review and Sabbath Herald* 102 (46):15.

"Father Which Seeketh in Secret, The." 1892. *Advent Review and Sabbath Herald* 69 (2):20.

Figuhr, R. R. 1960. "The President's Page." *Advent Review and Sabbath Herald* 137 (1):3.

Finke, Roger, and Rodney Stark. 1992. *The Churching of America 1776–1990: Winners and Losers in Our Religious Economy.* New Brunswick, N. J.: Rutgers University Press.

Flowers, Karen. 1989. "The Role of Women in the Church." *Adventist Review* 166 (39):14–18.

Ford, Desmond. 1977. "The Truth of Paxton's Thesis." *Spectrum* 9 (3):37–45.

———. 1979. "Daniel 8:14 and the Day of Atonement." *Spectrum* 11 (2):30–36.

Fowler, John. 1990. *Adventist Pastoral Ministry.* Boise, Idaho: Pacific Press Publishing Association.

Froom, LeRoy E. 1961. *The Prophetic Faith of Our Fathers.* 4 vols. Washington, D.C.: Review and Herald Publishing Association.

Gardner, Robert W. and Gerald R. Winslow. 1986. "Welcoming Back the Divorced and Remarried." *Spectrum* 18 (2):27–34.

Geertz, Clifford. 1983. "From the Native's Point of View: On the Nature of Anthropological Understanding." In *Local Knowledge: Further Essays in Interpretive Anthropology,* ed. Clifford Geertz, 55–70. New York: Basic Books.

General Conference. 1905. "To His Excellency President Roosevelt." *Advent Review and Sabbath Herald* 82 (21):33.

———. 1983. "Official Report of the 1973 General Conference Council on Women." *Spectrum* 15 (3):9–11.

———. 1984. "Symposium on the Role of Women in the Church." Washington, D.C.: Biblical Research Institute Committee.

Geraty, Lawrence. 1980. "A New Statement of Fundamental Beliefs." *Spectrum* 11 (1):2–13.

Gerstner, John H. 1989. *The Teachings of Seventh-day Adventism.* Grand Rapids, Mich.: Baker Book House.

Ghazal, Chamoon Hessen Camille. 1989. "Attitudes of Male Administrators toward Hiring and Promoting Female Administrators in the Seventh-day Adventist Educational System in the North American Division." Ph.D. dissertation, Andrews University.

Gilbert, Donald F. 1990. "Faithful Stewards." *Adventist Review* 167 (28):20–24.

Goldstein, Clifford. 1990. "Communists, Catholics and Adventists." *Adventist Review* 167 (3):5.

"Good Mother, A." 1873. *Advent Review and Herald of the Sabbath* 42 (20):155.

Gordon, Mary. 1985. "Should Women Be Ordained to the Gospel Ministry? Yes." *Adventist Review* 162 (10):6–12.

Gordon, Paul A. 1993. "How Shall We Warn the World?" *Adventist Review* 170 (26):13–15.

Graham, Edith. 1915. "A Special Work for Women." *Advent Review and Sabbath Herald* 92 (49):14.

Graveson, Roy G. 1983. "A Physician Reviews Adventist Sexual Advice Books." *Spectrum* 15 (1):19–23.

Graybill, Ronald D. 1975. "Adventist History." *Spectrum* 7 (4):46–47.

———. 1978. "Millenarians and Money: Adventist Wealth and Adventist Belief." *Spectrum* 10 (2):31–41.

———. 1981. "Kenneth Wood on the State of the Church." *Spectrum* 13 (2):19–24.

———. 1983. "The Power of Prophecy: Ellen G. White and the Women Religious Founders of the Nineteenth Century." Ph.D. dissertation, Johns Hopkins University.

Greenwalt, Glen. 1988. "The Gospel according to *Seventh-day Adventists Believe*." *Spectrum* 20 (1):24–28.

Greig, Stella Ramirez. 1985. "Women Elders: The Education of Pioneer Memorial Church." *Spectrum* 17 (2):14–19.

Gros, Paul E. 1891. "Christian Family Relations." *Advent Review and Sabbath Herald* 68 (7):101.

Guy, Fritz. 1972. "Contemporary Adventism and the Crisis of Belief." *Spectrum* 4 (1):19–28.

———. 1977. "The Shaking of Adventism? A View from the Outside." *Spectrum* 9 (3):28–31.

———. 1980. "The Church and Its Future: Adventist Theology Today." *Spectrum* 12 (1):6–14.

H., S. M. I. 1897. "The Father's Office." *Advent Review and Sabbath Herald* 74 (4):54.

———. 1899a. (No title). *Advent Review and Sabbath Herald* 76 (2):21.

———. 1899b. "The Woman's Work (Compiled Writings of E. G. White)." *Adventist Review and Herald of the Sabbath* 76 (23):357.

———. 1899c. "First at Home." *Advent Review and Sabbath Herald* 76 (39):617.

Habada, Patricia A., and Beverly J. Rumble. 1981. "Women in Adventist Educational Administration." *Journal of Adventist Education* 43 (3):12–13, 46–48.

———. 1992. "Women in SDA Education Administration." In *A Woman's Place: Seventh-day Adventist Women in Church and Society,* ed. Rosa Taylor Banks, 100–112. Hagerstown, Md.: Review and Herald Publishing Association.

Hackett, W. J. 1975. "The Church's Terrible Ordeal." *Review* 152 (2):4–5.

Hackleman, Douglas. 1978. "GC Committee Studies Ellen White's Sources." *Spectrum* 10 (4):9–15.

———. 1976. "Preserve the Landmarks." *Spectrum* 8 (4):39–40.

Hallock, Larry. 1989. "Adventists and Homosexuality Revisited." *Spectrum* 20 (8):38–41.

Haloviak, Bert. 1980. "Ellen White and Doctrinal Conflict: Context of the 1919 Bible Conference." *Spectrum* 12 (4):19–34.

———. 1984. "The Adventist Heritage Calls for the Ordination of Women." *Spectrum* 16 (3):52–59.

———. 1985. "Route to the Ordination of Women in the Seventh-day Adventist Church: Two Paths." Unpublished paper, Berrien Springs, Mich., Andrews University Archives.

———. 1987. "Ellen White Endorsed Adventist Women Ministers." *Spectrum* 19 (5):33–37.

———. 1988. "Longing for the Pastorate: Ministry in 19th Century Adventism." Unpublished paper, Berrien Springs, Mich., Andrews University Archives.

Harris, Deborah. 1992. "A Network of Caring." In *A Woman's Place: Seventh-day Adventist Women in Church and Society,* ed. Rosa Taylor Banks, 142–54. Hagerstown, Md.: Review and Herald Publishing Association.

Harrison, John W. 1980. "SAWS Expands Its Focus." *Spectrum* 12 (3):15–21.

Harter, Maud. 1925. "The Home." *Advent Review and Sabbath Herald* 102 (49):15–16.

Harwood, Ginger. 1989. "Ellen White, Feminist Theologian." *Ponderings* 2 (3):2–4.

Hasel, Gerhard F. 1975. "Equality from the Start: Woman in the Creation Story." *Spectrum* 7 (2):21–28.

Haskell, S. N. 1900. "Employment of Holy Women in Bible Times." *Advent Review and Herald of the Sabbath* 77 (46):726.

Hayton, Ruth Haskell. 1930a. "The Ethical Relation of the Home, the Church and the School—I." *Advent Review and Sabbath Herald* 107 (54):22.

———. 1930b. "The Ethical Relation of the Home, the Church and the School—II." *Advent Review and Sabbath Herald.* 107 (55):15.

Hegstad, Roland R. 1970a. "Especially for Men." *Adventist Review* 147 (2):10.

———. 1970b. "Especially for Men." *Adventist Review* 147 (7):11.

———. 1970c. "Especially for Men." *Adventist Review* 147 (50):12.

"Her Husband Also, He Praiseth Her." 1905. *Advent Review and Sabbath Herald* 82 (13):13.

Herndon, Booton. 1960. *The Seventh Day: The Story of the Seventh-day Adventists.* New York: McGraw Hill.

Heuback, Paul. 1955. "Job's Wife." *Advent Review and Sabbath Herald* 132 (29):4–5.

Hersley, Michael. 1989. "SDA Women Threaten Tithing Practice." *Spectrum* 21 (1):43.

Holbrook, Betty. 1970. "Especially for Women." *Review and Herald* 147 (14):9.

Holbrook, Frank B., ed. 1989. *Doctrine of the Sanctuary: A Historical Survey.* Silver Springs, Md.: Biblical Research Institute.

Hollock, Wilfred M. 1972. "Need for Organizational Change in the Adventist Church." *Spectrum* 4 (3):24–32.

Holmes, Raymond C., and Douglas Kilcher. 1991. *The Adventist Minister*. Berrien Springs, Mich.: Andrews University Press.

Hoopes, L. A. 1900. "Woman's Ministry." *Advent Review and Herald of the Sabbath* 77 (19):293.

Houck, Fannie. 1987. *Beyond Baptism: What the New Believer Should Know about the Adventist Lifestyle*. Washington, D.C.: Review and Herald Publishing Association.

Howe, C. B. 1965. "Omens of the End." *Advent Review and Sabbath Herald* 142 (35): 4–6.

Hoyt, Frederick. 1985. "Trial of Elder I. Dammon Reported for the *Piscataquiss* Farmer." *Spectrum* 17 (5):29–36.

Hull, Mark. 1989. "Admonishment" (letter to the editor). *Ponderings* 2 (6):18.

Hull, Moses. 1862. "Two Laws and Two Covenants." *Advent Review and Sabbath Herald* 19 (24):189.

Hymowitz, Carol, and Michaele Weissman. 1980. *A History of Women in America*. New York: Bantam Books.

Inter Ocean. 1895. "Are Wives Mendicants?" *Advent Review and Sabbath Herald* 72 (43):678.

James, Ashley. 1986. "Notes from the Diary of an Abused Wife." *Spectrum* 18 (2):16–19.

Jay, Nancy. 1992. *Throughout Your Generations Forever*. Chicago: University of Chicago Press.

Jewett, Dick. 1978. *Orientation for New Adventists*. Nashville, Tenn.: Southern Publishing Association.

Jewett, Paul K. 1980. *The Ordination of Women*. Grand Rapids, Mich.: William B. Eerdmans Publishing Co.

Johnson, Benton. 1957. "A Critical Appraisal of Church-Sect Typology." *American Sociological Review* 22 (1):88–92.

Johnson, Ida M. 1955. "The Far-Reaching Influence of Christian Women." *Advent Review and Sabbath Herald* 132 (4):12–13.

Johnson, Leonore. 1987. "Sexual Attitudes on SDA Campuses, circa 1978." *Spectrum* 19 (3):27–34.

Johnson, Paul E. 1978. *A Shopkeeper's Millennium: Society and Revivals in Rochester, New York 1815–1837*. New York: Hill and Wang.

Johnsson, William G. 1980. "Overview of a Historic Meeting." *Adventist Review* 157 (41):4–15.

———. 1985. "Should Women Be Ordained to the Gospel Ministry?" *Adventist Review* 162 (10):5.

———. 1988. "Women in Adventism" (editorial). *Adventist Review* 165 (Feb. 4):4.

———. 1990. "The Just Community—3." *Adventist Review* 167 (9):4.

Johnston, Madeline S. 1985. "Making Home, Making Church." *Adventist Review* 162 (22):11–12.

Jones-Haldeman, Madelynn. 1990. "Tired of Waiting?" *Adventist Review* 167 (48):6–7.

———. 1992. "Family Systems in the SDA Church." In *A Woman's Place: Seventh-day Adventist Women in Church and Society,* ed. Rosa Taylor Banks, 123–41. Hagerstown, Md.: Review and Herald Publishing Association.

Jordan, Anne Devereaux. 1986. *A History of the Seventh-day Adventists.* New York: Hippocrene Books.

Jorgenson, Alfred S. 1975. "What I Understand by Righteousness by Faith." *Adventist Review* 152 (Jan. 23):7.

Judd, G. E. 1891. "An Ideal Home." *Advent Review and Sabbath Herald* 68 (23):357.

Judd, Wayne. 1984. "From Ecumenists to Come-Outers: The Millerites, 1831–1845." *Adventist Heritage* 11 (1):3–12.

———. 1987. "William Miller: The Disappointed Prophet." In *The Disappointed: Millerism and Millenarianism in the Nineteenth Century,* ed. Ronald Numbers and Jonathan M. Butler, 17–35. Bloomington: Indiana University Press.

K., M. E. 1895. "The Woman's Congress." *Advent Review and Sabbath Herald* 72 (12):183.

Kanter, Rosabeth Moss. 1977. *Men and Women in the Corporation.* New York: Basic Books.

Kaufman, Debra Renee. 1991. *Rachel's Daughters.* New Brunswick, N.J.: Rutgers University Press.

Kistler, Robert C. 1973. "Social Science and Religion." *Spectrum* 5 (1):100–102.

———. 1984. *Adventists and Labor Unions in the United States.* Hagerston, Md.: Review and Herald Publishing Association.

———. 1987. *Marriage Divorce and . . .* Washington, D.C.: Review and Herald Publishing Association.

Kohler, Mrs. Walter J. 1955. "The Men and Women Who Do the Most Important Work in the World." *Advent Review and Sabbath Herald* 132 (33):12–13.

Knechtle, Emilio, and Charles J. Sohlmann. 1971. *A People Ready for the Return of Jesus.* Mountain View, Calif.: Pacific Press Publishing Association.

Kramer, Ardis Jaeschke. 1965. "This Business of Being a Parent." *Advent Review and Sabbath Herald* 142 (29):10–11.

Kress, D. H. 1950. "The Influence of a Godly Mother." *Advent Review and Sabbath Herald* 127 (19):14–15.

Kubo, Sakae. 1980. *Theology and Ethics of Sex.* Washington, D.C.: Review and Herald Publishing Association.

Kuehnert, Lori. 1987. "Women Pastors Baptize and Perform Marriages in North America." *Spectrum* 19 (1):51–54.

Kuzma, Kay J. 1975a. "The Church and Childcare." *Review* 152 (May 1):12–14.

———. 1975b. "The Loma Linda Children's Center." *Review* 152 (May 8):10–12.

———. 1992. "Home and Family." In *A Woman's Place: Seventh-day Adventist Women in Church and Society,* ed. Rosa Taylor Banks, 113–22. Hagerstown, Md.: Review and Herald Publishing Association.

Kwiram, Alvin L. 1975. "How the General Conference Election Works." *Spectrum* 7 (1):17–22.

———. 1976. "Can Intellectuals Be at Home in the Church?" *Spectrum* 8 (1):36–39.

L., F. 1940. "What Makes a Seventh-day Adventist?" *Advent Review and Sabbath Herald* 117 (1):6–7.

———. 1945. "When the Boys Come Home." *Advent Review and Sabbath Herald* 122 (29):2–3.

Land, Gary. 1975. "Providence and Earthly Affairs: The Christian and the Study of History." *Spectrum* 7 (4):2–6.

———. 1977. "Faith, History and Ellen White." *Spectrum* 9 (2):51–55.

———. 1978. "From Apologetics to History: The Professionalization of Adventist Historians." *Spectrum* 10 (4):89–100.

———. 1986a. "The SDA Theological Seminary: Heading toward Isolation?" *Spectrum* 18 (1):38–42.

———. 1986b. "Coping with Change, 1961–1980." In *Adventism in America: A History,* ed. Gary Land. 208–30. Grand Rapids, Mich.: William B. Eerdmans Publishing Co.

———. 1986c. "Shaping the Modern Church." In *Adventism in America: A History,* ed. Gary Land. 139–69. Grand Rapids, Mich.: William B. Eerdmans Publishing Co.

———, ed. 1986d. *Adventism in America: A History.* Grand Rapids, Mich.: William B. Eerdmans Publishing Co.

Larson, David R. 1983. "Sexuality and Christian Ethics." *Spectrum* 15 (1):10–18.

Lawson, Ronald. 1982. "Beyond the Seventh-day Adventist Fringe." *Spectrum* 14 (2):47–49.

———. 1997. "When Immigrants Take Over: The Impact of Immigrant Growth on the Trajectory from Sect to Denomination in American Seventh-day Adventism." Unpublished paper presented to the Society for the Scientific Study of Religion, San Diego, Calif.

Lee, Rosalie Haffner. Nd. "A Brief History of the Role of Women in the Church." Unpublished paper. Berrien Springs, Mich., Andrews University Archives.

"Lesson for Girls, A." 1879. *Advent Review and Herald of the Sabbath* 53 (12):91.

Lewis, C. C. 1915. "School for Mothercraft Offers New Profession for Women." *Adventist Review and Sabbath Herald* 92 (5):14.

Lian, Alex. 1987. "Lewis Walton and SDA Fundamentalism." *Spectrum* 19 (1):55–58.

"Life Sketches of Mrs. C. C. Lewis." 1915. *Advent Review and Sabbath Herald* 92 (24):14–15.

Lindén, Ingemar. 1978. *The Last Trump: An Historico-Genetical Study of Some Important Chapters in the Making and Development of the Seventh-day Adventist Church.* Frankfurt: Peter Lang.

Lloyd, Ernest. 1945. "Juvenile Delinquency and the Church." *Advent Review and Sabbath Herald* 122 (51 [Dec. 20]):11.

———. 1950. "I Want My Mother." *Advent Review and Sabbath Herald* 127 (12):14.

Londis, James. 1981. "Is a Dissident an Apostate? A Pastor Looks at Church Discipline." *Spectrum* 13 (3):17–23.

———. 1986. "Waiting for the Messiah: The Absence and Presence of God in Adventism." *Spectrum* 18 (3):5–11.

———. 1987. "The Gospel Demands Equality Now." *Spectrum* 19 (5):38–42.

Longacre, C. S. 1955. "The Case of Juvenile Delinquency." *Adventist Review and Sabbath Herald* 132 (46):12–13.

Loughborough, J. N. 1892. *The Second Great Advent Movement.* Battle Creek, Mich.: General Conference Association of Seventh-day Adventists.

Loveless, Edna Maye. 1972. "Comments." *Spectrum* 4 (3):64–65.

Lowe, Alice. 1980. "What the Child Needs from You . . . Is You." *Adventist Review* 157 (32):11–12.

Lugenbeal, Edward. 1984. "The Conservative Restoration at Geoscience." *Spectrum* 15 (2):23–31.

Lunday, Bernice. 1960. "Please Stay Home with Me!" *The Advent Review and Sabbath Herald* 137 (21):12–13.

Mallory, Lucia. 1940. "Echoes." *Advent Review and Sabbath Herald* 117 (8):15.

———. 1945. "After College." *Advent Review and Sabbath Herald* 122 (15):15.

Marcus, Eric. 1993. *Is It a Choice? Answers to 300 of the Most Frequently Asked Questions about Gays and Lesbians.* New York: HarperCollins.

Martin, David. 1962. "The Denomination." *British Journal of Sociology* 13:1–14.

Martin, Ralph. 1990. "The Church in Changing Times." *Adventist Review* 167 (1):7–9.

Mazat, Alberta. 1983. "Adventists and Sex: A Therapist's Perspective." *Spectrum* 15 (1):2–9.

McAdams, Donald R. 1978. "Shifting Views of Inspiration: Ellen G. White Studies in the 1970s." *Spectrum* 10 (4):27–41.

———. 1984. "The Scope of Ellen White's Authority." *Spectrum* 16 (3):2–7.

McArthur, Benjamin. 1978. "Where Are Historians Taking the Church?" *Spectrum* 10 (3):9–14.

McMillan-Prinz, Sheryll. 1989. "Dancing Sarah's Circle." *Ponderings* 2 (2):4.

Medley, Carlos. 1990. "Women's Issues Spark Debate." *Adventist Review* 167 (Aug. 2):13.

"Memories of a Father." 1965. *Advent Review and Sabbath Herald* 142 (24):12–13.

Ministerial Association. 1988. *Seventh-day Adventists Believe.* Hagerston, Md.: Review and Herald Publishing Association.

Mitchell, David. 1958. *Seventh-day Adventists: Faith in Action.* New York: Vantage Press.

"Modern Religion." 1873. *Advent Review and Herald of the Sabbath* 42 (25):194.

Moore, Marvin. 1978. "Divorce, Remarriage and Church Discipline." *Spectrum* 10 (1):20–22.

———. 1990. "Happy Homes Require Equal Effort." *Adventist Review* 167 (26):18–19.

Moore, Mary H. 1915. "Why Have Mother's Meetings?" *Advent Review and Sabbath Herald* 92 (41):11–12.

———. 1925. "Household Drudgery." *Advent Review and Sabbath Herald* 102 (45):13.

Moore, Raymond S. 1950. "Preparing Homemakers and Breadwinners." *Advent Review and Sabbath Herald* 127 (48):13–14.

Moore, Roberta J. 1975. "Fact and Fiction about Women and Work." *Spectrum* 7 (2):34–39.

Morrison, H. A. 1910. "Young Womanhood." *Advent Review and Sabbath Herald* 87 (1):11–12.

Morton, Eliza H. 1885. "To the Sisters Everywhere." *Advent Review and Sabbath Herald* 62 (31):484.

Mustard, Andrew G. 1988. *James White and SDA Organization: Historical Development, 1844–1881.* Berrien Springs, Mich.: Andrews University Press.

N., F. D. 1935. "Will Adventists Alone Be Saved? Part I." *Advent Review and Sabbath Herald* 112 (1):6–7.

Neall, Beatrice S. 1986. "Major Chinks in Bacchiocchi's Armor." *Spectrum* 18 (1):54–56.

———. 1987. "A Theology of Woman." *Spectrum* 19 (5):14–28.

———. 1992. "A Theology of Woman." In *A Woman's Place: Seventh-day Adventist Women in Church and Society,* ed. Rosa Taylor Banks, 13–40. Hagerstown, Md.: Review and Herald Publishing Association.

Neil, Richard, L. 1988. *His Coming.* Washington, D.C.: Review and Herald Publishing Association.

Neitz, Mary Jo. 1987. *Charisma and Community: A Study of Religious Commitment within the Charismatic Renewal.* New Brunswick, N.J.: Transaction Books.

Nelson, Debra Gainer. 1984. "Commission Postpones Decision on Ordination of Women." *Spectrum* 16 (2):32–38.

Nembhard, Judith P. 1983a. "Women Pastors Begin Baptizing." *Spectrum* 15 (2):7–13.

———. 1983b. "National Conference Petitions Church Leaders on Role of Women." *Spectrum* 15 (3):5–9.

Newman, Phyllis. 1975. "The Liberated Woman." *Adventist Review* 152 (Nov. 20):8–9.

Newville, Goldie. 1925. "Home." *Advent Review and Sabbath Herald* 102 (19):11.

Nichol, Francis D. 1940. "Should Women Speak in the Church?" *Advent Review and Sabbath Herald* 117 (41):9, 15.

———. 1960. "Higher Education—Bane or Blessing? (Commencement Address, Andrews University, June 2, 1960.)" *Advent Review and Sabbath Herald* 137 (32):4.

———. 1964. *Why I Believe in Mrs. E. G. White.* Washington, D.C.: Review and Herald Publishing Association.

———. 1965. "How Literal Are We?" *Advent Review and Sabbath Herald* 142 (49):12–13.

Nicoll, Joanne. 1990. "Hugs and Hellos." *Adventist Review* 167 (9):18–20.

Niebuhr, H. Richard. 1929. *The Social Sources of Denominationalism.* New York: Henry Holt and Company.

Numbers, Ronald L. 1992 [1976]. *Prophetess of Health: A Study of Ellen G. White.* Knoxville: University of Tennessee Press.

Numbers, Ronald L., and Jonathan M. Butler. 1987. *The Disappointed: Millerism and Millenarianism in the Nineteenth Century.* Bloomington: Indiana University Press.

Numbers, Ronald L., and Janet S. Numbers. 1992. "Ellen White: On the Mind and the Mind of Ellen White." Afterword to Ronald L. Numbers, *Prophetess of Health: Ellen White and the Origins of Seventh-day Adventist Health Reform.* Knoxville: University of Tennessee Press.

Odom, Martha Montgomery. 1950. "Encouragement for Mothers." *Advent Review and Sabbath Herald* 127 (52):14.

Olsen, M. Ellsworth. 1926. *A History of the Origins and Progress of Seventh-day Adventists.* Washington, D.C.: Review and Herald Publishing Association.

——. 1930. "Some Busy Marthas and What They Yearn For." *Advent Review and Sabbath Herald* 107 (12):15.

Olson, Albert Victor. 1966. *Through Crisis to Victory: 1888–1901.* Washington, D.C.: Review and Herald Publishing Association.

Olson, Robert W. 1981. *One Hundred and One Questions on the Sanctuary and on Ellen White.* Washington, D.C.: Ellen G. White Estate.

Osborn, Richard C. 1978. "The First Decade: The Establishment of The Adventist Forum." *Spectrum* 10 (4):42–58.

Oswald, Helen K. 1955a. "Happier Homes in 1955." *Advent Review and Sabbath Herald* 132 (1):12–13.

——. 1955b. "Father's Part in Homemaking." *Advent Review and Sabbath Herald* 132 (6):12.

——. 1955c. "Mother's Beautiful Place." *Advent Review and Sabbath Herald* 132 (9):12.

——. 1955d. "Home, a Palace of Peace." *Advent Review and Sabbath Herald* 132 (20):12–13.

——. 1955e. "Keeping Home Attractive for Adolescents." *Advent Review and Sabbath Herald* 132 (28):12–13.

Otis, Rose. 1970. "Take Time to Be a Mother." *Review and Herald* 147 (8):9.

"Our Daughters." 1893. *Advent Review and Sabbath Herald* 70 (9):133.

Pearson, Michael. 1990. *Millennial Dreams and Moral Dilemmas: Seventh-day Adventism and Contemporary Ethics.* Cambridge: Cambridge University Press.

Pease, Norval F. 1983. "The Truth as It Is in Jesus: The 1888 General Conference Session, Minneapolis, Minnesota." *Adventist Heritage* 10 (1):3–10.

Peebles, E. M. 1920. "The Home-Keeper." *Advent Review and Sabbath Herald* 97 (18):22–23.

Peebles, H. 1887. "Separation from the World." *Advent Review and Sabbath Herald* 64 (18):274.

Perez-Greek, Ramona. 1992. "Women's Leadership, 1971–1992: The Expanding Years." In *A Woman's Place: Seventh-day Adventist Women in Church and Society,* ed. Rosa Taylor Banks, 85–99. Hagerstown, Md.: Review and Herald Publishing Association.

Peters, Madison C. 1915. "The Mother: Her Responsibilities." *Advent Review and Sabbath Herald* 92 (6):16–17.

Peterson, Stella Parker. 1925. "An Allegory." *Advent Review and Sabbath Herald* 102 (7):15.

Phillips, Larry. 1986. "Children of a Greater God." *Spectrum* 18 (1):2–4.

Pierson, Robert H. 1978. "An Earnest Appeal from the Retiring President of the General Conference." *Review and Herald* 155 (Oct. 26):10.

Pope, Liston. 1942. *Millhands and Preachers: A Study of Gastonia.* New Haven: Yale University Press.

Potomac Conference. 1983. "Potomac Conference Executive Committee Action. In Judith P. Nebhard, Women Pastors Begin Baptizing." *Spectrum* 15 (2):13.

Priddy, Luella B. 1910. "Women and the Message." *Advent Review and Sabbath Herald* 87 (2):11.

Provonsha, Jack W. 1969. "An Ethic of Responsibility." *Spectrum* 1 (2):5–13.

———. 1977. "The Christian, Homosexuals and the Law." *Spectrum* 9 (2):45–50.

Ralph, Neall E. 1988. *How Long O Lord?* Washington, D.C.: Review and Herald Publishing Association.

Raoul, Dederen. 1970. "An Adventist Response to the Seventh-day Adventists and the Ecumenical Movement." *Spectrum* 2 (4):19–25.

Rasi, Humberto M., and Fritz Guy, eds. 1987. *Meeting the Secular Mind: Some Adventist Perspectives.* Berrien Springs, Mich.: Andrews University Press.

Rea, Walter. 1982. *The White Lie.* Turlock, Calif.: M & R Publications.

Reavis, D. W. 1915. "Homemaking." *Advent Review and Sabbath Herald* 92 (43):13–14.

Rebok, D. E. 1955. "The Head of the Family." *Advent Review and Sabbath Herald* 132 (39):12–13.

Rebok, Florence K. 1955. "Mother and Her Teen-age Daughters." *Advent Review and Sabbath Herald* 132 (34):12–13.

Reed, Rebecca. 1888. "Cooperative Housekeeping." *Advent Review and Sabbath Herald* 65 (5):64.

Review and Herald Publishers. 1956. *Pioneer Stories Retold.* Washington, D.C.: Review and Herald Publishing Association.

Reynolds, K. J. 1955. "The Church in Graduate Education." *Advent Review and Sabbath Herald* 132 (31):15.

———. 1986. "The Church under Stress: 1931–1960." In *Adventism in America,* ed. Gary Land, 170–207. Grand Rapids, Mich.: William B. Eerdmans Publishing Co.

Reynolds, Louis B. 1984. *We Have Tomorrow.* Washington, D.C.: Review and Herald Publishing Association.

Rice, Richard. 1978. "Dominant Themes in Adventist Theology." *Spectrum* 10 (4):58–74.

———. 1985. *The Reign of God: An Introduction to Christianity From a Seventh-day Adventist Perspective.* Berrien Springs, Mich.: Andrews University Press.

"Rights of Home, The." 1875. *Advent Review and Herald of the Sabbath* 46 (3):19.

Rivers, Louise. 1985. "Should Women Be Ordained to the Gospel Ministry? No." *Adventist Review* 162 (10):6–12.

Robbins, B. F. 1859. "To the Female Disciples in the Third Angel's Message." *Advent Review and Sabbath Herald* 15 (3):21–22.

Roberts, Ives McCarther, et. al. 1982. "Women in the Seventh-day Adventist Church." Unpublished Report Prepared for the Office of Human Relations, General Conference of the Seventh-day Adventists. Tacoma Park, Md.: Institute of Church Ministry.

Robinson, Ella M. 1960. "Little and Unimportant?" *Advent Review and Sabbath Herald* 137 (6):12–13.

Rock, Calvin B. 1970. "A Better Way." *Spectrum* 2 (2):21.

———. 1990. "Dying Disappointed." *Adventist Review* 167 (46):15

Rose, Susan D. 1987. "Women Warriors: The Negotiation of Gender in a Charismatic Community." *Sociological Analysis* 48 (3):245–58.

Ross, Gary M. 1990. "SDAs: Conservative and Liberal." *Spectrum* 22 (5):56–58.

Rowe, David Leslie. 1974. *Thunder and Trumpets: Millerites and Dissenting Religion in Upstate New York, 1800–1850.* Chico, Calif.: Scholars Press.

———. 1987. "Millerites: A Shadow Portrait." In *The Disappointed: Millerism and Millenarianism in the Nineteenth Century,* ed. Ronald Numbers and Jonathan M. Butler, 1–16. Bloomington: Indiana University Press.

Rubencamp, Cosmas. 1970. "The Seventh-day Adventists and the Ecumenical Movement." *Spectrum* 2 (4):5–18.

Rudy, H. L. 1955. "Beware the Alien Yoke." *Advent Review and Sabbath Herald* 132 (5):4–5, 26.

Running, Leona G. 1972. "The Status and Role of Women in the Adventist Church." *Spectrum* 4 (3):54–62.

Rutherford, Joseph F. 1983. *Millions Now Living Will Never Die!* Brooklyn, N.Y.: International Bible Students Association.

Rydzewski, Ella M. 1973. "The World Council of Churches and Seventh-day Adventism." *Spectrum* 5 (3):33–41.

S., W. A. 1925. "Unto You, Young Men." *Advent Review and Sabbath Herald* 102 (9):13.

Sahlin, Monte. 1989. "Who Are North American Adventists?" *Spectrum* 21 (2):17–22.

———. 1990. "Large SDA Churches: Adventism's Silent Majority." *Spectrum* 22 (2):32–38.

Schwartz, Gary. 1970. *Sect Ideologies and Social Status.* Chicago: University of Chicago Press.

Schwarz, Richard R. 1978. "Reorganization and Reform." *Adventist Heritage* 10 (1):11–18.

———. 1979. *Light Bearers to the Remnant.* Mountain View, Calif.: Pacific Press Publishing Association.

———. 1986. "The Perils of Growth: 1886–1905." In *Adventism in America,* ed. Gary Land, 95–138. Grand Rapids, Mich.: William B. Eerdmans Publishing Co.

Scriven, Charles. 1987. "How to Keep the Sabbath." *Spectrum* 19 (1):47–50.

———. 1988. "The Debate about Women: What Happened? Why?" *Spectrum* 20 (5):25–30.

———. 1995. "World Votes No to Women's Ordination." *Spectrum* 25 (1):30–32.

"SDA Church Moves against Homosexual Support Group." 1988. *Review* 165 (Feb. 4):6.

Sel. 1890. "Consult Your Wife." *Advent Review and Sabbath Herald* 67 (14):213.

"Sensible Girl, The." 1889. *Advent Review and Sabbath Herald* 66 (32):501.

"Serviceman's Wife, The." 1945. *Advent Review and Sabbath Herald* 122 (9):16–17.

Seventh-day Adventist Yearbook. 1997. Washington, D.C.: General Conference of the Seventh-day Adventists.

Seventh-day Adventists Answer Questions on Doctrine: An Explanation of Certain Major Aspects of Seventh-day Adventist Belief. 1957. Washington, D.C.: Review and Herald Publishing Association.

"Shall Women Speak in the Church?" 1871. *Advent Review and Herald of the Sabbath* 37 (13):99.

Shell, Penny. 1992. "How Society Affects Social Change in Today's Church." In *A Woman's Place: Seventh-day Adventist Women in Church and Society,* ed. Rosa Taylor Banks, 155–67. Hagerstown, Md.: Review and Herald Publishing Association.

Shinn, Leroy I. 1930. "From Hearthstone to Heaven." *Advent Review and Sabbath Herald* 107 (44):13–14.

Shull, Robert L. 1974. "Ellen G. White in Adventist Theology." *Spectrum* 6 (3, 4):78–85.

Shupe, Anson D., and David G. Bromley. 1985. "Social Responses to Cults." In *The Sacred in a Secular Age,* ed. Phillip E. Hammond, 58–72. Berkeley and Los Angeles: University of California Press.

Shyrock, Harold. 1949. *Happiness for Husbands and Wives.* Washington, D.C.: Review and Herald Publishing Association.

Sider, Lucille, and Donald E. Dayton. 1975. "Women as Preachers: Evangelical Precedents." *Spectrum* 7 (2):15–20.

Smith, Uriah. 1858. "Christianity Requireth a Renunciation of the World, and All Worldly Tempers." *Advent Review and Sabbath Herald* 8 (10):73–75.

———. 1884. *Synopsis of the Present Truth: A Brief Exposition of the Views of Seventh-day Adventists.* Battle Creek, Mich.: Seventh-day Adventist Publishing Association.

Spalding, Arthur Whitefield. 1935. "Fathers in Israel." *Advent Review and Sabbath Herald* 112 (27):13–14.

———. 1949. *Christ's Last Legion: Second Volume of A History of Seventh-day Adventists Covering the Years 1901–1948.* Washington, D.C.: Review and Herald Publishing Association.

———. 1961. *Origin and History of the Seventh-day Adventists.* Vol. 1. Washington, D.C.: Review and Herald Publishing Association.

———. 1962a. *Origin and History of the Seventh-day Adventists.* Vol. 2. Washington, D.C.: Review and Herald Publishing Association.

———. 1962b. *Origin and History of the Seventh-day Adventists.* Vol. 3. Washington, D.C.: Review and Herald Publishing Association.

———. 1962c. *Origin and History of the Seventh-day Adventists.* Vol. 4. Washington, D.C.: Review and Herald Publishing Association.

Spangenberg, James L. 1974. "The Ordination of Women: Insights of a Social Scientist." *Spectrum* 6 (1,2):67–73.

Spectrum Editors. 1976. "An Adventist Creed? Introduction." *Spectrum* 8 (4):37–38.

———. 1979. "Must the Crisis Continue?" *Spectrum* 11 (3):44–57.

———. 1980. "Editorial Note." *Spectrum* 11 (2):i.

———. 1980. "Growing Up Gay Adventist." *Spectrum* 12 (3):38–46.

———. 1980. "Letters to the Editor on Homosexuality." *Spectrum* 12 (4):57–59.

———. 1981. "A Short Primer on Adventist Church Structure." *Spectrum* 13 (1):6–7.

———. 1982. "Policy on Discipline Adopted at 1982 Annual Council." *Spectrum* 13 (3):20–22.

———. 1984. "Women Licensed as Ministers, 1878–1975." *Spectrum* 16 (3):60.

———. 1988. "Speaking in Turn: Excerpts from Delegates' Speeches on the Ordination of Women." *Spectrum* 20 (5):31–36.

———. 1989. "Historians on Spectrum: Pioneering a Free Press." *Spectrum* 21 (1):23–27.

Staff of the Ellen G. White Estate. 1976. "A Biased, Disappointing Book." (Pamphlet written in response to Ronald Numbers' *Prophetess of Health.*)

Stafford, Ottilie. 1983. "On Mislaying the Past." *Spectrum* 15 (4):31–34.

Stanley, Caroline Abbott. 1900. "Home-Making: A Vocation." *Advent Review and Sabbath Herald* 77 (25):390–91.

Stark, Rodney, and William Sims Bainbridge. 1985. *The Future of Religion: Secularization, Revival and Cult Formation.* Berkeley and Los Angeles: University of California Press.

Stiles, Mary Lou. 1950. "My Mission Field." *Advent Review and Sabbath Herald* 127 (41):14.

Stirling, Maryan. 1990. "Don't Bury My Heart." *Ponderings* 3 (3):11.

Stone, Albert. 1886. "Separation from the World." *Advent Review and Sabbath Herald* 63 (15):227.

Stoner, Rebecca Bailey. 1925a. "A Twisted Point of View." *Advent Review and Sabbath Herald* 102 (12):10.

———. 1925b. "A Great Woman." *Advent Review and Sabbath Herald* 102 (43):12.

Strayer, Brian E. 1986. "Adventist Tithepaying—The Untold Story." *Spectrum* 17 (1):39–52.

Strong, June. 1975. "A New Kind of Women's Lib." *Adventist Review* 152 (Apr. 10):15–16.

Student Movement. 1985. "Ordaining Women: Andrews Faculty Responds." *Spectrum* 17 (2):20–38.

Sturges, Stanley G. 1972. "Ellen White's Authority and the Church." *Spectrum* 4 (3):66–70.

Sunday School Lesson Illustrator. 1925. "Her One Talent." *Advent Review and Sabbath Herald* 102 (17):14.

Stutzman, Arla. 1980. "Do You Really Love Your Wife?" *Adventist Review* 157 (12):11–12.

"Suggestions for Sisters." 1900. *Advent Review and Sabbath Herald* 77 (25):391.

T. 1895a. "The Man of the House." *Advent Review and Sabbath Herald* 72 (17):261.

———. 1895b. "True Womanhood." *Advent Review and Sabbath Herald* 72 (22):341.

———. 1895c. "The Wife and the Pocketbook." *Advent Review and Sabbath Herald* 72 (28):437.

———. 1895d. "Woman Suffrage a Success." *Advent Review and Sabbath Herald* 72 (36):565.

T., G. C. 1894a. "The Home." *Adventist Review and Sabbath Herald* 71 (33):517.

———. 1894b. "Marriage and Divorce." *Advent Review and Sabbath Herald* 71 (43):681.

———. 1895. "Husbands, Love Your Wives." *Advent Review and Sabbath Herald* 72 (2):21.

Tabor, A. E. 1894. "How Shall We Dress?" *Advent Review and Herald of the Sabbath* 71 (50):789.

Tarling, Lowell. 1981. *The Edges of Seventh-day Adventism.* Australia: Galilee.

Task Force Report. 1982. "A Call for an Open Church." *Spectrum* 14 (4):18–24.

Taylor, Arlene. 1990. "The Superwoman Syndrome." *Adventist Review* 167 (45):14–16.

Taylor, Kathleen. 1989. "I'm Single and It's Saturday Night." *Spectrum* 21 (5):8–11.

Teel, Charles Jr. 1970. "On Church Structures, Change and Unity." *Adventist Review* 147 (21):4–6.

———. 1980. "Withdrawing Sect, Accommodating Church, Prophesying Remnant: Dilemmas in the Institutionalization of Adventism." Unpublished paper presented at the 1980 Theological Consultation for Seventh-day Adventist Administrators and Religion Scholars. Loma Linda University, Heritage Room, La Sierra Campus.

———. 1984. "Bridegroom or Babylon? Dragon or Lamb?: Nineteenth Century Adventists and the American Mainstream." *Adventist Heritage* 11 (1):13–25.

Tenney, George C. 1892. "Woman's Relation to the Cause of Christ." *Advent Review and Herald of the Sabbath* 69 (May 24):26.

Theobald, Robin. 1980. "The Role of Charisma in the Development of Social Movements: Ellen G. White and the Emergence of Seventh-day Adventism." *Archives de Sciences Sociales des Religions* 49 (1):83–100.

———. 1985. "From Rural Populism to Practical Christianity: The Modernization of the Seventh-day Adventist Movement." *Archives de Sciences Sociales des Religions* 60 (1):109–30.

Thompson, Alden. 1985. "Letting the Bible Speak for Itself." *Adventist Review* 162 (44):12–15.

Tobler, Lorna. 1984. "A Reformer's Vision: The Church as a Fellowship of Equals." *Spectrum* 16 (2):18–23.

Todd, Sharen R. 1985a. "When Mother Goes to Work." *Adventist Review* 162 (8):11–13.

———. 1985b. "When Mother Stays at Home." *Adventist Review* 162 (19):10.

Troeltsch, Ernst. 1932. *The Social Teachings of the Christian Churches.* Trans. Olive Wyon. Vol. 1. New York: Macmillan Company.

Tyrell, Ruth. 1930. "Work Women Can Do and Are Doing." *Advent Review and Sabbath Herald* 107 (3):5–6.

V., L. R. 1980. "Where Academic Freedom Ends." *Adventist Review* 157 (12):18.

Vail, Wayne R. 1980. "Dear Mary." *Adventist Review* 157 (43):11–12.

Van Pelt, Nancy. 1979. *The Compleate Marriage.* Nashville, Tenn.: SPA Press.

Vandevere, Emmett K. 1986. "Years of Expansion: 1865–1885." In *Adventism in America,* ed. Gary Land, 66–94. Grand Rapids, Mich.: William B. Eerdmans Publishing Co.

Various Authors. 1970a. "Homemaker's Exchange." *Adventist Review* 147 (3):10.

———. 1970b. "Homemaker's Exchange." *Adventist Review* 147 (21):12.

Vasquez, Manuel. 1990. "Emerging Voices in the Church." *Adventist Review* 167 (1): 12–13.

Veltman, Fred. 1976. "Some Reflections on Change and Continuity." *Spectrum* 8 (4):40– 43.

Venden, Morris L. 1984a. *Uncommon Ground: Foundations for Faith/2.* Boise, Idaho: Pacific Press Publishing Association.

———. 1984b. *Higher Ground.* Boise, Idaho: Pacific Press Publishing Association.

Vernon, Julia. 1985. "Husbands in the Imitation of Christ." *Adventist Review* 162 (45): 12–13.

Vick, Edward W. H. 1976. "Against Isolationism: The Church's Response to the World." *Spectrum* 8 (3):38–40.

———. 1982. "Must We Keep the Sanctuary Doctrine?" *Spectrum* 14 (3):52–55.

Vyhmeister, Nancy. 1983. "Women of Mission." *Spectrum* 15 (4):38–43.

W., K. H. 1970. "Capitulation to Culture." *Adventist Review* 147 (1):13–14.

———. 1975. "Avoid Linguistic Sexisms." *Adventist Review* 152(January 30):2.

———. 1980. "The Home Is in Big Trouble." *Adventist Review* 157 (2):3.

Wallenkampf, Arnold V. 1985. "Mothers: The Keepers of the Springs." *Adventist Review* 162 (19):5–7.

———. 1989. "Challengers to the Doctrine of the Sanctuary." In *Doctrine of the Sanctuary: A Historical Survey* ed. Frank B. Holbrook, 112–37. Silver Springs, Md.: Biblical Research Institute.

Walters, James W. 1989. "Ellen White in a New Key." *Spectrum* 21 (5):12–17.

Walton, Lewis R. 1981. *Omega.* Washington, D.C.: Review and Herald Publishing Association.

———. 1986. *Advent: World Events at the End of Time.* Washington, D.C.: Review and Herald Publishing Association.

Watts, Kit. 1990a. "Let's Do the Right Thing." *Adventist Review* 167 (10):5.

———. 1990b. "Women Support One Another, Church." *Adventist Review* 167 (37): 22–24.

———. 1990c. "Adventist Women Regain a Voice." *Adventist Review* 167 (53):5.

———. 1992. "Ellen White's Contemporaries: Significant Women in the Early Church." In *A Woman's Place: Seventh-day Adventist Women in Church and Society,* ed. Rosa Taylor Banks, 41–74. Hagerstown, Md.: Review and Herald Publishing Association.

Wayland, Lois Atterberry. 1935. "Fitting Housework to Make You Fit." *Advent Review and Sabbath Herald* 112 (26):17–18.

Weber, Max. 1963. *The Sociology of Religion.* Boston: Beacon Press.

———. 1968. *On Charisma and Institution Building,* ed. S. N. Eisenstadt. Chicago: University of Chicago Press.

Weiland, Robert J. 1985. *Will Marriage Work in Today's World?* Kenilworth: Southern Publishing Association.

Weiss, Harold. 1972. "Are Adventists Protestants?" *Spectrum* 4 (2):69–78.

———. 1984. "Formative Authority, Yes; Canonization, No." *Spectrum* 16 (3):8–13.

———. 1987. "The Sabbath in Matthew, Mark and Luke." *Spectrum* 19 (1):33–39.

Welcome, S. C. 1860. "Shall Women Keep Silent in the Churches?" *Advent Review and Sabbath Herald* 15 (14):109–10.

Welebir, Douglas. 1977a. "Church Settles Court Case." *Spectrum* 9 (2):2.

———. 1977b. "Is the Church above the Law? God and Caesar in the California Lawsuits." *Spectrum* 9 (2):6–15.

Welter, Barbara. 1976. *The Cult of True Womanhood: 1829–1860.* Athens: Ohio University Press.

Wentland, R. H. 1950. "Come unto Me." *Advent Review and Sabbath Herald* 127 (10):9.

West, Nancy Richard. 1955a. "A United Front." *Advent Review and Sabbath Herald* 132 (14):12–13.

———. 1955b. "Home—A Little Heaven on Earth." *Advent Review and Sabbath Herald* 132 (16):12–13.

Westphal, Wilma Ross. 1950. "Thoughts on Child Training and Discipline." *Advent Review and Sabbath Herald* 125 (5):15–16.

White, Ellen G. 1857. "Communication from Sister White." *Advent Review and Sabbath Herald* 7 (15):118.

———. 1864. *Appeal to Mothers.* Battle Creek, Mich.: Seventh-day Adventist Publishing Association.

———. 1868. "The Dress Reform." *Advent Review and Sabbath Herald* 31 (18):278–79.

———. 1878. "Address and Appeal, Setting Forth the Importance of Missionary Work." *Advent Review and Sabbath Herald* 52 (25):190–91.

———. 1879. "Address and Appeal, Setting Forth the Importance of Missionary Work." *Advent Review and Sabbath Herald* 53 (1):1–2.

———. 1884. "Separation from the World." *Advent Review and Sabbath Herald* 61 (2):17.

———. 1885. "The True Standard of Righteousness." *Advent Review and Sabbath Herald* 62 (34):65.

———. 1889. "The Open Door." *Advent Review and Sabbath Herald* 66 (13):193.

———. 1891. "The Mother's Work." *Advent Review and Sabbath Herald* 68 (36):545.

———. 1892. "Friendship with the World is Enmity with Christ." *Advent Review and Sabbath Herald* 69 (34):529.

———. 1894a. "Be Separate." *Advent Review and Sabbath Herald* 71 (46):721.

———. 1894b. "Fellowship with the World Forbidden." *Advent Review and Sabbath Herald* 71 (48):753.

———. 1895a. "No Union between the Church and the World." *Advent Review and Sabbath Herald* 72 (9):129.

———. 1895b. "The Duty of the Minister and the People." *Advent Review and Sabbath Herald* 72 (28):433–34.

———. 1895c. "A Word to Parents." *Advent Review and Herald of the Sabbath* 72 (29):453.

———. 1910. "Separation from the World." *Advent Review and Herald of the Sabbath* 87 (34):3.

———. 1911 [1888] *The Great Controversy.* Mountain View, Calif.: Pacific Press Publishing Association.

———1913 [1890] *Patriarchs and Prophets.* Mountain View, Calif.: Pacific Press Publishing Association.

———. 1915. *Life Sketches of Ellen White.* Mountain View, Calif.: Pacific Press Publishing Association.

———. 1946. *Evangelism.* Washington, D.C.: Review and Herald Publishing Association.

———. 1952. *Welfare Ministry.* Washington, D.C.: Review and Herald Publishing Association.

———. 1965. "Disciplining Children." *Advent Review and Sabbath Herald* 142 (13):12–13.

White, James. 1851. "The Seven Last Plagues." *Advent Review and Sabbath Herald* 2 (1):1–4.

———. 1897. "Women in the Church." *Review and Herald* 45 (May 29):74.

Whitney, E. H. 1895. "Responsibility of Motherhood." *Advent Review and Sabbath Herald* 72 (22):341.

Widmer, Myron. 1990. "For Fathers Only." *Adventist Review* 167 (7):4.

———. 1993. "When the Pope Came to Town." *Adventist Review* 170 (36):4.

"Wife's Power, The." 1881. *Advent Review and Herald of the Sabbath* 57 (4):54.

Wilcox, A. R. 1894. "Home." *Advent Review and Sabbath Herald* 71 (40):628.

Wilcox, Francis McLellan. 1936. *Seventh-day Adventists in Time of War.* Takoma Park, Washington, D.C.: Review and Herald Publishing Association.

Williams, A. H. 1930. "Working for the Women of India." *Advent Review and Sabbath Herald* 107 (39):18–19.

Willes, Joyce. 1970. "Housewife or Homemaker?" *Adventist Review* 147 (35):7.

Wilson, Bryan. 1959. "An Analysis of Sect Development." *American Sociological Review* 24 (1):3–15.

———. 1967. *Patterns of Sectarianism*. London: Hienemann.

———. 1970. *Religious Sects*. Wallop, Hampshire: BAS Printers, Limited.

———. 1975. "Sect or Denomination: Can Adventism Maintain Its Identity?" *Spectrum* 7 (1):34–43.

———. 1981. *Religion in Sociological Perspective*. Oxford: Oxford University Press.

———. 1990. *The Social Dimensions of Sectarianism: Sects and New Social Movements in Contemporary Society*. Oxford: Clarendon Press.

Wilson, Halcyon. 1990. "My Journey . . . " *Ponderings* 3 (3):9–10.

Wilson, Neal C. 1980. "This I Believe about Ellen G. White." *Adventist Review* 157 (12): 8–10.

———. 1983. "Statement on Association of Adventist Forums and Spectrum." *Spectrum* 15 (4):25–27.

Winslow, Gerald. 1975. "Divorce, Remarriage and Adultery." *Spectrum* 7 (2):2–11.

Wittschiebe, C. E. 1970a. "Love and Sexuality." *Review and Herald* 147 (9):2–4.

———. 1970b. "Toward a Theology of Sex." *Review and Herald* 147 (11):4–6.

"Womanly Ministries in the Church." 1875. *Advent Review and Herald of the Sabbath* 46 (17):131.

Wright, Clara Nosworthy. 1965. "Cheating Your Children." *Advent Review and Sabbath Herald* 142 (28):12–13.

Wright, William. 1976. "Adventism's Historic Witness against Creeds." *Spectrum* 8 (4):48–56.

Yinger, Milton J. 1961 [1946]. *Religion in the Struggle for Power*. New York: Russell & Russell, Inc.

Yob, Iris M. 1987. "The Transcendent Human Being: Life beyond Gender Stereotypes." *Spectrum* 19 (5):43–45.

———. 1988. *The Church and Feminism: An Exploration of Common Ground*. Englewood, Colo.: Winsen Publications.

———. 1989. "Adventist Women Adopt Common Action Plan." *Spectrum* 21 (1):41–43.

———. 1992. "Living beyond Gender Stereotypes." In *A Woman's Place: Seventh-day Adventist Women in Church and Society*, ed. Rosa Taylor Banks, 168–83. Hagerstown, Md.: Review and Herald Publishing Association.

Yonge, C. M. 1880. "Strong-Minded Women." *Advent Review and Sabbath Herald* 56 (17):262.

Yost, Donald F. 1990. "Archives and Statistics." *Adventist Review* 167 (July 17):28–31.

Young, David M. 1975. "When Adventists Became Sabbath Keepers." *Adventist Heritage* 2 (2):5–10.

Zervos, Bryan. 1995. "A Sacred Moment at Sligo." *Spectrum* 25 (1):33–36.

Index

LAURA L. VANCE teaches sociology and anthropology at Georgia Southwestern State University.